The
JERRY
IZENBERG
Collection

ALSO BY JERRY IZENBERG

Championship: The NFL Title Story
At Large with Jerry Izenberg
The Rivals
How Many Miles to Camelot?
The Proud People
The Greatest Game Ever Played

Series Editor, Carlton Stowers

The
JERRY
IZENBERG
Collection

Introduction by
BUDD SCHULBERG

TAYLOR PUBLISHING COMPANY
Dallas, Texas

For all those Knights of the Late Night Road
who shared with me the dust of Zaire, the beauty
of Malaysia, the frozen-food locker that
Green Bay, Wisconsin, can be, and the cerebral
density of those special cop clones whose
vocabularies always seemed limited to "No, you
can't go in there. The Jets is praying."

Copyright © 1989 by Jerry Izenberg

Published by Taylor Publishing Company
1550 West Mockingbird Lane
Dallas, Texas 75235

The columns included in this collection
originally appeared in *The* (Newark) *Star-Ledger.*
Reprinted by permission. All rights reserved.

Library of Congress Cataloging-in-Publication Data

Izenberg, Jerry.
    The Jerry Izenberg collection / introduction by Budd Schulberg.
        p. cm. — (The Sportswriter's eye)
    "The columns included in this collection originally appeared in
the Newark star-ledger"—T.p. verso.
        Includes index.
        ISBN 0-87833-632-X : $14.95
        1. Sports—United States. 2. Sports. 3. Newspapers—Sections,
    columns, etc.—Sports. I. Title. II. Series.
    GV583.I96 1989   88-28634
    070.4'49796'0973—dc19   CIP

Printed in the United States of America
0   9   8   7   6   5   4   3   2   1

Introduction

At dinner with a group of fellow writers the other evening, Barney Rosset, eminent publisher of the long-established avant-garde Grove Press, was reminiscing about Fidel LaBarba, who had been his neighbor in a Hollywod bungalow court fifty years ago.

"Did you ever know LaBarba?" he asked.

Answer: "Barney, Fidel (Flyweight champion of the world, who beat some of the greatest flys, bantams, and featherweights, including the late Kid Chocolats) was not only one of my childhood idols, he was a dear friend, best man at my marriage to Geraldine Brooks."

Since Fidel's post-boxing ambition was to become a writer, discussion inevitably led to the traditional affinity between boxing and writing—boxers drawn to writing, from Gene Tunney to Jose Torres, and writers drawn to fighters, like Jack London, Ernest Hemingway, Nelson Algren, Norman Mailer, and the undersigned. Which prompted Rosset to share with the group his conviction that the best and most creative writing in almost any American newspaper comes from its sports pages. He called an impressive roll of literary successes whose work originated in sports reporting: Ring Lardner, Paul Gallico, Damon Runyon, and Red Smith, who, although he never ventured into fiction, wrote so exquisitely that his peers awarded him all the prizes long before he won the Pulitzer.

As Rosset held forth, I realized that he was providing me with the springboard I had been seeking for my introduction to this welcome collection by Jerry Izenberg, a veteran observer who works in the heady tradition of Ring to Red, a writer who brings immaculate care and caring to a world he is sentimental enough to admit loving, while avoiding the precarious slide into sentimentality that runs along the road straight and narrow of good, honest, clean, and affecting sportswriting.

In the early pages of this anthology, which can be read as an insightful essay on the sports world of the past twenty years, Izenberg reminds us that sportswriting, for all its tribulations and discomforts, is "a license to do what others have to steal time from work to enjoy."

Of the "little giant" of sportswriters, Red Smith, Izenberg writes: "We owe him the greatest debt of all. He earned for us the right to write sports without being afraid to use the English language.

"He gave us dignity. It was up to us to take it. If we failed, the failing was ours and not his."

I'm here to assure you that Izenberg has not failed Red or the thousands who follow Izenberg's pieces and now have an opportunity to read many of their favorites back to back.

Whether he is describing the troubled giant Mike Tyson sobbing for his lost mentor Cus D'Amato, or Irish featherweight champion Barry McGuigan, the Belfast Catholic sick of his Island's internecine bloodshed, who wears a dove on his trunks in lieu of a harp; whether he is paying tribute to genuine sports heroes from Jackie Robinson to Jeff Blatnik, or exposing the fraud and corruption of phonies who demean the purity of athletic competition, Jerry Izenberg brings to his work at play, his play at work, a humanitarian involvement frequently laced with cutting humor expressed in images unmistakably his own.

Although he can describe impeccably "The Greatest Game Ever Played," that epic 16-inning Game Six between the Mets and the Astros, he also has eyes and time and heart to notice former light-heavyweight champ Jose Torres leaning against the wall of the Chicago Hilton lobby, shaken by the '68 riot raging outside. A born ringsider, Jerry was there making mental notes on Torres saying:

"I walk all over the Loop today and I think if only he were here the Latins would have someone. Bobby Kennedy was not afraid of poor people. He was not afraid to put out his arms and touch you. I really think he was the only rich man who knew how it really is in this country with Puerto Ricans or with black men."

No, it's not all fun and games, Jerry is telling us. Though without fun and games, life would be one unrelieved disaster. Which is why he chooses to end this book on a note of wry humor, bringing us the Kentucky Derby as seen through the eyes of the only trainer with a no-chance plodder.

So, not to worry about failing Red Smith, Jerry. He would have been proud.

Budd Schulberg

Contents

CONTENTS

CONTENTS

The Faces of Courage / 211

On the Road Again and Again and Again / 237

Preface

I had just come home from Chicago—Chicago of the bloody pavements, Chicago of the shattered windows and the guttural curses hurled down night streets filled with too many people who themselves were filled with too much hate as it all hung there on the mace-and-tear-gas-scented air. In Chicago, right there on the staircase inside the building where the Democratic Convention was in session, a cop, who by then had no more taste for the job than I did, swung his nightstick casually, almost with a sense of boredom. The only things he hurt were my ego and my watch, each of which seemed to shatter into a million pieces.

And so I brooded and, although my boss never knew it, I came perilously close to quitting my job. By then, the way I saw it, I had spent close to two decades chasing outfielders, who might or might not agree to talk to me, getting belted by special cops outside of fight dressing rooms, ruining my digestion, feeding a chronic inner-ear infection on cross-country airplane flights through three time zones, wearing out suitcases, and opening letters from people who would never dare question their plumber or their milkman but who knew exactly what I was doing wrong.

It was, I suppose, the kind of restlessness that builds in all of us at one time or another but it fed on what had happened in Chicago and I suddenly found it intolerable. I had gone to Chicago, as I had gone to three other national political conventions before it, to write what managing editors call "offbeat" columns. I was, after all, a sports columnist, and there is no greater spectator sport than our politicians at play.

But it shook me because this was the setting against which a man who might become president had been nominated, and so, in a very real sense, this was the real world. It seemed to pinpoint for me just how meaningless that other world in which I was grinding out roughly 1,000 words a day, five times a week, really was.

I thought about it and thought about it and had just about made up my mind to shove it when I discovered I couldn't do it. I kind of doubt the readers benefited from that decision but

I know I sure as hell did. I know the things I had a chance to see, the places I had a chance to go, and the people I've been lucky enough to get to know.

But still, a man always has to rationalize—if only to himself. It is ludicrous to say that any of these labors in this, the newspaper's toy department, has ever changed anything that matters in the real world. And when it comes to the idea that we create literature, well, the knowledge that this morning's column will line tonight's garbage pails tends to restrain even the largest of egos among us.

Still, there was a time, when I was defending the right of a boxer named Muhammad Ali to the protection of the same U.S. Constitution as the rest of us, that I struck paydirt. Hundreds of letters poured in from around the country, all of which began with the greeting, "Dear Commie Jew Bastard."

About six months later, I had occasion to take Ali to task about some oratory he had unleashed during his brief but boorish you'll-be-struck-dead-if-you-don't-agree-with-me period. Again the mailman almost developed a hernia. This time, the salutations read, "Dear Fascist Jew Bastard."

It occurred to me that any time you can get the extreme Left and the extreme Right to agree on two out of three things, you just might be making a contribution at that.

In any event, I know I'm lucky because my job affords me a license to do for a living what others have to steal time from work to enjoy. I have met some of the finest people and some of the absolute worst who share the planet with us. If you read on, then I hope you will get to know them, too. When I was a kid, my old man once told me that a lot of good things and a lot of bad things were going to happen to me when I grew up, but that the thing to bear in mind was to learn something from each experience. That helped in this business, too. Years later, as I cowered on the floor next to the ring in Madison Square Garden while some people who did not like the decision in the fight just completed stripped the fire axes off the wall, threw the organ over the side from the mezzanine, and generally ran amok in what management insisted was not a riot, I recalled his advice. That was the night that I learned cheap wine bottles shatter and cheap rum bottles do not.

And finally, the best friend, teacher, and disciplinarian I ever had in this business was a remarkable man named Stanley

Woodward. I worked for him on two newspapers and there will never be another like him. He had read both *The Iliad* and *The Odyssey*—in Greek. He could outfight you, outdrink you, and outsing you—if you stuck to Welsh mining songs. He could beat you at anagrams, crosswords, or arm wrestling. He used to say journalists are fellows who wear a Phi Beta Kappa key, touch-type at a frightening rate of speed, and should never be permitted to write about anything except the Federal Reserve System.

He also said something else: "A professional—a skilled performer whether paid or unpaid—is the only person who counts. The amateur is just a clumsy son of a bitch."

If you don't like what follows, therefore, the fault is clearly with the writer and not the reader.

The Honest Workmen

THE FIGHTER

MARCH 1965

Mostly his old man worked the docks, and on Friday, which is when New Orleans collects its bread for the week, the old man would come home to the walk-up on Chartres Street with a big nine bucks in his pocket, and that was the bankroll for the next seven days.

They lived over a little Italian grocery store and one night the old man discovered a trap door in the living room and after that he'd hook all these contraptions and lower them into the grocery store and go fishing.

"He'd just take enough for supper," Willie Pastrano remembered. "Like, you know, he'd never make a big score and wise the guy up . . . just enough for a meal. One night he pulled up this great big ham and my mamma started hollering, 'Put it back . . . they're going to miss it.' But my old man he just got tired and said the hell with it and we ate it . . . we even had potatoes with it. That's the way it was, man.' "

It was down in the Quarter and the river was only a block away. "It wasn't mean poor," Willie Pastrano remembered. "Man, I been places that were mean poor. No, it was more tough poor. You grew up fast."

In the Quarter, money was tight and if life is a race, it didn't take the kids on Chartres Street long to learn that you don't go in expecting to win. All you look for is a shot to make the finish.

When he was twelve years old, Willie Pastrano was five feet tall and he weighed 185 pounds and the kids on the block called him Moe Fat and Dumb Dumb and he wouldn't go swimming in the river because he was ashamed of the way he looked in a bathing suit.

"I hated myself," he said, leaning back in his chair and looking at the ceiling. "I hated my body. I played the role, man, you know what I mean? I was the village idiot. I was the original nothing. And all the while I kept looking at myself in the mirror and hating the whole scene."

In the streets, he ran with a kid named Ralph Dupas, who was later a good, workmanlike fighter who never made the big money. They ran together and they fought together and every Saturday night they slept together.

Every Saturday night, Ralph Dupas would come to the door and holler up for Willie and he would stand there in the street with tears streaming down his thirteen-year-old face and he would say, "Man, it's fight night again. The old man is half in the bag and he's beating up the old lady. You got any room, Fats?"

"He was a big thing in my life," Willie Pastrano said. He wore dark slacks and a T-shirt and his bare feet were crossed. He is the light heavyweight champion of the world and he will make a beautiful pay night next Tuesday when he goes against José Torres at the Garden and now he is at Kutsher's Country Club training.

He remembers Ralph Dupas because they lived together and stole bananas from the freight yards together and because Ralph Dupas could punch like hell at the age of thirteen and had a wisdom far beyond his years.

"He did it for me," Willie said. "He said to me: 'Hey, man, you want to be a fat slob all your life? Do you want that?' " And Willie Pastrano used to say, "Get off my back," but deep inside he wanted Ralph Dupas to keep after him because he hated his body and he hated the way the kids laughed at him and he hated being the neighborhood punching bag.

So Ralph Dupas took him outside on Chartres Street one day and he said, "Now we are going to run, Fat. Now we are going to get you down to looking like a human."

"Oh, man," Willie Pastrano said, "was I ever fat. I ran one block and I turned red and the blood was rushing to my head and I couldn't breathe. Every day we ran a little more. Then he took me over to St. Mary's Italian CYO gym and I worked out there, but I was so fat my belly kept bouncing and everyone laughed at me.

"So Ralph had a key to the gym and I would come in after everyone left and I would work with him and then I'd go home and eat salad and I did it for a year and it drove my mother crazy because I always had a cold and I was always coughing.

"When the weight started to go, kids would stop me and they'd say, 'You sick, man?' and I'd say no but inside I'd be real proud because they didn't call me Fat anymore and I went looking for some of those guys who used to get on me and we evened up a lot of scores."

Willie Pastrano lost sixty pounds that year and he learned to fight and when he was fifteen he went out and fought for money and when he was eighteen, he had no job and a pregnant wife and he went to Miami, where Angelo Dundee started to move him.

They said he wasn't a banger and they said he couldn't punch but he won a lot of fights and he got nowhere and he couldn't make enough decent paydays and then one night in 1960 he fought Jesse Bowdry, who was then on the way out, and nothing happened.

"I mean nothing, man," Willie remembered. "I was just a body, you know. The concentration was gone. It was like I was fighting slow motion and he banged me pretty good. I said the hell with it."

But it didn't stay that way. He tried the sporting-goods business. He went out and borrowed five grand and every night he would pick up hot dogs and mustard and rolls and he would walk in the door and look at his wife, Faye, and say, "Momma, here's supper."

Six months later he went down to the store and he saw this big truck loading up and he went to his partner, Smiley, and he said, "Some order," and Smiley, who was into three loan sharks and had run out of time, just looked at him and said, "We lost the business."

So he went back. He kept boxing the only way he knew how and then he got a title shot against Harold Johnson as a substitute and now he waits to go again.

"I got a tiger by the tail now, man," Willie said. "I like it . . . the championship part. But at 6 A.M., well, I been fighting fourteen years. You know whether you're exercising or doing road work, it gets a lot tougher to get out of bed when you're wearing silk pajamas."

THE LEGEND RETURNS

SEPTEMBER 25, 1980

His right foot teetered on the edge of the wooden bench and as he bent to his task, the golden crucifix around his neck dangled back and forth like a pendulum ticking away the measured beat of so many hours in so many countries for so many years. When he thinks about it, he will tell you that along the way he has missed Iceland and Greenland and the North Pole. Everywhere else the bouncing ball went, Pelé was probably the foot behind it.

Now he held the flesh-colored bandage in his left hand and with his right, he slowly began to fashion the figure-eight wrap . . . under the callused sole . . . across the ridge where the scarred ankle met the foot itself . . . farther and farther back and then upward. For nearly a quarter of a century the ritual had been the same.

His name is Edson Arantes do Nascimento. That's what it is this morning . . . that's what it was yesterday morning . . . but for one glorious evening . . . from the instant he raced out of the traffic and into the Cosmos' locker room a half hour later, he was Pelé once again.

"Look, look," Vladislav Bogicevic, the big midfielder, hollered across the room as Pelé looked up from his bandaging. "The rookie is here. See . . . see . . . he does not yet shave. His contract is only one day old. I predict he will be a star one day."

And then Pelé smiled. It was the smile that won the heart of Brazil. It was the smile that brought a floodlit stadium to heel twenty-two years ago in Sweden when a seventeen-year-old kid changed the face of soccer forever. And it was the smile that came to the heartland of the baseball barbarians and won a nation, starting with the little old ladies with their Instamatics up in a Rochester parking lot and moving all the way through the guys with timetable minds on Madison Avenue.

Now he had pulled on the shirt and the white shorts and

he was snapping a set of white socks between his hands almost like a man breaking the seal on a twenty-five-year-old bottle of Napoleon brandy. A slice of him made small talk as the Cosmos came to him one by one.

But the other side of Pelé was deep in thought. When he walked out of Giants Stadium on October 1, 1977, after that incredible afternoon when, at his request, 75,000 people rose and repeated after him "Love . . . Love . . . Love," he had never expected to play again.

Yes, there was that strange moment in Lagos, the following year, when he was invited to perform an honorary kickoff and had wound up playing a half of soccer against the Nigerian national team in response to a plea from that country's president. And there had been the brief charity appearance in Rio. But it was over and he knew it and when a man asked Edson Arantes do Nascimento how Pelé had played, he had laughed and said, "Pelé played like Edson."

But then a month ago, sitting in his East Hampton home with his friend Professor Julio Mazzei, the subject of Franz Beckenbauer's retirement had come up. "Pelé," Mazzei had said, "a great player like Franz . . . it would be an honor for him . . . . why don't you play in that game."

"No, no, professor. I feel . . . I think . . . ." And then he had jumped out of his chair and walked back and forth across the room. After an eternity of silence, he stopped and said, "You ask Franz. If he wants it, well, we shall see."

Beckenbauer sent back word that it was, indeed, what he wanted. "I think I shall play goalie," Pelé told Mazzei. "I am a very good goalie and nobody knows it. I shall surprise them. Then it will not be so much like Pelé but it will still have the meaning."

"It won't," Mazzei said. "If you do it in respect to Franz, you must show you are serious."

And so it began. The hour run each morning through Central Park on forty-year-old legs that bear the visible scars of too many wars on too many 120-yard battlefields . . . the steady work in the gym . . . five hours of brutal roadwork each weekend on the sands of the Hamptons.

But last night as Pelé walked into the locker room in a wine-colored leather jacket, a pink turtleneck, and dark slacks, there was apprehension.

"At first I wanted to come to pay honor to Franz—only that. But then they made the announcement. Then sixteen countries bought television rights. Then I thought of the people who will expect to see Pelé tonight and I remembered that I once said, 'Better to quit while they still want you to play than to play when they want you to quit.'

"I have nerves tonight."

Then there were more players around him and with a marvelous sense of timing that separates Pelé from all others, he turned to Giorgio Chinaglia and deadpanned: "Giorgio, do not spare me. Tell me the truth. Have I changed so much? How do I look for a man of seventy?"

The answer came an hour later. As Pelé scored against the NASL All-Stars and the crowd offered a mighty salute. It was as though he had never been away.

HANDYMAN

MARCH 1965

POMPANO BEACH, Florida—It was not exactly the social highlight of the 1964 baseball season. All year long, Gil Hodges, the Senators' manager, had been watching Don Zimmer fool around with the catcher's glove and for a lot of that time he had been threatening Zimmer with the chance to put up or shut up.

This was no small thing to Don Zimmer. He is thirty-five years old and he will do anything this side of the Sullivan Law to win a game and keep his job. In 1953, for example, he matched his head against a fast ball thrown by a young pitcher named Jack Kirk. The ball won and Don Zimmer damn near died.

Now, six major league clubs later, he had already played six positions for the Senators and when Hodges challenged him to play the seventh, Don Zimmer figured that his ability to do it just might keep him working.

So in the eighth inning of the final game of the season at Boston, Gil Hodges gave Don Zimmer a catcher's glove and sneaked him behind the plate for the first time in his life. It was a very nice affair.

A man named Buster Narum was coming in from the bull pen and Zimmer walked out to meet him.

"About the signals . . . " Don Zimmer began.

"Yes," Buster Narum prodded, "about the signals?"

"Well, one finger is a curve. Two is a fastball, and three," Don Zimmer stumbled, "three is a what?"

"Yes," Buster Narum replied, "three is a what but let's call it a slider."

There followed a large pause as Buster Narum waited patiently on the mound and the batter waited patiently in the batter's box and finally someone suggested Don Zimmer go back to the dugout and get a catcher's mask, which is the way most catchers in the Western world do it.

Now Zimmer was ready. He crouched. The batter tensed and Buster Narum waited . . . and waited . . . and waited . . . .

"Now what's wrong?" Zimmer wondered. "Hey, Zim," Hodges yelled from the dugout, "you are supposed to give him a target."

"Oh," Don Zimmer said.

The next inning the leadoff batter popped a high foul behind the plate. Zimmer reacted . . . oh, how he reacted. Instead of following the ball, sliding off his mask and dropping it, Zimmer reached up, ripped the mask away, and flung it behind him. It hit umpire John Flaherty in the head.

Still, it was a successful debut. Zimmer did not kill the umpire. After it was over, Gil Hodges called him aside, told him that by learning to catch he might prolong his career, and offered him a chance to learn at Tampa in the Winter Instructional League.

"You wouldn't believe it," Zimmer said yesterday, near the batting cage at Pompano. "You wouldn't believe the things that have happened to me since then."

"Try me," a fellow suggested.

"Well, I'm thirty-five years old," Don Zimmer began, "and after five games down there I couldn't move. I'd go home at night and lay on the couch while my wife, Jean, massaged my ankle. I was numb.

"And the games, oh boy, the games were beautiful. It was ninety degrees and we didn't get any rain and the ground was like concrete. Then we had them wild kids trying to find the plate and the damned games lasted three and a half hours. They were beautiful."

After a week or so, Don Zimmer could finally straighten out and walk without looking like a lowercase N. He had also progressed in other directions. No longer was it necessary for Haywood Sullivan, the ex-catcher who managed Kansas City's instructional club, to shout down to Zimmer from the coaching box: "Hey, you forgot the chest protector this time."

And no longer were things happening like the first game at Tampa when the umpire said to Zimmer, "Get lower, get lower. I can't see the pitches."

"I'm trying," Don Zimmer said.

"Listen," the umpire asked, "don't you know how to catch?"

"Don't ask," Don Zimmer mumbled. "Don't ask."

All of that was behind him, and when Hodges finally saw

him catch at Tampa, he was suitably impressed. "Now I'm not afraid to use him if we have to," the manager said. "He will probably add some years to his career like this."

When practice began yesterday, there was only Rube Walker, an old-time catcher, deliberately throwing terrible pitches to Zimmer on the empty practice field. They bounced in the dirt on both sides of him and he dove and scrambled, leading an uninformed spectator to say, "Either that #24 is a lousy pitcher or that #23 is a great catcher. What's it all about?"

"You wouldn't believe it, friend," an eavesdropper said, "you wouldn't believe it."

INSIDE MIKE TYSON

JUNE 1988

The heavyweight champion of the world cried yesterday.

He sat stripped to the waist in his dressing room behind the showroom at the Trump Plaza Hotel, where he is training for his title defense against Michael Spinks later this month, and he fought hard to swallow but for all the good it did there might as well have been a basketball stuck in his throat.

And then the tears came.

They streamed down both cheeks.

But they could not wash away the pain of the one loss that still cuts so deeply into the core of his very soul.

And for that single moment, Michael Tyson, the man-child whose very presence in the ring has become a new synonym for awesome, was more human, more mature, and more dead honest than any athlete I have ever known.

He was remembering Cus D'Amato.

"In the morning when I run," he had explained earlier, smiling warmly at the thought, "I can still hear his voice and see his face and sometimes with what is going on all around me and the way my world has changed I wonder what he'd tell me to do. We came together when I was a little kid and day after day he would tell me, 'Pay attention. Learn. Listen to me. One day I won't be here any more, Michael. One day you are going to have to do it all for yourself.' I miss him so much."

As he spoke, he conjured up another man's memories of the old man with the white hair and the passionate voice and a guy could picture the way it must have been between them in those moments that nobody else shared. There was always a touch of the hypnotist deep inside Cus and for those who grooved along the same intense wave-length with him, there was a heavy learning experience.

A lot of folks didn't like him. A lot of other folks thought he was the ultimate teacher. But both groups had one thing in common. Nobody ever ignored him. Yes, Cus taught Mike Tyson how to fight. And, yes, he gave him a purpose and a self-respect. But with all that swirls around this young millionaire, who will not reach his twenty-second birthday until after this title defense, we are inclined to forget the most important thing of all.

It was Cus D'Amato who guided Mike Tyson through his adolescence. Cus was past his eightieth birthday and half blind by then. All his life he was a teacher in search of a disciple and it was almost as though once destiny had sent this kid his way, Cus, who knew exactly how ill he had become, was not going to waste a single precious moment.

Yesterday Tyson conceded that he always knew one day he would have to finish climbing the rest of the mountain, which Cus had shown him, all by himself. But when you are a kid, time is relative. It was as though he knew it would happen but for so long he refused to believe it.

"It [boxing] was so much fun back then with Cus and Jimmy [Jacobs, his original co-manager] around then. It wasn't about money so much with everyone having his hand out like now. I know that's hard to believe but then you had to know Cus to understand this. The man was broke. He gave money away to people who needed it.

"The world was so much fun when we were together. It's one of the reasons I run alone in the morning. I can think about him. I can wonder if Cus was around what would he do . . . what would I do? He tried to teach me so much. I just wish I had listened to him more."

"Forget boxing for a moment," a man suggested. "Forget the jab and the right hand and the way he taught you to cut off the ring. What's the one thing he said that sticks in your mind the most?"

"It's so simple," Tyson replied, "but it says so much. He used to say to me every day that no matter what you have to face, no matter how hard it looks like it's going to be, don't ever forget that nothing is as bad as it seems once you face it. He was right. The fights? It's the getting ready that's so hard on you. Not the fighting. Once you get into the ring, the unknown is gone. Now it's reality and you can deal with that."

"When he was here," a man pointed out, "he was always pointing you toward the future . . . looking ahead to the goal . . . trying to see you were ready. But now, well, he's gone and you're there at the top. How do you keep going when the goal is passed?"

"You have to take it to another level," Tyson said. "I don't know exactly . . . win a lot of fights . . . set a lot of records . . . I'm not sure exactly what the level is but I'm sure it's out there."

And then Mike Tyson started to say something else but it never got out. I don't even remember the question that prompted the silence but he was clearly struggling with himself. There are those who will say that perhaps the emotional moment was generated by the frenetic world into which he suddenly has been catapulted.

But they're wrong.

It's not who's here but who isn't. Cus D'Amato touched Mike Tyson deeply and permanently. He became his measuring stick for all things. He still grieves for him.

Twice he opened his mouth as if to speak. Nothing came out and he swallowed hard instead. It was at that point, Kevin Rooney, his trainer, walked to him and gently touched his shoulder. Kevin was shaped by Cus, too.

And then the single tear started to form and finally the words came pouring out between sobs with a lonely passion that few ever share with strangers as he revealed a strange, private truth.

"I . . . I didn't want to fight . . . not really . . . it's what he wanted for me . . . I . . . wanted so desperately to make him proud of me." The words were a blend of love and pain.

Ten minutes later, he was down in the ring doing the things Cus had taught him.

COURAGE IS RIDING OUT A 1,600-POUND TORNADO

NOVEMBER 29, 1985

This was a couple of nights ago, when the beers were short and the talk was long and the veterans were trying to single out the most courageous feat they had ever seen from the safety of a press box. This is, of course, an impossible task.

On the other hand, it brought to mind Mr. Freckles Brown, simply because nobody else at the bar had seen or heard of him, and it opened the wellspring of memory just enough to make a man think that no matter how you rate his sport, he is worth a mention any time the subject of sheer competitive courage surfaces.

Freckles was a rodeo bull-rider. His career, which incredibly did not reach its zenith until he was forty-six years old, was a throwback to the time when real cowboys spent the entire winter in the line camps, curled up in their soogans (which were unwashed but well-inhabited quilts), dreaming of canned peaches and free women and the beautiful return of spring, which would send them off the ranch and back to the arenas.

The calendar, and the modern truck (which eliminated the need for a line camp), dictated that Freckles missed that slice of life but, emotionally, he was clearly one of them. So when rodeo moved into a new world where the band played "Georgie Girl" instead of "Home on the Range," Freckles never paid much attention to the new breed of cowboy that came out of rodeo schools and supermarket checkout jobs.

The first time a man met him was back in 1967 at the national finals in Oklahoma City, where, just four years short of his fiftieth birthday, he had come to ride a bull.

Some things do not change.

The bull was a big, ugly, red-and-white-faced Braford—a strange cross between a Brahma and a Hereford. A rodeo bull is no family terrier, turning on the neighborhood kids because they have tied a can to his tail. Hit-and-run is not his ball game. He will throw you, and then keep on coming back at you until the rodeo clown jumps in front and sticks out his butt to draw the bull's attention.

So, on that night one man will never forget, here was old Freckles, and here was Tornado, who weighed 1,600 pounds. They had sent 300 cowboys out of the chute on Tornado's back during his career, and none of them had survived the six-second whistle.

Freckles was going out to ride him at an age when most of us have put taking out the garbage under the heading of strenuous exercise. He was going to ride him for two reasons: The first was to protect the mortgage on 500 acres over on the Muddy Boggy River in Soper, Oklahoma.

Nobody handed Freckles the down payment on that acreage. It was paid for with three decades of riding the Tornados of his world, one broken neck, and enough broken legs to stock the spare-parts department at the Mayo Clinic.

He was also going to ride him because nobody else in the world ever had—and in Freckles's mind this was, therefore, his Super Bowl, his World Series, and his heavyweight championship.

When the chute banged open, Freckles was looking down at that big, red hump of a neck, and he was telling himself over and over to remember that this was what the cowboys call a "spinner," and that sooner or later he would jerk that huge body to the right, rip backward, and try to nail the man on his back.

Freckles fought him. He rode him past the whistle, and when it blew, everyone in the joint was standing and shrieking as Freckles cut clear. Then he was walking away.

Freckles's walk was his signature. He was so bow-legged that if you stood him next to somebody who was knock-kneed they would have spelled "ox." He was walking away, and waving his hat, and 12,000 people had seen a miracle.

The next day a man told him that he almost expected his grandchildren would see Freckles at work one day. "Not likely," Freckles drawled, but you could see the thought intrigued him.

That night, he announced his retirement. A rodeo official named Dave Stout laughed in his face. "Freckles, you ain't gonna quit," he said, and then turned to another man and explained: "He can get up on a bull and do something very few folks in the world can do. Last week he told me that when he comes out of the chute, sittin' on the bull's back, he feels just like the emperor of Japan. No, I'd say catch him after he's turned fifty, and he'll be doin' exactly what you saw him do last night."

When a man next saw him again, four years later, Freckles, indeed, was fifty. Some retirement. Just six months earlier, in a place called Lenapooh, Oklahoma, a bull with the imaginative name of Number 46 caught him leaning the wrong way and smashed his ankle.

He and Ronnie Bowman drove fifty miles that night to where Freckles had parked his car. Then Ronnie packed the ankle in ice. Freckles drove the remaining 200 miles.

When he limped through the door, Edith Brown, who was the resident Soper, Oklahoma, expert on Freckles, through marriage, shook her head and said, "Damn, Brown, you done it again."

Finally, he quit. There don't seem to be any more Freckleses around the sport these days. The Old West is dead, along with people like Pete Knight, who once lay dying on the hard dirt floor of a tiny arena in Hayward, California, after a bronc named Duster had kicked a piece of rib into his lung. The year was 1937; ironically, it was the first year Freckles Brown went off to ride bulls for money.

When the first man to reach him asked Pete if it hurt, he replied, "You're damned right it does. Now help me get the hell up, because this is downright embarrassing."

Once, in a quiet moment, a man asked Freckles if he'd been afraid back in Oklahoma City on the night he went out to master Tornado.

"Hell," Freckles said, "only two kinds of folks don't have the sense to be afraid—the first are crazy and the second are dead. It's the way you handle it that counts."

Case closed.

THE PROMOTER

He sits at his desk and stares through the unwashed window at the gray lump that is 44th Street. It is beginning to drizzle outside but most of the good that might have come from last night's show was already mortally wounded. It had begun to die in the early-morning dampness.

Now it is early afternoon and in three hours he will pick up the bulky envelope filled with tickets and he will lock the iron-gray wall cabinet and he will walk down the dirty fourteenth-floor corridor to the elevator. He will drive out to Sunnyside Gardens and he will have all night to think of the people who will not be there.

He has been thinking about them for two days now but he will forget them when the dawn breaks in on his next sleepless night. He will forget them and start worrying about the ones who will not be there the next time he goes.

Irving Cohen is a fight promoter. Once he was a manager and his eyes change ever so slightly when he ticks off the names . . . Rocky Graziano . . . Walter Cartier . . . Irish Bob Murphy. That was in another world. Now he is his own promoter and his own matchmaker and sometimes his own ticket-taker and his own usher.

The operation runs every Tuesday but this week he has a bonus show on Friday night because the circus is in the Garden and the big television camera has to live somewhere and they are giving him his shot. It is the only show of the season on which he will make money.

The rest of the time Sunnyside Gardens will die its weekly economic death. It has as much chance in the modern world as a buggy-whip factory but it trains young fighters and so Madison Square Garden picks up the deficit and helps Irving Cohen make his weekly nut.

Last night he had José Torres in the main event and he should have sold out the joint but yesterday it rained and Irving Cohen knew right then that he was hurting.

17

"We got three types of customers at Sunnyside," he said yesterday afternoon, turning away from the dirty window and his weather watch. "We charge $1.50, $2.50, and $3.50. The $1.50 guy, he comes because it is Tuesday and there is a fight and this is what he has to do. But when the weather is lousy, well, the $3.50 guy, he doesn't come. He is a businessman. He won't go across the street to see a fight if it rains. He can stay home and watch television. Tonight, he will stay home."

This is the way it is and Irving Cohen knows it. He also knows that he has had a lot of rainy Tuesday nights this season, which began last October and will run through the first week in May. He has an option to pick up five more dates but he will not exercise it. He says he is very tired.

On Monday night, the night before he had Torres going for him, he watched the late show and he watched the late late show and then he watched something else but he is not sure what it was.

"You worry. You worry that tomorrow you will go to the office and there will be a phone call and one of your fighters is going to cancel out. God forbid he should be a star bout fighter. Then you're dead. Monday I found a substitute in Paterson and another in New York but they were on the undercard. Where do you find a substitute for a main event the day of the fight?"

So all night long Irving Cohen tossed and turned and around 4:30 he dozed off and his wife, Jean, tiptoed out of bed and shut off the television. At 8 A.M. yesterday he was awake and he looked out the window and he felt the dampness and saw the wet streets and he still felt lousy.

"Where you going?" Jean Cohen asked him.

"I gotta go to the office."

"So," Jean Cohen said, "sit and have coffee. Sit and eat something. You don't eat now, you wouldn't eat later. Sit down."

Irving Cohen is sixty years old and has been over this course so many times before and he will be over it again so many more times. So he sat and had coffee.

"I get to the office and nobody canceled out, thank God. So then I go to the commission for the weigh-in. You gotta hope they all make the weight but mostly you gotta hope they all show up. We don't pay Garden prices. A four-rounder gets $50 with us. At the Garden he gets $150. A six-rounder gets $100 with us. At the Garden he gets five times that. So you want to know about the heartaches of a small promoter? So that's it. From 10:45 until 12:15 it's hell. The commission office is on West 47th, and you stand by that elevator hoping and praying until every last one of them shows. Then all you got to do is hope they show that night at Sunnyside."

It has been a long season for Irving Cohen. He needs $3,000 to break even and an average show draws $2,200. He will tell you that his small club is an artistic success and he will point to kids like Johnny Persol, who jumped from Sunnyside to a main event at the Garden. He will also tell you that business is lousy, which it is, and then he will look at the rain.

The television card this Friday is the saver. Last year, he had three of them. This year, he has one. There is a thin white stubble on his face because he did not shave yesterday morning and, as he says, he looks tired.

"You worry," he says, sitting in the middle of all those fight posters in his office. "You worry about the weather and the fighters and the customers and you worry about the decisions because the people will blame you for that too.

"Back when I was a manager," he says, "a small promoter could do all right because then you had the neighborhood rivalries. Now you don't even have the neighborhoods."

And then he turned around and looked out the window again.

"Today is gone, I hope it don't rain Friday."

THE OMEN

LEXINGTON, Kentucky—It was laid out there on the table for all the world to read . . . a kind of blueprint for the night the mosquito savaged the elephant . . . but then fairy tales are difficult to take seriously and there was not a one among the listeners who didn't smile to himself and think, "You can make it sound real but the truth is that the last thirty-seven times the beautiful princess kissed the frog all she had to show for it was a wart on her lower lip."

But on Sunday, even as the army of tourists searched for a drink they couldn't legally buy and the surviving players sought to think about something other than the game they couldn't forget, Horace Broadnax, a Georgetown guard out of Plant City, Florida, reflected on what he considered the key to the Hoyas' final step toward their place in the life and times of great college basketball teams.

It was as though he was reminding himself of the faint possibility of a terrible truth.

"We can't let up," he said of Villanova and the game that the world had begun to view more as a coronation than a contest. "They have come back so many times in this tournament. It's like, well, it's like when you step on a bug and then you move your foot and you look down but the bug is still there."

Or, to put it in less prosaic language, you could turn to the poet laureate of Queens, Louis Carnesecca, who, when asked if there was any possible way known to man or Kentucky basketball fans that Villanova had the slightest chance of beating Georgetown, reduced the proposition to its lowest common denominator by replying, "I thought that's why they are playing the game."

Roughly thirty or so hours later, as the noise rattled the ceiling of Rupp Arena and the victorious Villanova basketball team swarmed over, around, and on top of their coach, Rollie Massimino, he was thinking of what it must be like at that very moment back home in Philadelphia and shouted back at them, "You didn't win a ring tonight. You won a city."

So look out, world, because from this morning forth and for every morning, noon, and night until they get together for the next version of this marathon dribble down in Dallas next year, his Golden Mosquitoes are the kings of college basketball.

Much to his horror, they have made Horace Broadnax a reluctant entomologist with honor.

They had said they needed the perfect game for this one and they came about as close as you can get to it. They had said something else, too. Specifically, it was Rollie Massimino who said it after advancing to the finals by eliminating Memphis State back on Saturday. He was speaking about the role of Patrick Ewing in the Georgetown master plan.

"When it comes down to the critical last four minutes and you have to make decisions, he is involved in every one of them." The "you" he was talking about was the rival coach and Ewing's own coach, John Thompson, because his presence means that much to a ball game.

But a funny thing happened while the mosquitoes were stinging holes in Georgetown's wall-to-wall fly swatter. They had stolen the tempo of this game and, as hard as Ewing played, the crunch moments did not come down to him . . . not even a little bit . . . which explains a hell of a lot about what happened here in Rupp Arena on Monday night.

And there was one other thing that Massimino said before they finally got around to playing the game. "When it comes down near the finish and we are one point ahead, we like to think that we have enough to win."

Since Rollie had a two-point cushion at that stage, all the citronella in the Western world could not have put Georgetown back together again.

What follows, then, is a reprise to a theme that dominated Villanova's incredible march to the national championship.

Here was Villanova, out-rebounded in all five tournament games when it came up against Georgetown and playing the stunned Hoyas to a 17-17 tie in that department. Here was Villanova, taking the long way home and still getting there. Here was Rollie Massimino all through this tournament in every press conference repeating a credo, which would simply come off as a hollow cliché—if you didn't know this team and its coach:

"Good things," he said over and over again, "come to people who work hard."

He is his own best example. At age thirty-four, he had still yet to coach in college when he applied for the Harvard job and was among the three finalists. "What happened," he will tell you, "is that the new athletic director at SUNY over in Stony Brook, Long Island, took the losing finalists and interviewed us. I got the job. But I didn't want to go. I had every kid coming back on my team. I thought we could win the state title. I might not have left but my wife [Mary Jane] reminded me that it was what I'd always wanted. So I left Lexington [Massachusetts] High and we did okay."

He won the Knickerbocker League title and took the team to the NCAA's small-college tournament.

"Now I get a call from Chuck Daly at Pennsylvania. He tells me to meet him at Newark Airport and he offers me an assistant's job. My wife says it's a step toward where I want to be. So here I am. I lose $7,000 in the deal. I'm making $13,000 and I don't have a car and I have five kids."

But he was chasing a dream. When he finally got the head job at Villanova, it wasn't the end of the trip. It was simply that he had finally come to a place where he could start to really begin.

If you want to know how tortuous, how cruel, and how frustrating that journey can be, then there are probably a thousand or so high-school and small-college coaches who can tell you all about it.

If, as the old Hollywood musicals told us, there's a broken heart for every bulb on Broadway, you may rest assured that there's also one for every dribble in a thousand high-school gyms you never knew existed.

The story is enough to make a lot of hungry coaches keep on keeping on.

NOW, THE SILENCE

FEBRUARY 1972

You can trace the substance of what he was and the places he had been through the sounds of his life. There were the roosters, crowing in the fresh, clean dawn of a Nigerian village that never knew the belch of a smokestack or the squeal of hard rubber tires against a macadam surface.

He was born Richard Ihetu and he was an Ibo and he stayed an Ibo forever after. Years later, when the sounds had become the confusion of the first city he ever saw or the low-pitched groan of the foghorns along the Thames or the rat . . . tat . . . tat . . . of the speed bag in a hundred gymnasiums or the full-throated crescendo of the customers from out in the darkened arenas, he was still an Ibo.

When he stripped in the narrow confines of Lord knows how many little cubicles and bent to pull on the protective cup and the other pieces that fit together to make the uniform of his profession, you could see the raised ridges of the criss-crossed tribal initiation scars glowing against the burnished ebony of his chest.

Still later, when the sounds turned to gunfire and screams and flames in the tortured after-birth of a new country in turmoil, Richard Ihetu remained an Ibo and no matter how you look at it, the Ibos lost the war in the new government house and lost the war in the body count that followed and in the crackling sounds of African villages aflame.

He was born Dick Ihetu and when he ran from the village at age fifteen—more from boredom than hardship—he left the name behind. He went into the gymnasium in Aba and they liked the way he moved and they put him into four-rounders once a week at the local movie theater against guys with names like Super Black Power and Willie the Lion. He called himself Dick Tiger and it is the name by which most will now remember him.

Light years away from Aba, Dick Tiger won the middleweight championship of the world. He was a walk-in, straight-ahead fighter with a punishing left hook and the hook was, for a time, too good and so they ducked him, which is why it took him so long to fight for the title. He won the middleweight title and he gave Joey Giardello a shot and Joey boxed his ears off in Atlantic City and took it away from him. When it ended, they embraced and Joey said that he would do the same for Tiger but Dick Tiger spent a long time chasing that rematch.

The calendar and his waistline cut him down and made it impossible for him to fight middleweights, but he was a professional fighter and a professional has to do what he can and so Dick Tiger became a light heavyweight simply because they were the only people left who would fight him. He won the light-heavyweight championship, too.

The noise and the money and the crowds lasted for twenty-one years. Actually, the money gave out first because he was an Ibo and the Ibos lost the war back home and lost much of what they had when a country (which never really became a country) called Biafra was hammered back into Nigeria. He lost the apartment houses and the beauty shop and the other tangible things he had earned mostly in the prize rings of the United States.

But while it lasted, it was always the same. He would fight the same fight, that straight-ahead-don't-back-up-look-for-a-place-to-land-the-hook kind of fight. And he always came to fight it in the same way.

They would sign the thing by mail or telegram and for perhaps a week, Chickie Ferrara, who always worked as his cut man, would drop by the Garden publicity office and open the lower drawer of the filing cabinet in Tommy Kenville's office. It would be empty and he would chat for a while and leave.

Then one day, Chickie would slide the drawer open and there would be a large, dirty old shopping bag inside stuffed with a set of gym shoes and a protective cup and a set of worn trunks and Chickie would step back and say, "He's here."

And they would go to work.

He was a man with a soft voice tinged with the flavor of an English accent, and the amenities meant much to him in terms of what was proper and what was not, and when he would climb through the ring ropes and they would announce him, he would always turn toward each side of the arena and bend slightly in an Oxonian bow of acknowledgment. Then, for as long as he could, he would fight like hell.

If you pressed him, he would speak about home—which was really two places at once. Home was Aba and home was also the state of mind he carried around inside him because a long, long time ago he had told a man that the war was coming and that fear seemed to multiply geometrically instead of arithmetically.

When it came, he went home and he put the only thing he had into Biafra, perhaps suspecting even then that the new country was stillborn and that he would lose it all.

If you pushed him about the business of fighting he would tell you with great logic that he neither liked nor disliked it . . . that it was simply his job and long ago he was taught that when you have a job you do it the best way you know how.

On the morning after he lost a very close decision to Emile Griffith in his pursuit of the lost middleweight championship, he sat in an anteroom at the Garden. Most people thought he had won that fight even though the other guy got the duke.

"Go ask him," he said with absolutely no bitterness. "Maybe he will tell you but I know I win the fight. It is only the decision I lose."

That was a long time ago and now the sounds are over . . . the arenas are empty . . . the crowds are gone. He died yesterday in Aba.

He was the kind of boxer Hollywood will never understand.

MOMENT
OF TRUTH

MARCH 1975

RICHMOND, Ohio—And so Chuck Wepner remains the heavyweight champion of Bayonne, New Jersey. Do not treat that lightly, stranger. It is a title as old as time, as battered as Abel and as scarred as the cracked brown leather on a withered old catcher's mitt.

The other title, the big one . . . the one with all the money and the one that requires all the skills . . . still belongs to Muhammad Ali. He put it back in the safe at 2:41 of the fifteenth round as referee Tony Perez stopped it with Wepner staggering rudderlessly, blood pouring from cuts above both eyes, legs jellied, eyes cloudy, but courage laid naked to the world never to be questioned by generations as yet unborn in the folklore of Bayonne, New Jersey.

Muhammad Ali had it virtually all his way on the scoreboard. And the truth is even though he was the victim of a ninth-round knockdown that would have done credit to the Bolshoi Ballet (a right to the short ribs by Wepner as Chuck trod tenderly on Muhammad's foot at the same time), there was never any real thought that Ali could lose this thing.

But then that truly was not the issue. The thing itself was a three-act play. Act 1 featured Muhammad in a kind of Dance of the Sugar Plum Fairies, baiting his opponent, fighting almost casually but conquering referee Tony Perez almost immediately in Act 2.

That came when they battled and wrestled and tugged on the ropes. Wepner bashed Ali behind the head and Ali retaliated nicely with three forearms to the Adam's apple. In the corner it caused trainer Angelo Dundee to remark with great candor, "Forget the rabbit punches. You don't need it against this guy. Come on, be the champion."

He was every bit of that. He was the champion of the world

in general, Wepner in particular and Perez for good measure. He had put up a leg on that last title during the second Frazier fight and last night Perez without question was intimidated on several occasions . . . shouting, "Come on, Chuck, break," as Muhammad was doing the breaking on Wepner's neck. Late warnings to Ali still did not tie that score.

And Act 3—well, Act 3 was something else. Wepner was bloody from the eighth round on, but long before that it became obvious that Muhammad could nail him with a left hook any time he chose and as often as he chose. In truth the jabs were not the machine-gun tattoos they used to be but they were sufficient.

It was the right hand that was silent most of the night and in the corner between rounds Ali indicated that it was hurting him. There is doubt that it was injured but there is no doubt that he thought it was. From this last, both the length of the fight and its conduct begin to make more sense.

But in its way this was really Chuck Wepner's night. It began in the long, narrow dressing room beneath the stands here at the Coliseum. Tucked heavily into the folds of his red, white, and blue bathrobe, he sat on the rubbing table while the pathetic figure of Jerry Quarry staggered across the television screen.

Ron Delaney, the ex-fighter who is the chairman of the Richfield (Ohio) Boxing Commission, a body somewhat inanimate and just seven days old and that includes two plumbers and a hairdresser among its members, leaned against the wall.

They were waiting for Angelo Dundee to witness the bandaging of Wepner's hands. Dundee walked through the door wearing a red cardigan with MUHAMMAD ALI in block letters across its back and then Chuck said, "Don't touch the set." He came forward and sat silently peering at the screen while Braverman began to wrap the gauze. He put on two rolls and then he started into the taping.

"One roll of tape," Angelo said.

"No, two," Braverman said. "What the hell's the difference? You can do the same with your guy."

"What, do you make up your own rules? I hate this crap . . . don't give us any crap."

"All right, be picky," Braverman said.

Delaney said nothing.

And on the screen Jerry Quarry was being bombed out by Kenny Norton, losing yet another major fight in an endless soap-opera kind of career. "Hey, Angelo," Wepner said to the enemy trainer, "you ever work with Quarry?"

"No," Angelo said, "only against."

Wepner nodded. And then Angelo left and moments later Chuck Wepner took his concrete chin and his wall-to-wall heart down the runway and into the arena. He looked pasty in the harsh house lights. He did not draw a great deal of applause. An organist tried to play the Richfield, Ohio, version of the "Marines' Hymn," and it came out sounding like "An Ode to a Herniated Bellows."

And so it began as it was expected to begin, even as Ali himself had indicated it would at breakfast yesterday morning. It was a game of sorts and Ali had come to play it and he did more playing than fighting at the outset.

But something happened. It was something that could not possibly change the preordained fate that Wepner would not win . . . that, in fact, Wepner would come crashing down at the finish . . . that more than his eyes would betray him on this night. In truth everything—or the lack of it—would betray him . . . everything but his heart.

But the something that happened was this. In Round five—as he had earlier—Ali talked to Chuck. He hollered, "Keep pitchin', sucker," he leaned over his shoulder and hollered to his corner, "I'll let the sucker punch himself out" . . . he, in fact, made Wepner look something of the buffoon.

And as the bell rang, Chuck Wepner turned and shot Muhammad Ali a look that was for the moment heated fury and transient hate. He knew he would not win. He knew he could look bad. But he did not come here to play the fool.

And it was then that the heavyweight championship of Bayonne, New Jersey, took on a bright, shiny meaning. He is awkward and he doesn't punch very well but he had a pride that said, "I will chase you and the punches I throw will come up short and you will bloody my face but don't mess around with my dignity."

He goes home with honor.

IN SEARCH
OF A FATHER

DECEMBER 30, 1980

He was a sixth-grader in a little town called Warner Robins, Georgia, and each day when school let out he could see the front door of his house half a block away from the schoolyard. On this particular afternoon, there was this big truck parked in the front yard and Ron Simmons hollered over his shoulder at the half-dozen brothers and sisters trailing behind, "Come on, y'all, we're gettin' somethin' new."

And they all began to run. Maybe fifty feet from the house, he noticed that the men weren't taking anything inside. They were bringing the furniture out . . . the beds . . . the sofas . . . the tables . . . the dressers. As the Simmons kids stood there silently, afraid to ask, and the men worked silently, embarrassed to talk, Ron Simmons's father pulled up in his 1965 Pontiac.

"What are they doing, Daddy?" Ron Simmons asked. "Where are they takin' my bed?"

The elder Simmons stood there for a moment watching his life file by from the house to the truck. His wife had died two years earlier. Then he took one long look at his seven kids and slowly walked away. He stepped back into the car and drove out of his children's lives forever.

On Thursday night, Ron Simmons and his Florida State teammates meet Oklahoma in the Orange Bowl, and, if Notre Dame beats top-rated and unbeaten Georgia in the Sugar Bowl, it is possible the national championship will go to the second-ranked Seminoles. There will be football and fireworks and marching bands. More than 70,000 people will be there. Ron Simmons hopes desperately that his father will be one.

"I don't even know if he's dead or alive," the huge senior nose guard will tell you. "He just got fed up. He lost his wife and his belongings and, I guess, he just couldn't take it any more. So he left. But if he is alive, then in my heart I'm pretty sure he's aware of what I'm doing."

What Ron Simmons is doing, of course, is playing some spectacular defensive football despite an ankle that says with every drop of fluid and with every jolt of pain that he ought not be playing at Florida State at all.

His ankle is not the only thing that says it. You could suggest that his track record wasn't particularly noteworthy and in his favor. When his father left, Ron Simmons and his older brother moved in with an uncle in Warner Robins. The other five Simmons kids went on to Detroit to be raised by an aunt.

Enter Bill Franklin into the life of Ron Simmons.

Bill Franklin never went to Florida State. He played his college football at a place called South Georgia Junior College. The coach there was a man named Bobby Bowden, who, of course, subsequently moved on to FSU. Franklin owned a battery shop in Warner Robins and Ron Simmons went to work for him. While Simmons was working, he was growing and growing. Franklin, a football fan, permitted the kid to fit high-school football into his work schedule. By the time graduation rolled around, more than a hundred colleges wanted Ron Simmons. They were not attracted by the thought that he might one day discover a cure for the common cold, and Ron Simmons knew it.

With no parents to guide him . . . with the slickest of the slick college recruiters promising a golden world . . . with an inherent sense of self-preservation that told him he needed someone . . . Ron Simmons turned to Bill Franklin.

"He was like a father to me," Simmons will tell you. "He had lived through everything I had lived through—no mother, no father. He had gone to school on a football scholarship and he had to work for everything he ever got. He corrected me. He gave me guidance. He was the reason I chose Florida State and Coach Bowden."

For three seasons, Ron Simmons was damned close to being the best head-to-head defensive player in the country. Now it was the autumn of 1980 and a year of popcorn, tinsel, and toy balloons almost turned to ashes the first crack out of the box. In the first quarter of football in this season's opener at LSU, Simmons stopped to change direction. His body kept going but his cleats locked. The diagnosis was a severe ankle sprain. It has been with him ever since. He missed two games. Nothing has helped . . . hot packs or cold packs . . . medicine or plastic supports. The theory is that the only thing that can help is time.

For a time—until he said the hell with it and played without thinking about it—he became, in the words of an anonymous Florida State assistant coach, "just another lineman." In every game, they have gone for his lower legs and he feels it is deliberate but he will tell you, "There's just nothing you can do but live with it."

On Thursday night, he must be at his best or the Seminoles will have no chance against Oklahoma. He knows that, too. Ahead is the big pro contract. Ahead is the hope that one day he can reunite all his sisters and brothers.

And ahead is that big Orange Bowl stadium filled with people and that repeated ritual of despair when, for a brief instant, he will look at that mass of humanity, searching vainly for a single face that he barely remembers.

THE SCOUT

JUNE 1988

Judging from the very beginning, if a little help from "above" is necessary for a big-league scout to find his ultimate prospect, then Ralph DiLullo, the seventy-four-year old supervisor of the New York—New Jersey major-league scouting pool, may be a divine cinch to sign his future Hall of Famer.

A little history about the start of his lifelong love affair with baseball is in order here. Times were tough sixty-eight years ago in the little mountain village of Caprocatta between Rome and Naples. When Ralph was six, DiLullo's father died. Later that year, when a letter from an old friend in America proposing marriage arrived for his mother, she took what little she had and they sailed away to Ellis Island.

So this is how Ralph DiLullo first came to a life in baseball, which took him to dozens of minor-league parks as a player and manager and which moves across a landscape of postage-stamp-sized fields on which he sees 500 games each year between February and October—not with a Little League uniform and not with a set of major-league bubble gum cards but through an event that arguably may have been triggered by the ultimate in guidance counselors.

The family settled next to St. Anthony's Church in Paterson, New Jersey. One day when he was seven and still struggling to learn English, the parish priest called to him, "Hey, I am going to make you an American. Take this bat and see if you can hit this ball." On the third try, DiLullo made contact. The ball sailed out of his yard and through the window of the nunnery next door.

The crash of glass was still echoing when the mother superior came racing down the steps. "Grab that boy, Father. He just broke our window."

"What's she saying?" DiLullo asked.

"What she's saying," the priest said, translating into Italian, "means you better start running."

He took off with the bat in his hand and has been running

to and from baseball games ever since. Starting as a sixteen-year-old catcher playing sandlot ball against thirty-five-year-old men, then as a minor-league player and manager, and now as a kind of dean of surviving scouts, he has seen just about everything you can see in a baseball park.

Sunday, after an unusually heavy schedule had taken him to four different games the day before, he was in Plainfield to watch a pair of semi-pro teams comprised of college kids play a doubleheader.

"I don't care who you are and it doesn't matter that the entire concept of scouting has changed now that each club can also draw upon pool reports. One thing never changes. Whether you're as old as I am or whether you are scouting your first game, the dream is the same.

"Some day, somewhere, you want to be able to say that you signed a future Hall of Famer."

So he squints out at the sun-drenched infield where there are no Hall of Famers-in-waiting and he makes his mental notes. The catcher from Duke is wearing glasses when he bats. He didn't last year. The outfielder from Rutgers, who tore up his knee playing football last fall, is running as well as he ever did. The kid at third from New York Tech used to be a shortstop.

"The switch could help," he notes. "It requires less range in the field and more power at bat."

He has had more than his share of signees, an impressive number of whom made it to the big leagues. Along the way he lost a few, too. He talks about both ends of that spectrum and the way it was when (before pool scouting) the job was fiercely competitive.

"I was out in a little town called Mount Joy, Pennsylvania, and they had this tournament there. This pitcher had an average fastball, a pretty good curve, and he managed to keep it around the plate. But nobody paid much attention to him. There were too many others that day with big reputations.

"Afterward, I went over to introduce myself and we shook hands. What got me was the fingers. I felt his grip and I looked at the size of his fingers and I thought coaching can make this kid some kind of pitcher. I signed him that day for $500. His name was Bruce Sutter."

"All he did was win the Cy Young Award. You didn't sign him," a guy suggested. "You stole him."

"Well, it cuts both ways. Let me tell you one with a different ending."

"I could have had my Hall of Famer a long time ago. There was this lifeguard on summer vacation from the University of Cincinnati and I saw him pitch out in Queens one Sunday morning. Al Campanis was there for the Dodgers. I was with the Cubs then and I called Chicago that afternoon and told them he was the best I had ever seen. But the Cubs' roster was filled and they wouldn't listen. The Dodgers cut a player to make room. That's how I lost Sandy Koufax."

There are two things that keep DiLullo in this business where the travel grinds down men two decades younger. One is the quest for that rare player and the other is the game itself, whose shared beauty can sometimes command a higher loyalty.

Once when he was managing Albany, Georgia, the manager of the Thomasville club asked him if he could help with a future big-league catcher named Hal Smith, who was having throwing problems. DiLullo spent the next morning with him. That night, he threw out one of DiLullo's base runners.

"I'd do it again. The kid got to the bigs, didn't he? It wasn't about money or franchises," the scout recalled. "It was about baseball."

Death Be Not Proud

DEATH BE NOT PROUD

DECEMBER 15, 1977

Once, in another world during the heat of an Israeli summer, he looked down at his students in the Wingate Institute and thought to himself that this was not exactly the way a college classroom was supposed to be. The faces were wrong . . . they were young and they were eager but they were marked as perhaps no other student body in the world. Innocence belonged to somebody else's children.

This was the generation that grew to manhood and womanhood before its time . . . soldiers in a war with no boundaries and no rules and, like most wars, with no real explanation. They were the students that childhood forgot.

The lecture on sports medicine continued and then Jimmy Bryan, the teacher, a man who had come from the United States to share knowledge with a student body that never could seem to get enough of it, thought about the cool of the school cafeteria, his wife, Mickey, who would be there, and his friend Moshe, the wrestling coach, who would always seem to find a way to help a visiting Christian make an end run around the school's dietary laws.

But that was in another world.

Moshe Weinberg is dead these five years now. So, perhaps, are some of the students in that classroom. Dr. James Bryan continues to teach. Now the classroom is in Petersburg, Virginia, at a school called Virginia State where the students have that same eagerness but where innocence still lives.

Moshe Weinberg was one of eleven Israeli Olympic coaches, athletes, and officials who died in the hell of the Munich Olympics of 1972. Jimmy Bryan, who is not an Israeli . . . who is, in fact, a black American . . . barely missed dying along with him. On Sunday, the American Friends of the Hebrew University will hold their second annual scholarship dinner in honor of the Munich Eleven.

Yesterday, therefore, was a time for Jimmy Bryan to remember.

36

Long before he earned his Ph.D., Jimmy Bryan was a trainer of athletes . . . the girls who came out of Tennessee State, ran like ebony-tinted Greek goddesses, and called themselves the Tiger-belles . . . in New York at Columbia University . . . with amateur athletes of all shapes and sizes and of both major American skin pigmentations.

If the Israelis wanted to learn, then Jimmy Bryan was going to see that they had a chance, which is how he wound up on the faculty at Wingate that summer of 1971. His next-door neighbor was Moshe Weinberg.

They were an odd couple, these two . . . the muscular, dark Jew who spoke constantly of next year's Olympics and the green kids he would take there and the hope that one of them might show something right from the start . . . and the black man from across the ocean who spoke no Hebrew and who saw life with more balance and who felt something stir each time he thought of those same green kids and the beauty of Olympic competition that awaited them.

In the airless summer nights they would sit together in an outdoor cafe called The Nathayna and drink beer and argue training methods. Sometimes, on weekends, Jimmy Bryan would leave Mickey back at the apartment and the two of them would go down to Tel Aviv to the cafes of Dizengoff Street, where a man could get a stimulating argument going on everything from wrestling to cross-pollination.

When the semester ended, they gave Jimmy Bryan an honorary degree and he promised he'd see them again at Munich, where he had already signed on to help train the West Germans but where there would always be time to help old friends and to share a beer or two.

And so they met again. Jimmy Bryan took his magic hands and his miles of tape over to the Israelis. "You know," he remembers, "I'd tape an ankle or two or give a weight lifter a massage or slap on a Band-Aid here and there."

The Israelis—except for a sprinter named Esther Shacha-morov—fell early victims to their inexperience. The West Germans no longer needed Bryan at that stage. He began to think of going home.

In the bar at the Bayerischer-Hof Hotel he and Moshe sat down to a night when the beers were short and the conversation was long. "We just need to get more experience," Moshe told him. "But we'll be back."

They saw each other just once more. In the Olympic Village two days before the massacre began, Jimmy Bryan told Moshe that he was thinking of going home. Moshe encouraged him. "Shalom," Moshe said as they embraced. "See you at the Maccabiah Games next year."

Two days later, Jimmy Bryan was home in bed. Mickey was in the kitchen making coffee and the clock radio was reaching out and pulling him from his half-sleep at 6:30 with the words: "One of the dead Israelis has been positively identified as Moshe Weinberg, the wrestling coach."

And then Jimmy Bryan remembers that for one of the few times in his life he screamed. Mickey came running into the bedroom and she heard him say again and again, "Mune is dead . . . Mune is dead." And hearing the pet name that only she and Jimmy and Moshe used among them, she began to weep uncontrollably.

"He was supposed to see his mother after the Games," Jimmy Bryan said yesterday. "She was living in Munich but he hadn't had time to get around to visiting her. I think about him often. I think that, well, I could have been with them that night but I don't think about that part very often.

"This summer I ran into Esther Shachamorov in Europe. We talked about her new marriage and her running but neither of us mentioned Moshe."

In his mind's eye, Jimmy Bryan still sees his friend. Mostly he sees his strength . . . the sheer physical power of him and how he must have fought when he tried to hold the door against killers who never even knew the men they sought.

And then he sees the laughter . . . the beautiful laughter on those lunch hours at Wingate when Moshe winked and slipped Mickey into another part of the dining room so a girl could have a glass of milk with her meat since that was the way she was raised.

Sunday night they will speak of Moshe Weinberg again at dinner at the Waldorf and he will live in a different way through those speeches.

"He was my friend," Jimmy Bryan said.

He hesitated just enough that it seemed as though he yearned to substitute "is" for "was".

A DIFFERENT DRUMMER

MAY 1966

Each man, Henry Thoreau said, must march to his own tune no matter how distant the drummer. For Eddie Sachs, the drummer danced on coal black skid marks. He flitted from the treacherous dirt track at Langhorne to the fairgrounds in Trenton to the desperate brrumph . . . burrumph . . . burrumph of the Offys and the Lotus Fords, belching down the straightaway at Indianapolis.

The drummer was a crapshooter and a liar and a cheat. He said, "Next year . . . next year . . . next year," and Eddie Sachs heard him above the bands and above the crowds. He heard him above the clatter of wrenches along Gasoline Alley. He heard him above the little popping sound his jaw made in Trenton when they had pieced him together in a hospital bed last year and above the dull drone of antiseptic routines when he lay on his stomach in other hospitals' beds while they carved shreds of skin from his rump and used them to patch the other burns.

The drummer was a fraud but he played loudly and Eddie Sachs heard him in the hot Indianapolis sun last year as he sat on top of a golf cart with another guy and he said, "If I win it, I'll quit."

He had said it before. In Trenton four years ago he said, "If I win it, I'll quit. I'll never drive again. I'll even hire a chauffeur to drive me to work."

He had said it in bars and on telephones and in a plush motel in Indianapolis. He had said it the night of the funny money. They had held this big parade in Indianapolis, as they always do, and Eddie Sachs had said it was his birthday and it might have been but it really didn't matter because every day was a ball with Eddie Sachs. It is that way when the drummer is your roommate.

And so there had been this party. "I am going to win it," Eddie Sachs had said, "and then I am going to quit and we are all going to be millionaires." And then he had started throwing the funny money around. It was small and greenish and it had funny pictures on it and it was as phony as Eddie Sachs's distant drummer, and he had said, "You got kids? Give it to your kids. Happy birthday."

And he had gone out that year and he had not won the race but Eddie Sachs's drummer never stopped hammering away at him and still the refrain came echoing: "Next year . . . next year . . . next year."

Once he almost made it. Once he had licked the field and the odds and the drummer but he came up with a bum tire with two laps to go and he could see that big white line burning through the rubber, which means it is time to make a decision even the drummer cannot obscure. Eddie Sachs had chosen wisely. He had taken the pit stop and lost the big money but he was still alive.

And he figured to stay that way. He was a laugher. Some guys called him a big mouth but when Parnelli Jones had left a stream of slippery oil on the Indianapolis track last year, Eddie Sachs had had the guts to say what nobody else would tell Parnelli and Parnelli had flattened him with a punch.

"See if you can get me and Parnelli in a six-rounder at the Garden," Eddie Sachs had said while he was mending in a Trenton hospital last year. "If I'm gonna take a punch at least get me a price."

He was a laugher and a liver and when a guy had asked him if the plastic jobs on his rump bothered him, he had said, "I can't knock it because my face could use the skin. More people get to see my face. They've taken so much off my backside for patch-up jobs that I'm the only man in the world who disappears when he turns around."

He said a lot of things and then one day out at Indianapolis he said something else. He had sat on top of a golf cart loaded with tires with that baseball cap cocked on his head and his overalls more grease than material and he had swung his feet back and forth against the side of the truck while the hot Indiana sun blistered him and listened while a guy asked, "What makes it different from a road race, you know, from a Grand Prix or even from drag racing on a highway?"

"The escape route," Eddie Sachs had said. "When you get in trouble here, the only way out is over the wall."

And a year later there had been bands and crowds and noise. There had been a flaming car in front of him and there had been no way out and the drummer hammered one last measure. Then there was the explosion. Then there was the silence.

Why do they do it? Why does a man climb mountains or test airplanes or drive in the Indianapolis 500?

This is not a harangue for the abolishment of speedways or auto races or anything else. A man is grateful that the schedule falls the way it does. He is grateful that there is the fight coming up in Las Vegas and the U. S. Open in Washington and the schedule was so crowded that he could not get to Indianapolis. He is grateful that he was not there to see Eddie Sachs's drummer play the last measure.

They can run the Indianapolis race from now until infinity and it doesn't matter any more. The drummer is finished and you know that you are never going to go back there again.

The drummer was a crapshooter and a liar and a cheat. He killed a very good man.

OTHER VOICES

CHICAGO—The city is a bitter kaleidoscope of hectic days and violent nights and the raw truth of what is happening here is painfully obvious. The bitterness between the two principal candidates has degenerated into a city-wide trail of name-calling and ridicule. Subtlety is dead.

The cops are out to set a mid-America record for reporters beaten all the way into the emergency wards. The Yippies fling venom and rocks at anyone who stands in front of them.

A huge black woman from Alabama, with the face of eternal patience, stands in the Hilton lobby and sings of love and of Jesus. But the mob with its pins and straw hats sweeps past her and her sign, which says, "Hunger . . . the 51st State." It rushes toward a Hubert Humphrey discotheque called the Huberet.

There are Lord knows how many people doing their thing in the heart of Chicago's Loop. And then there are the other people . . . people like Ty Fain of McLean, Virginia, and Chuck Nau of Indiana and Mrs. Cordelia Sanchez of Albuquerque, New Mexico, and the people like them who have been drawn to this convention by the sound of another voice and the sadness of time remembered.

They are here and because of their presence so is Robert F. Kennedy. Make no mistake about that. Robert Kennedy's image hovers over this convention from the Sherman House, where twenty-one-year-old Chuck Nau sits on a bed in Mike DiSalle's suite and recalls the crowds and the laughter and the hot, gut-filling dust of an Indiana motorcade, all the way to McGovern headquarters at the Blackstone, where Ty Fain, who ran three state campaigns for Bobby Kennedy, continues to work with the remnants of the tough young deputies who expected to be doing a different job here this August . . . the Sorensens . . . the Salingers . . . the McGraths.

Chuck Nau is the vice president of the student body at Notre Dame. He stood next to Bobby Kennedy in the big student union building and introduced him, he rode in the motorcade that started on the campus and inched a dusty, slow route through the flat Indiana farmlands and down to Gary's blast furnaces.

Now he's one of the field leaders in the Draft Ted Kennedy movement. On Sunday night he walked into DiSalle's room and said he wanted to go to work. Yesterday he was waiting for a man "who will be here to sell us buttons at an outrageous price."

He is the kind of kid nobody ever seems to write about any more. "People forget how many of us there were," he said yesterday. "I miss Robert Kennedy. It was a personal thing and that's why I'm here now. Robert Kennedy is why I'm here. It's why Terry Curley is here and Chris McGrath and so many others. They're over at the Blackstone with McGovern but Bobby Kennedy brought them here."

Chris McGrath was an advance man for Bobby Kennedy. "In Indiana, he had on this expensive business suit and it was very hot and I remember it very well," Chuck Nau said. "Chris McGrath got the signs printed and then he went around with us and nailed them up. He set up the reception at the airport and he rode on the hood of Bobby's car and he was always throwing himself between Bobby and the people and then throwing himself back onto the grimy hood of the car. He went forty-eight straight hours. You don't forget people like that."

Over at the Blackstone, Ty Fain was talking to Mrs. Cordelia Sanchez. She is a schoolteacher and a housewife and her first contact with politics was when Bobby Kennedy came along. She chaired the New Mexico Citizens for Kennedy. She is here as a delegate. She is trying to help McGovern but it was Bobby Kennedy who really brought her here halfway across the country.

Ty Fain used to work in the American Embassy in Mexico. He met Bobby Kennedy at the unveiling of the JFK housing project in Mexico City less than a year after John Kennedy's assassination. And when Bobby Kennedy declared for the presidency, Ty Fain quit a good job in the Inter-American Bank in Washington to work for him as an organizer in the Southwest.

"He put people into politics who never dreamed they'd be there. The reason I went was that Bobby Kennedy made me feel that I was a middle-class dropout with my house in the lily-white suburbs and my, I don't know, I guess you could call it noninvolvement.

"They sent me to Texas and because I speak Spanish they also gave me New Mexico and Arizona.

"All they gave me was Ralph Yarborough's telephone number and a ticket to Austin. That's the way Bobby Kennedy was. He set such standards of excellence that people automatically assumed anyone around him had to be an expert. So you became one . . . you made yourself one . . . because you were pledged to who he was and where he was going."

"We had this storefront headquarters in Albuquerque and there were 300 people there and we heard his victory statement from California. Then I got in my car to drive back to the hotel. I heard it on the car radio. I bought a ticket to Washington. I had to change at Dallas. When I got to Dallas all I could think of was the hospital in Los Angeles so I cashed in my ticket and flew to L.A.

"I was out there when he died. I just hung around the hospital. There were a lot of people like me. Somewhere all of us had made a commitment. Two days before the convention I told my wife, Janet, that I thought we should go. Bobby Kennedy is why I'm here."

In the lobby of the Hilton, José Torres, who was once the world's light-heavyweight boxing champion, leaned against the wall and watched the hollering and shouting and said, "I walk all over the Loop today and I think if only he were here the Latins would have someone. Bobby Kennedy was not afraid of poor people. He was not afraid to put out his arms and touch you. I really think he was the only rich man who knew how it really is in this country with Puerto Ricans or with black men."

They are a strange, leaderless army. Perhaps they are waiting for something rare and wonderful when the roll is called. Perhaps they are here because for them there is nowhere else to go. As Chuck Nau said, "People forget how many of us there were."

FAREWELL, RED SMITH

JANUARY 16, 1982

He was writing about Willie Pep, a featherweight boxer who served as living proof that no matter what the self-styled beautiful people and critics say, you do not need a paintbrush or a palette knife or a typewriter to qualify as an artist. He was writing about Pep grown older and wiser and, yes, in some ways better, and to make the point he needed a word or two.

Most of us couldn't even have begun to do it with a paragraph. But because he was Red Smith, two words were really all he needed. So he reached back into that private land of imagery, which was so basic and yet so beautiful that the self-styled "tell-it-like-it-is-real" reporters couldn't have understood it without a course in English-as-a-second-language.

The words he chose said it all. The words he chose were "autumn wine."

Of course, they described what Pep had become in the twilight of a brilliant career. But, Lord knows, they were so much more applicable to the writer than the subject. Long before the day I first met him, he had already become that magic blend of maturity and unique sensitivity, what the rest of us in this business only dare pose at being on rare occasions.

Red Smith is gone . . . the phone call late yesterday afternoon said so . . . so do the obituaries today . . . so do the spoken electronic words of those who never knew him. And, of course, there will be more than a few printed words written by the same people who in their self-proclaimed wisdom never missed a chance to whisper among their smug coterie that Red's time was long past.

The last group doesn't count. They never had to sit at ringside and make a slice of history come to life while bottles flew at them from the balcony . . . they never had to look into the eyes of a bloodied linebacker in a losing locker room and form the questions that hurt sensitive people as much to ask as they did the guy who struggled to answer. They never tried to write with the wind in their teeth or the rain sweeping in across their copy paper—in the days before all press boxes were enclosed and electronic wonder-machines took the place of typewriters.

Their triumphs were all linked from newspaper office to press box by telephone. Their wisdom was the wisdom that they knew to be true by virtue of their lofty office and the television set at their white-shirted elbow. Their truth was the truth that enabled them—and them alone—to understand that a columnist is a drone and a drone cannot possibly understand the nuances of an Olympic boycott measured against the battle of Afghanistan.

It was their truth, for example, which killed a column in which Red expressed his views about the boycott and Afghanistan. Their truth is measured in titles. What they lost is hardly worth mentioning. You cannot identify what has no meaning in the first place.

If the loss had meaning to them, Red Smith would have won his Pulitzer long before he got into their little club, which controls such things. As it was, the award didn't thrill some of them.

But the rest of us . . . who learned under him . . . who loved him . . . or who may never have written a word but learned the beauty of the language simply by reading him . . . he was ours . . . and we were his people.

The *Herald-Tribune* is long dead . . . but not the long nights at the saloon downstairs when he sat with Stanley Woodward and Jess Abramson and Harold Rosenthal and Tommy Holmes, and Tom O'Reilly, et al.

It was a strange sports staff. It was a sports staff comprised of people—right down to the lowest among us—who learned by walking the sidelines at football games and by collecting horse manure on the soles of their shoes along the backstretch.

In our era—but not just on our paper because Woodward never permitted us the stupidity of arrogance—there were four giants:

There was Frank Graham, Sr., who taught us all the beauty of pure dialogue purely reported . . . there was Jimmy Cannon, who made the mood part of the deed. There was Stanley Woodward, who gave integrity a meaning no other sports section could ever hope to match.

And then there was Red.

He paid his dues in St. Louis and Philly long before I ever

met him. We owe him the greatest debt of all. He earned for us the right to write sports without being afraid to use the English language.

He gave us dignity. It was up to us to take it. If we failed, the failing was ours and not his.

Of all the shared nights and places and events and saloons and plane rides, one instant will remain forever in the mind's eye about this man, who never threw his weight around and who never was too busy to help the least among us.

It was 1961 and we had returned to his hometown of Green Bay, Wisconsin, for a football game. Now it was late and the bar was closed and we headed for the elevator in the local hotel.

"Once upon a time," Red said, "I made some money one summer running this old thing." Then he pointed to the row of newly installed self-service buttons. "As you can see, I've been replaced in the interest of efficiency."

Later that week, the elevator stuck between floors.

Forevermore I will always believe there was a message in that.

He never said, "good night," as long as I knew him. Each time, his last words were simply, "God bless."

I know there's a message in that, too.

A BOY FULL OF HOPE

MARCH 1972

CAROLINA, Puerto Rico—Maria Isabel Caceres stands in the courtyard at Julio Vizcarrendo Coronado School. She has taught history there for thirty years. The world changes in Puerto Rico, too. Now the kids are different.

"I must be mother and father and priest and policeman to some of them," she says. But there is love in her eyes. Just twenty minutes earlier, a visitor had listened to her lecture on the history of the abolitionist movement in Puerto Rico. The lecture was in Spanish and the visitor's Spanish was twenty-four years removed from the classroom. But when Maria Isabel Caceres runs a class she runs a class, and even the visitor could hear enough to know that if these kids will remember one thing years from now, it is going to be Maria Isabel Caceres.

She is that kind of teacher.

Now she is standing in the sunlight and the kids are moving all around her. She is wearing a black dress with white trim for the visit and a kid who has to be no more than fifteen walks by and winks at her and says, "Ay, que linda."

And then everyone laughs.

Roberto Clemente was thirty-eight years old when he died but the last time she saw him, which was back in early December, he still called her "teacher."

There are people in this world who move mountains and they are the ones you hear about. There are people in this world who shape young minds. And they are the ones you never hear about. Maria Isabel Caceres, teaching virtually all of her adult life in Carolina, Puerto Rico, has been an anonymous shaper of minds.

There are perhaps 125,000 people in Carolina today. The high school now services 2,400 kids. But when Roberto Clemente was growing to young manhood in Carolina, the population was 25,000 and the school was one small building and nobody ever knew him any better than Maria Isabel Caceres.

"He was so shy," she said. "I remember the very first day he came to my class. I had known his father because my father had a grocery store in Carolina and Roberto's father used to come there.

"He walked into the room and he took the very last seat he could find. He was a boy with a fierce pride and a fierce ambition. He wanted to be an engineer. He would sit there and he would never speak unless I called on him. He would look down at the floor, but when he would smile he would light up the whole room.

"I taught all three Clemente boys. I taught Vera, who would become his wife. I even recall that I was there the day he met her . . . but I think," she said with a wise, joyous smile, thinking of a time when Puerto Rico was still the land of the chaperon, "I think he knew her before that.

"We were in the pharmacy and she came in and he saw me and he asked me if I knew her and I said, 'Roberto, you watch it. That girl is in my class. She is my pupil. You watch it.'

"They were married here in Carolina. She is a beautiful woman but then Roberto was a beautiful man. You know, he was like a son to me."

It was Maria Isabel Caceres to whom Roberto turned when Pedron Zarrilla offered a contract with the Santurce team and he had to choose between professional baseball and the hope of an engineering career. It was Maria Isabel Caceres to whom Roberto turned when he had spent that first long year with the Pirates . . . homesick . . . afraid . . . and lonely.

"Teacher," he told her on the day he returned from his full season in 1955, "play some music on the phonograph for me. Play the music of home. I missed it."

"I would tease him about his English in the beginning," she said. "I wanted him to study more and feel more comfortable with the language. And he did."

Each year, he would come back to the school to speak. Each year, he would talk with her about his dream of a boys' village and his own hopes for his family and himself. She knew his pride. She knew his fears.

And once when her back was troubling her, Roberto came to visit.

"Where is the teacher?" he asked her stepdaughter.

"Her back hurts. She is in the bed."

"Teacher," Roberto shouted, "you get dressed. We are going to the doctor."

"He came every day for fifteen days," she recalled. "He had to carry me in his arms like a baby to the car. He took me for the treatments. And when they ended and I tried to pay the doctor, the doctor told me I could not because Roberto had taken care of everything."

Later that afternoon, we drove through the crowded narrow streets of Carolina.

"Do you wish to see the town cemetery?" she asked.

We were passed through the gates by the attendant, who had been dozing in the sun with a transistor radio ablare at his side.

We walked down the narrow road to the rear of the cemetery. There was a great silence. People die in Carolina as they live. Space is a luxury. Amid a crowd of stone crosses, the crypt sits empty. He had purchased it just two months before the mercy flight.

"It was ironic," Maria Isabel Caceres said. "His father, you know, has been quite ill. I think Roberto had that in mind at the time."

She is a strong woman on an island of strong women. She is the face and heart of all the pride and all the good that all of us seek among our teachers.

"I will remember him," she said as we walked back to the car, "as a little boy . . . with hunger and ambition. He is, for our people, a great symbol because of what he accomplished. I know what they say about him as a baseball player.

"But I will remember him as a little boy . . . a boy so full of hope."

THE MAN THEY CALLED COACH

MARCH 29, 1985

LEXINGTON—From the moment the wish became the deed out in Denver last Sunday, they have been asking him about Patrick Ewing and the Georgetown press and the Big East with an intensity that would lead you to believe that he wasn't Lou Carnesecca about to coach a basketball game, but Patton, poised to cross the Rhine.

But the truth is that he has only now begun to think about the task at hand. During the first half of this week, his mind was much on the man who never took a team to the Final Four, who is not here now but who shaped the coach in such a way that nothing can sever the bond that links them.

Joe Lapchick has been gone almost fifteen years. Every coach has a coach and every student has a teacher and forever in Lou Carnesecca's mind Joe Lapchick will remain both.

Theirs is a bond forged on transient winter nights in places like Milwaukee and Chicago and Buffalo, when the wind hurled itself against the ancient faces of carbon-copy hotels and the sound of the overworked radiators served as background to the teacher's voice.

Lou Carnesecca can tell you what those nights meant to him. He remembers the way Lapchick would shamble across the room to the cumbersome window, raise it just enough to slip a hand out into the cold and pull in one of the cans from the six-pack he had stowed on the sill that afternoon.

"He would talk," Carnesecca said, "and I would listen. Sure, he taught me basketball. He was a great player with the early pros and he was a great coach. But he taught me a lot more than that and I will never forget him. Last week in Denver with five seconds left I looked up at the clock and I thought, 'Well, it's happened. We're really going.' And a part of me was thinking about Coach, who never got there, and it was thinking that everything he gave me was going right along with us."

They were an odd couple—the tall old man from Yonkers, who had dropped out of high school at fifteen to follow a dream and a bouncing ball, and the onetime gym rat, who never played college basketball but who became the hand-picked successor of the man he loved so much.

Lapchick would laugh about the way he had first come to St. John's after a career of what he referred to as tin-canning, which got its name from the battered old cars that he and his people rode as they fulfilled contracts with as many as three pro teams in three different leagues in a single week. He would tell you how he didn't know how to coach because the Original Celtics, with whom he had become a name for the making of legends, never had a coach.

He would tell you how he didn't know to set up a pregame drill because the Celtics never had one. He would tell you he was awed and a little tongue-tied the day he first met "my college men" because he was from the streets and the best lessons he learned in life had been taught to him by the Old Celts on long, lonely highways, in packed gyms and taprooms.

And whatever he learned in the years that followed, he ultimately passed on to Carnesecca. "As sentimental as he was, he was a realist. He used to say that the inevitable end of coaching was failure," Carnesecca recalled. "It took me a long time to understand that but I do now.

"We are playing in the biggest tournament of all this weekend but five years from now most of the players' names will be forgotten. You can win and you can lose and as close as you can come to success is not about that as much as it is about how you handle it. He taught me to be myself and enjoy it. He saw the way the demands were changing this game and the men who coach it and he told me that the longer you coach, the worse it can get—and it does. It gets to mean so much.

"He went through all that coaching is. He had great teams and great players and wherever he went people knew it. I remember one year when I was his assistant we played a tournament game against Duke and 9,000 people stood up and cheered him. If he were here now, I know he'd smile and he'd say, 'Well, coach, now you are going to walk with kings. Let's see how you handle it.'

"I guess you might say, I'm not alone here."

They were that close. Lapchick breathed a lot of maturity into the "student" who came to him as an assistant after a brilliant career coaching in New York's competitive Catholic high-school league. "He gave me a chance to learn. A lot of head coaches are afraid to do that. He let me organize practices. He let me analyze scouting reports. One night when we were down by sixteen at halftime against Michigan and Cazzie Russell, I asked if we could press full court. We did and we won but we didn't win because of the trap. We won because he was willing to listen to an idea that wasn't his. Try that with some other head coaches."

There is, of course, so much of Lapchick in Lou Carnesecca. The difference is more in style than content. "Hey, he was Polish. I'm Italian. I'm naturally more emotional," said Carnesecca. "But maybe the biggest lesson of all is the way he handled the time my mother used to call, 'il solo tramonto.' It means the sun sets. But she used to use it about that time in life when you look back and try to see yourself as you were and as you are, because by that time the sunset takes on another meaning for you."

Nobody is quite sure when Joe Lapchick had the first heart attack. He once told a man he thought it happened just before halftime on a night when St. John's was beating NYU. Lou Carnesecca recalls a bitter cold morning in Madison, Wisconsin, when they were on their way to Mass and suddenly Lapchick grabbed his chest and bolted out of the wind and into an open doorway, and again in the dressing room down in Miami, and each time Lapchick told him it was nothing much. But that figured. Later, when it became fact, he told a man, "You have to beat the fear. The fear will kill you. You have to stay on your own route. Me? I've got my pills. I gotta have the wind in my face, a golf club in one hand, and a stinger in the other."

"He was a coach and a teacher and a friend," Carnesecca said. "I wish he were here."

REST IN PEACE, ROGER

DECEMBER 19, 1985

Near the end, when the battle none of us win forced him to the wall, Roger Maris did the kind of thing people who really knew him would have expected. He went to the medical research center in Franklin, Tennessee, where they planned to take some of the cancerous nodes from his body in the hope of developing some kind of antibody to slow the obscene course of the disease.

They told him the process would take four to six weeks. Roger didn't have that kind of time and both he and the doctors knew it.

"If I'm gone before then," he asked one of them, "what happens?"

"Well," the doctor replied almost cautiously, "we would use it to try to help someone else."

"Do it," he said.

Pat Maris told the story without emotion over the telephone yesterday. She is a strong woman—as tough as the North Dakota winters in which she and Roger grew up and as warm as the people of Fargo, who have opened their hearts to her since she brought Roger's body home to where it all began.

"He died the way he lived," she added, explaining his conversation with the doctor in Tennessee. "Strong, private, and doing what he thought was right. He was at peace with himself and his God."

They will bury Roger Maris in Fargo today. "There was never any question about this," Pat Maris said. "This is our home and these are our people. We moved away in 1957 but our hearts were always here."

Today, the sun is expected to shine and the temperature will creep up toward twenty after yesterday's below-zero windchill reading, almost as though the snow-covered frozen tundra of Holy Cross Cemetery, which will receive him, was trying to offer a modest gift of its own.

They will leave the red brick front of St. Mary's Cathedral, where Father Moore, who taught religion to both Roger and Pat Maris at Shanley High School, will be one of three priests assisting in the ceremony. As the procession creeps past the snowbanks that line this middle-class neighborhood, Shanley will be a block to its left.

"Everything centered around the high school and the church," Pat Maris said, summoning up a time when their world was young. "There were only 250 students. The Friday night dances were held in the gym or the cafeteria and you either went there or to the movies. He lived on the North Side and I lived on the South Side, so we didn't meet until high school."

She remembers the night of the senior prom.

"The boys wore suits—nobody in this town could afford to rent a tuxedo," she said. "Roger borrowed his dad's old beat-up car."

She remembers the way Roger Maris looked when he came up the steps with that same nervous half-smile that he would muster years later in the middle of the confusion and the pressure of so many locker rooms during "the year of the record." He was self-conscious in his suit and in his right hand he held a box containing the first corsage Pat Maris received.

Moments past Shanley, the funeral procession will swing by the new public high school. Once, the land on which it stands was called Barnett Field, and on frosty North Dakota nights more than thirty years ago, his name rose from the old wooden bleachers and carried out across the football field again and again.

Sid Cichy, who will be among the mourners, will think his own private thoughts in that moment. The year Roger and Pat came to Shanley as freshmen, he was hired to coach three sports and teach five subjects.

"The nuns were understanding," he said. "They always gave me Mondays off in hunting season."

Shanley played its games in the state's smallest division and Sid Cichy was waiting for Maris. As a college student at North

Dakota State, Cichy helped out in summer American Legion ball in Fargo. Even then he marveled at the gifted twelve-year-old kid with the blond crew cut.

"We didn't have a baseball team because of the weather, but he played football and basketball and ran track for me."

He remembers that Roger was a fair shooting guard in basketball but a ferocious catalyst on defense each time Shanley went to a full-court press. He will tell you Roger ran dashes and led off two relay teams, was his best long jumper, and could even pole-vault.

But what he really remembers is the kid in the red jersey with the white numerals and the white pants and the red-and-white helmet. "How could I forget him?" he will tell you. "He ran out of the single wing and nobody ever stopped him. On defense, he would come up from the secondary to cut down the ball carrier for no gain on one play and intercept a pass twenty-five yards downfield on the next. We'd run him in motion as a blocking back and then bring him back to crack block on the linebacker—it was legal back then—and if you ever saw him hit, you'd know how the block got its name."

In Shanley's state-championship year, Roger Maris ran sixty-five yards to score on a reverse against Valley City on the first play of a big game under the myopic lights of Barnett Field.

And then there was Devil's Lake. In 1951, Cichy took his kids from the tiny downstate parochial school up to Devil's Lake, North Dakota, just an hour's drive from the Canadian border. On a Tinkertoy field in the teeth of a wind that could only have been born somewhere north of Hudson Bay, Roger Maris caught four kickoffs and returned each of them for touchdowns.

"Most people don't know it, but that's still a national high-school record today," Cichy said. "Afterward, when we had won it big, their coach told me he was hoping they wouldn't score at the end because he was tired of watching Roger take the kickoffs in."

But the way Cichy talks, he will probably remember none of these things when they move past the site of old Barnett Field today.

"His honesty (which never left him in later years) was the thing," Cichy said. "One day we were running a ridiculous drill in practice. I was a young coach back then. The drill was dumb. We ran it too long. And then Roger said something about it.

Well, you don't want to hear that when you are a young, self-important coach. But he was right. I called it off."

Don Gooselaw, who will be among the mourners, will remember the way his father, the barber, cut their hair. Dick Savageau, who grew up with both of them, will remember Roger and Pat together the way they were. Ever since the funeral plans were announced in this town, businessmen and doctors alike have taken off work to pick up mourners at the airport and to help with arrangements.

Fargo has opened up its heart. Today it will weep. He is not a fallen celebrity. He is family.

FOR VINCE

SEPTEMBER 1970

They had begun to gather early and as the day warmed they filled the wide expanse of concrete opposite St. Patrick's Cathedral, spilling backward toward the huge statue of Atlas, which fronts Fifth Avenue. They stood in soft, quiet queues, their morning-long vigil relatively motionless because yesterday was Labor Day and there was no flow of pedestrians to compound the wait.

Inside the huge cathedral, His Eminence Terence Cardinal Cooke was quoting from Corinthians: " . . . but when this mortal body puts on immortality, then shall come to pass the word that is written: death is swallowed up in victory. Oh, Death, where is your victory? Where is your sting?"

On Thursday, Vincent Thomas Lombardi died at Georgetown University Hospital. Yesterday the city that had always been so much a part of his life said good-bye to him.

It was the city where he was born, and played both high-school and college football. It was the city to which he came with five of Red Blaik's Army teams as an assistant coach, and later ran the offense for the first New York Giants football team to win a world championship in eighteen years. It was the city to which the Giants tried to call him back just a year after he left for Green Bay and to which, had his own sense of honor been any the less, he would have returned.

But he was a man with an obsessive sense of obligation and he had given his word to the people out in Green Bay and so, in the end, it is the city where he never coached the team he most wanted to lead as head coach.

Yesterday, the ones who couldn't get inside, where the men who had played with him and for him and against him were saying good-bye, stood quietly in the warm sunshine against the wooden police barriers up and down Fifth Avenue and waited.

At roughly 12:30, some three and a half hours after the early arrivals had first taken up their vigil, the huge doors to the cathedral swung open and the men who had been so much a part of the sum total of Vincent Lombardi's life began to form a wide corridor from the top of the massive steps to the pearl-gray hearse at the curb below.

It had begun with the eight honorary pallbearers but they had been joined by others; together, these were the people whom Vince Lombardi was all about. Inside the cathedral there had been John Lindsay and Ethel Kennedy and Louis Lefkowitz and a lot of other front-page faces. They were mourners, too, but the silent lines of men who now waited as a final guard of honor were really Vince Lombardi's people.

They were his people even as the people against the wooden barriers across the street felt that this city was somehow always his. You could search the faces during the brief wait before the simple, highly polished casket left the cathedral and in each one there was a mirror to a piece of Vince Lombardi's life.

There was seventy-five-year-old George Halas, standing erect and squinting into the sunlight despite his tinted glasses. It was Halas who got the telephone call from Dominic Olejniczak in what surely must seem like another world. The Packers were disintegrating at the box office and hopeless on the field and they looked as though they might blow the franchise. And Olejniczak, who was and still is the club president, pleaded with Halas, "What can I do?"

"You can hire Vince Lombardi, that's what you can do," Halas told him, and he did.

That was eleven years ago and that very fall in his first game as a head coach anywhere Vince Lombardi, who was already forty-fix years old on the day of his debut, beat George Halas out of a football game. Halas had stomped into the Packer locker room afterward and had stared at him for an instant with those safecracker eyes of his and then he stuck his hand out and said, "You're going to be a great one but don't get careless. I still plan to beat hell out of you."

Across from Halas yesterday there was Colonel Earl Blaik, who stood tall and proud and whose thoughts surely were of an earlier time. It was Blaik who brought Lombardi out of the total anonymity of the freshman coaching job at Fordham and made him an assistant coach at West Point. It was Blaik who once lectured his assistant coach because he had flung his peaked cap in a burst of rage when somebody on the field had failed to do the job Vince knew he should have done. It was Blaik who first knew Vince Lombardi as a talent and as a very human man with a very human temper.

Down the line there was Willie Davis. The Cleveland Browns said Willie Davis never would be a football player. Lombardi said he would. And he was. And the two of them—each in his own way—grew to a kind of maturity together out in Green Bay. Across the way there was Paul Hornung and next to him stood Bart Starr.

Lombardi was, after all, a football man and a teacher. And it is perhaps Bart Starr who is proof that this man with the great driving force, who came to greatness at a time when most men stagnate in their careers, may be the finest football coach ever.

They said that Starr couldn't throw, and, indeed, it seemed he could not. They said he couldn't run a ballclub and handle complex defenses. The throwing came first. After Lombardi handled that, he worked day and night on the "audible" (the changing of a play at the line of scrimmage that is the difference between mediocre and great quarterbacks). Starr won a title for him but still he was not polished.

Then one day against the Cleveland Browns, at a time when he thought he had learned all he thought there was to learn, he looked across the scrimmage line and suddenly all the hours Lombardi had spent with him took on new meaning.

"Everything he had been trying to teach me," Starr once told a man, "suddenly it all seemed so easy. Suddenly, I knew I could do anything he told me I could do."

They stood there . . . Pete Rozelle and Art Rooney and Lamar Hunt and Edward Bennett Williams, who brought him down to Washington, and the others. These were the people to whom he had meant so much and their stories are his story as much as his story was theirs.

At 1:40, the casket was carried slowly down the stone steps and placed in the hearse. Then, one by one, the big, black limousines pulled into the curb and prepared to begin the long, slow journey through the Lincoln Tunnel, away from the city and down to Mount Olivet Cemetery in Middletown Township, New Jersey.

Across the street, they stood behind the wooden barriers until the very last car had left.

DEATH OF
THE BOMBER

APRIL 13, 1981

LAS VEGAS—They were crushing against each other in the narrow makeshift aisles of the Sports Arena at Caesar's Palace Saturday night—arguing over seats, spilling the beer from their paper cups, struggling to be seen rather than to see—when suddenly the ring announcer interrupted his endless drone with the only announcement capable of silencing a mob scene or a crap game: "Ladies and gentlemen, seated here at ringside—a resident of Las Vegas—the all-time greatest in the history of heavyweight boxing, the Brown Bomber—Joe Louis."

They were standing then, those who had come to see Larry Holmes successfully defend his heavyweight crown against Trevor Berbick, craning their necks to catch a glimpse of the sixty-six-year-old legend. What seemed like a thousand cameras began to click at once. The noise was deafening.

From his wheelchair, Louis raised his arms, his palms interlocked in the symbol of triumph in which they had been seen so many times. He was smiling.

Maybe it was the lighting. Maybe it was the moment. But the strain was gone from his face. People who saw him day after day in this town say he looked better than he had looked in months.

So we made a date for Sunday. Freddy Sommers, who first met Louis in 1932 when he was an amateur in Detroit, picked me up at 8:30.

As he nosed the white Buick out of the parking lot and into the traffic along the Vegas Strip, Sommers spoke about the way Louis was responding since they had put the pacemaker in him in Houston last December 23.

"I brought Irving Ungerman [a Toronto fight manager] out to see him on Friday and Joe loved it," said Sommers. "They kidded about the time Irving brought him up to Toronto to convince everyone that George Chuvalo [a courageous but lumbering heavyweight] could fight.

"Joe understood everything that was going on. Irving has a poultry slaughterhouse up in Canada and when I brought him into the house, Joe laughed and said, 'I know you. You the chicken man.'

"Believe me," Sommers said, "you'll be surprised at the way he reacts."

Then we had turned into Desert Inn Road. It was a picture-postcard day with the mountains catching the sunlight on the horizon. The conversation was interrupted by the scream of sirens on the soft morning air.

As Freddy pulled to the side of the road, an ambulance and a paramedic truck roared past. By the time we were moving again, both vehicles had vanished.

Seminole Drive is a well-manicured cul-de-sac just off Desert Inn Road. The Louis family lives at 3333, the third house on the right. It is a low-slung functional home with a small black wrought-iron fence fronting it. Immediately in back of it is a small set of swings and other children's playthings, a reminder of the four youngsters whom Joe and Martha adopted.

A kidney-shaped swimming pool is visible just beyond the glass doors leading from the family room to the side of the house.

Wayne Newton once lived here and after that Johnny Carson, from whom Joe and Martha bought the house.

As Freddy swung the car onto Seminole Drive, the sight of the two emergency vehicles, parked obliquely in front of the Louis home, the door of the paramedic truck still open, choked off all conversation.

"Oh, God," Freddy said. "Go look."

The door was open and Martha Louis stood there in that stunned kind of limbo that grabs all of us when we know a terrible thing is happening and we have expected it for so long that the shock does not quite sink in.

"It's Joe," she said. "He's not breathing. They're inside trying to work on him now."

So much of the dignity that Joe Louis was able to maintain for so long is directly traceable to Martha Louis. She is a lawyer who commutes several days a week to her Los Angeles office.

During the painful period when Joe Louis needed medical

and emotional help, she fought the battles to keep him from succeeding as his own worst enemy. She is a remarkable woman.

Now she was sitting down, a small blue telephone book in her lap, making the first painful telephone calls to people who were entitled to know.

Lillian Holmes, who works for the Louises, was trying to ride herd on three of the four children in one of the back rooms.

A nurse named Ruth was trying to find out what was going on with the medical team working over Louis. With them was a physical therapist named Noel Latimore from Desert Springs Hospital.

Almost every morning either Latimore or Keith Klevin, who is also Larry Holmes's physical therapist, got to the house early in the morning.

They helped prepare Louis for the day ahead and also worked with him on a variety of light exercises designed to keep his once-great body from atrophying.

Yesterday morning, Latimore had arrived around 8:40. Louis had wanted to arise earlier, but Martha and the nurse had convinced him to wait. He had wanted to eat breakfast before we arrived.

Latimore took Louis into the bathroom as he always did. He was going to assist him into the whirlpool that is part of the deep brown marble bathtub.

There was no warning sign. Louis simply keeled over.

"I was just sitting here thinking about going to church," Martha Louis said, facing the huge oil portrait of Louis, painted when he had won the world title in 1936, "when I heard Noel call for Ruth to get help."

It took the paramedics and the ambulance less than five minutes to get there, but during that time Latimore and the nurse kept up a frantic, nonstop ritual, administering CPR treatment to Louis.

"I don't know whether or not he ever actually regained consciousness," Latimore would say later in the emergency room.

As he spoke, he was clearly stunned by what he and everyone else knew to be inevitable but what none of them had ever really convinced themselves to expect.

John John, one of the Louis children, sat next to him on the hospital green couch. Latimore's arm was around him.

Earlier Martha Louis had sat in her living room, quietly making the necessary calls. "I better try to get Dr. Ericson down in

Houston," she had said. "They have a computer printout to see if the pacemaker is still all right."

"But he looked so well," Freddy Sommers said.

"Nobody plans these things, Freddy," Martha Louis replied. "You don't have any messages from God that one day you won't go into the bathroom and suddenly die. Oh, so many times he was . . . well, when it happens, you just can't believe that it really is happening."

Then the medical team had wheeled Louis out of the back of the house, moving swiftly to the ambulance.

Martha Louis waited then for another nurse named Jaye, who would go with her to the hospital.

She put her home in order, leaving instructions about the children with Lillian Holmes. Then she said good-bye and walked slowly to her brown Mercedes with Jaye, drove out onto Seminole Drive and off toward Desert Springs Hospital.

A few moments later, we were back in Freddy Sommers's car, preparing to take the same route. As Sommers began to back out, Lillian Holmes rushed to the doorway and began to scream, "Freddy . . . Freddy . . . he's gone . . . he's gone."

Martha Louis had telephoned her with the news.

Moments later, Latimore was sitting with John John in the emergency room and Martha Louis was talking softly to someone on the pay phone.

Somebody in the group said something about the press and the television people coming to the hospital and Martha Louis said, "I don't want to see anyone. And I don't want to fight with anyone because of that on this day. I'm going to do the things that have to be done now. There's no time for anything else. You do the things you have to do for people when they're alive. That's what's really important.

"I'm going home now," she said with great dignity.

THE COACH

NOVEMBER 1963

The projector whined softly in the darkened room and on the screen the Giants were futilely chasing the Bears. Then the telephone rang and a man on the other end said that Stanley Woodward was dead and for the rest of the morning, the figures were a hollow blur and a man thought about all the things he could have said and should have said to Stanley, who was up in Connecticut a million miles away from the world he made.

So this is for Stanley, who would be embarrassed by it and who would surely wonder why a man isn't out trying to learn how Al Dark got the Kansas City job or how much money passed under the table in the pro football war this week or any of a dozen things that are supposed to be important in the fun-and-games department.

These things are impossible today. The typewriter is a liar now because whatever it says this morning, it will not be nearly enough. Once, when he was the sports editor of this paper, he sat maybe ten feet from where this is being written. His knees were already riddled with osteomyelitis and the cane, leaning against the wall, was a bitter reminder of the strength he had left in so many places on so many nights . . . in Bleeck's, the house bar two doors down from the *Tribune,* where he was twice sports editor and where the dawn had a habit of creeping up as Stanley hand-wrestled all challengers against the polished bar . . . in Miami, where he hated the heat and he hated a great many of the frauds that are Miami and where he took the second newspaper in town and tried to get it to hold up its head.

So much effort . . . so much time. The calendar was a fraud and a joke . . . a watch was a thing you kept beside you at a football game to remind you what time the bulldog edition locked up and at night you put it away and forgot about it. There was always time . . . time to drink . . . time to argue . . . time to sit down at the typewriter and tell it the way it was in clear, concise English.

Now there isn't any more time. Now a man thinks back on

all the time that Stanley put into this thing. All the people newspapering today are there simply because he was there and because he cared enough about them to demand the most from them and to fight like hell with anybody who made things difficult for the men who worked for him.

He was, of course, hipped on football, which is how he came to be called "The Coach." At Amherst, where he was the only college tackle with Greek and Latin behind him, he played the game violently. As a child he had been blind for a brief period and his glasses looked like twin milk bottles and before each game he would put on an old baseball catcher's mask and wrap the spokes with electrician's tape.

"I found this," he was fond of saying, "most discouraging to belligerent opponents."

"A guy could break his knuckles on you . . . he could get hurt," an employee once said, referring to the Amherst days.

"Yes," Stanley said, "couldn't he?"

Stanley Woodward couldn't sit still. Long before the long days and the longer nights were to take their toll, he had been rejected for military service in World War I and he had gone out and joined the merchant marine.

Twenty-three years later he would try again in another war and now his eyesight would be even worse and age would say he couldn't possibly be a soldier even though he was the strongest man I have ever known, a man who once ripped a bar away from the wall on a bet and whom I have never known to be afraid. So he went off to join the 82nd Airborne as a correspondent in Europe and when the Germans quit, he came home and picked up his laundry and went out to carry his own private war to the Japanese.

He was on the bridge of the *Enterprise* with Captain Tom Hamilton, the football coach at Navy and Pitt, when the kamikazes came in low and hard, screaming their high-pitched death whine, and years later when he would speak about the war, it would be a very personal thing. The Germans kicked it in while Berlin danced red with flames and the Japanese bowed politely on the deck of the *Missouri* and said, "So sorry," but Stanley Woodward never signed the armistice.

He would talk about the horror very precisely and if you told him that Germany was a neat, clean country and the Japanese were very industrious, he would look at you and tell you in two or three well-chosen words what he thought about that. And when the brothers were up in arms about the split-T and the interminable time it takes to play a baseball game Stanley Woodward would wonder if we were going to give the new German army nuclear warheads to play with.

You can speak about the giants in this business and the myths that grow up around them. Well, the Coach was a giant and there are no myths here. From the time he kicked the hell out of railroad graft as a cub reporter up in Worcester to the time he called it quits under some duress at the *Tribune,* he was direct and honest and the best we will ever see at this sort of thing.

"A professional," Stanley would say, "is a highly skilled performer whether paid or unpaid. He is the only one who counts in this world. An amateur is just a clumsy slob."

Rufus Stanley Woodward was a pro. When all of this was behind him, he went up to Brookfield Center, Connecticut, which is just this side of Danbury, and he built himself a house in the woods. He lived out the string there with his wife, Ricey. Now there was one heart attack and then another and the doctor said no whiskey and the days went by and down in New York the people shoved and pushed and the subways rattled and the glasses tinkled at Bleeck's and Stanley was all alone a million miles away.

The last time I saw him, he walked through the little den with the model of the *Enterprise* on the mantelpiece and we looked at pictures of the six grandchildren and then we talked about the times he hired me—there were two—and the times he was furious with me and the times we sat together and every drink he took on those nights was a yes-I-can challenge.

He recalled the day in Miami when a poor put-upon member of the opposition press (Stanley's opposition was always put-upon) said, "Stanley, why do you pick on my friend and I?"

"Friend," Stanley had told him, "when I pick on you, it will be in the objective case."

Then we walked out into the woods and he walked very slowly, cursing the wooden cane with every step, and he sat down on a big rock and we watched a deer scamper away.

"It's lonely here," Stanley said. It was the closest he ever came to a complaint that day.

Now it is over. He died yesterday morning. He was never one for sentiment but I wish I could have told it better. It's not his fault. He was a very good teacher.

A VERY
SAD STORY

MARCH 15, 1980

The mind's eye is a camera, sifting and sorting and filtering out the ugly images and saving forevermore the memories that are greenest. So it is with the memory of Lem Steeples. The twisted remnants of the Polish airliner that crashed and burned and killed within sight of the runway at Warsaw Airport cannot be the way to remember him.

He was, after all, just twenty-three years old, and the things he had seen and survived and the thought of the glorious future that was hard work's reward make that obscene moment when twenty-two American amateur boxers and team officials died all the more tragic.

You can run down the names on the passenger list and shake your head and tell yourself nowhere is it written that life has to be fair, but the thought won't change a thing . . . names like Paul Palomino, whose older brother Carlos was king of the welterweights . . . and Johnny Radisson and Bernie Callaghan, who were making the trip to Poland so there would be American officials to share the scoring . . . and Steeples and all the others. Yesterday Bob Sirkin, the AAU boxing official who helped put this trip together, sat in his office out in Illinois and spoke about those four.

His voice cracked often and you could almost reach out through the telephone line and touch the tears. "Carlos called me and asked me to put his brother on the team and so I . . . I . . . and Radisson and Callaghan went because I asked them to go . . . and Steeples was so decent and fine . . . and the team doctor took his wife along and now they left children behind and I . . . I . . . I just feel . . . oh, God, what can you do?"

And of course there is nothing you can do except to try to remember the best of what you saw and skip over the rest and realize that people die every day and horrible accidents happen every day, but in the end, it will not make it any easier because this time the faces are real and the names are not simply words on a list.

But the mind's eye is indeed a camera and the best of its photos remain evergreen.

So a man thinks back to the broiling July heat of Puerto Rico and a little mountain town called Trujillo Alto and it is, in truth, the only way to remember Lem Steeples.

There was only one ticket booth and there was no air-conditioning and inside the Coliseo de Trujillo, the air hit your lungs with all the impact of a branding iron. There were 2,500 fight-night customers jammed against each other sardine-tight. This is where they staged twelve Pan-American Games semifinal bouts. This is how and where I will most remember Lem Steeples.

They matched him with a Cuban of frightening reputation in what the amateurs call the junior welterweight division. José Aguillar had the reputation of a bomb-thrower. Like Steeples, he was a southpaw. He was out of that cookie-cutter mold that seems to be the wellspring of all Cuban fighters with the exception of heavyweight Teofilo Stevenson.

They are stand-up fighters who move with the grace of a wrecking ball in search of an abandoned tenement. Each of them has more scar tissue than an amateur deserves, which indicates that while they are pitching, they are also catching. They are fighters whose winning and losing are centered around the big punch.

Lem Steeples was climbing through the ropes on the other side of the ring now, wearing a blue tank top with "usa" on it and blue-and-red trunks. He was smarter in the ring than a fighter with no professional experience has a right to be. He did not have any scar tissue. He may not have pitched as hard, but he sure as hell made it his business not to catch at all.

There was a strong mellowness to this young man. Like Leon Spinks, he was raised in that concrete coffin the people out in St. Louis used to call the Pruitt-Igoe housing project. It won the Jungle of the Century award, and when even the Feds decide a place is so bad that you had best dynamite it and start over somewhere else—which they did—you do not need to know anything else about the things Lem Steeples began to see when he was very, very young.

On this night at Trujillo Alto, he was sheer poetry. He would come forward with that peculiar stoop-shouldered stride of his and then slide slightly to the left and the Cuban would set himself. Then he would slide to the right and the Cuban would have to reset himself. But by then, he would sting home three . . . four . . . five straight jabs . . . and the Cuban's nose would sting and little bells would ring and the Cuban would crank up the big punch, but by that time, there was nobody to throw it at.

It was a shutout. Afterward, with the gold medal just ahead, he told a man, "I'm just grateful for what God gave me. I'm grateful I have some kind of chance. There's the Olympics and then I'll turn pro. I don't want to be rude, but we can talk about me later. I really would like to get out there and see our other guys right now."

And the last time a man saw him, two nights later, they were playing "The Star-Spangled Banner" and they were hanging a gold medal around his neck and thoughts of Pruitt-Igoe were all but buried in his view.

The mind's eye is a camera, saving the best of its photos. I remember a night in Trujillo Alto and another in San Juan, and a winner's smile. I remember Lem Steeples.

AN ARTIST HITS THE CANVAS

AUGUST 13, 1982

In the beginning, he was like a thousand carbon copies of himself, who are drawn each day to the crowded, airless gyms of Mexico; young and passionately sure that with nothing more than their fists they can assault the kind of poverty that is a mother to the type of despair few of us north of the border can understand.

In the gyms of Mexico, the battle for living space never abates. They fight for a locker . . . they fight for a towel . . . but mostly, they fight to be noticed by the swarms of hustlers, who frequent the building and who, in some ways, are as desperate as they are.

The sparring sessions emerge as a kind of Philadelphia South—gym war without pay, where the prize is attention and the hope that one of the hustlers will offer them a fight for money is the spur.

The resemblance between Salvador Sanchez and an army whose movement was traceable solely to an empty stomach ends there. He did not become one of those squat, angry Mexican fighters whose managers never bothered to tell them that their courage too often sadly preceded their skills by a quarter of a mile. He became, instead, the kind of boxer who could have been deposited here by a time machine—so genuine were his skills . . . so out-of-time were his classic moves.

But that was later.

In the beginning, there was indeed the same kind of gym . . . the same kind of colleague . . . the same kind of day-to-day desperation. When he was sixteen years old, one of the hungry-watchers approached him and said, "You wanna make

71

money? Next Friday, you come to the bus station. Next Friday, you fight with the pros."

The bus trip was six hours. The hotel, where they waited, had twenty rooms and one toilet. The arena is not even worth discussing. The other fighter was named Al Gardeno and, in the first round, he broke the nose of Salvador Sanchez. In the third round, Sanchez knocked him out.

On the long bus ride back, he had difficulty breathing through all the swelling. The man who took him out there handed him 2,000 pesos. Three weeks later, he fought again.

That was the Salvador Sanchez whom none of us got a chance to know . . . who fought in places like Los Mochis and Misantla and Mazatlan . . . who even failed to win the Mexican bantam-weight title (the only loss on a record that stands forever at 43-1-1).

His roots conjure up the image of nameless gyms and fighters whose hearts are larger than the chins with which they lead. They conjure up the poverty of a place called Santiago Tianquistenco and the natural temper of an undersized, barefoot kid who reacted with his fists when his classmates called him niña—the ultimate epithet.

But his style . . . his own, unique loaded-with-class style . . . ah, his style conjures up something very different.

Salvador Sanchez was a fighter of the 1940s or the 1950s, operating in the vacuum of the 1980s, where guys with eleven fights get a title shot, where there are two titles for just about every weight division, and where only a very few ever learn their skills in a world populated by furriers, who are managers, and garment-center guys in softball warm-up jackets, who call themselves trainers.

To watch Salvador Sanchez at work was to watch the kind of artistry that is so rationed in this age of media-hype fighters and challengers of synthetic skills that people often did not understand what they were seeing.

He would work an opponent the way Miles Davis can work a horn until it builds the ultimate fugue . . . the way Hartack used to work a horse . . . the way a cool barroom Romeo works a wide-eyed squeeze.

On nights when Salvador Sanchez boxed, rounds were not simply fought to be won. They were fought to take advantage of the nuances of the three minutes that preceded them and the three minutes that would follow. And the doing was so professional in its performance that the victim rarely knew it was happening until the ultimate moment, when a tiny corner of his brain would light up and almost say, "Oh, that's why he was doing that," even as the referee was leading him away.

Do not remember Salvador Sanchez as some kind of storybook hero who becomes a folk model for a way out of poverty. Do not remember him coming up to that last turn of his life on a narrow, twisting Mexican highway.

Instead, remember Madison Square Garden—where he fought just once in his life. Remember now that the fight would be his last. Remember the stumpy opponent named Azumah Nelson, who had come to fight and who had offered resistance worthy of Salvador Sanchez's finest efforts.

Then remember the fifteenth round. Reach back in the corner of your mind and conjure up that textbook of a right hand followed by a hook, which caught Azumah Nelson even as he was falling. And remember that it was no more than Salvador Sanchez expected to do when the moment was the correct one.

He was one of the five or so best fighters in the world during his time. He was an artist who transcended the mediocrity around him.

He was not a 1982 fighter.

For those who understand that, no other words are needed. For those who don't, no other words can explain.

FOR SADYE

JULY 5, 1972

Long before they met, the man who would become her husband had been a second baseman . . . good enough with the bat to play as a paid ringer in a railroad league that followed the route of what is now the Erie Lackawanna . . . but not good enough with the glove to fuel the dream of a major-league career that haunted his youth.

The truth is that he was a second baseman long before he was a husband and a father. So they made a deal. She wouldn't bother him when the Giants were playing the Dodgers up at the Polo Grounds and he wouldn't bother her when she was making the decisions that kept the household running. It was the formula for a beautiful marriage.

Until the day he died, fourteen years ago this fall, she had never seen a football game or a basketball game or a prizefight. Once, he got her to a baseball park out in Wilkes-Barre, Pennsylvania, for a night game, but after they announced the winning lucky-number scorecard at the end of the fifth inning, she was ready to leave.

She had two children and they conspired together with the father on hot summer nights in the late 1930s to monopolize the old Philco radio on the screened porch, forcing her into an early bedtime while they listened and died with Carl Hubbell's every pitch, and one night she was properly embarrassed when the maiden lady across the street called the fuzz to protest because the stillness of a July night sent the roar of the crowd bouncing down the block.

When the cop who came to investigate stayed to listen to a couple of innings at the ex-second baseman's invitation, it was hard to tell whether she was angriest at the ex-second baseman, the maiden lady, or the policeman.

And she wasn't too pleased with Carl Hubbell, either, for starting the whole thing.

In the final analysis there were only three important things in her life—the ex-second baseman and the two kids. She managed the ex-second baseman's paycheck the way Casey Stengel used to platoon the Yankees. She squeezed here and she pinched there and once, when the daughter's senior year in college and the son's senior year in prep school came head to head on the fiscal calendar and she was out of financial bench strength, she sold her own mother's bracelet to make the payments.

And the daughter and the son grew older, with daughters and sons of their own, but the ex-second baseman never got to see any of the grandchildren make the double play. He was pretty much a shut-in at the end when the heart condition finally nailed him. The Giants had moved to California and all you could get on the tube was the Yankees. But the figures still danced across the television screen. As long as there was a ball game, the ex-second baseman was going to watch it. And as long as there was a ball game, the ex-second baseman's wife wasn't going to look at the set.

And then the ex-second baseman died.

A subtle change caught the ex-second baseman's wife and held her. In the morning, she turned to the sports section of the paper for which the son now wrote and with scissors at the ready she cut out his column each day.

"Well, you might need them some time," she told the son. And it went that way for years and the son knew the ex-second baseman's wife—or so he thought—so he was sure that the clippings went from newspaper to desk drawer with no stops in between.

And then one day the ex-second baseman's wife said, "That was a terrible thing that man who owns the Cardinals did to Mr. Kane."

"His name is Keane, Ma. Johnny Keane."

"Kane . . . Keane . . . what's the difference? Tell me, you think he can win with the Yankees? Are the Cardinals mad about what you wrote?"

And then one day the ex-second baseman's wife said, "It's not right what they are doing to that Mr. Ali. Tell me, do you think they'll let him fight again? Will you get in trouble for what you wrote?"

And another time she said, "What do you have against that Mr. Brindage?"

"It's Brundage, Ma."

"Brindage . . . Brundage . . . nobody could be as bad as you say he is."

"Brundage is."

"Why can't you ever write nice things about nice people?"

And another time she said, "The clippings are filling the desk. Stop cluttering my house."

"Well, then don't clip them."

"The least you could do is take them. They're cluttering the house. Why do I have to wait forever to hear from you? Your sister could come more often, too."

"She does."

"Don't change the subject. That was a nice story on the quarterback today. Have you got a warm coat to take to Green Bay?"

"Minneapolis, Ma, not Green Bay."

"What's the difference? Don't be so difficult. It's cold. I don't know who you take after. Sometimes I read the words and I have to look them up. My doctor says you're a very good writer. Call me once in a while."

The ex-second baseman's son is so smart that it only took him about five years to figure out that she never started a day without reading every word he wrote.

And then one day, she didn't feel well.

She had been a diabetic and now there was this lump and suddenly there was the hospital and when she came home it wasn't diabetes that worried the ex-second baseman's kids.

She was religious in a strange hyphenated way that to her was totally compatible. Her religion was a blend of Jewishness and Christian Science and need for prayer was deep within her. One day after she came back from the hospital, the ex-second baseman's son noticed two pieces of paper on her table. One was his column of that day. The other was a handwritten copy of the Twenty-third Psalm on the back of an old envelope.

The NBA playoffs were coming down the stretch by then and the son was at the game writing about them and the daughter, who had become a Knickerbocker freak, was visiting the mother, who turned on the game.

She had never done that before.

"Don't worry," she said, "the Knickers will win."

"It's Knickerbockers, Ma," the daughter said.

"Shh . . . shhh [Willis Reed had the ball]. God directs him."
With Willis, God, and Sadye Izenberg in the pivot, Wilt never
had a chance.

About a month later, she clipped a column for the last time.
And she went back to the hospital.

Her children thought she didn't know what she had. And she
let them think that. But she knew.

She died in her sleep on Sunday morning.

The Beautiful . . .

ARCEL LAURELS LONG OVERDUE

AUGUST 29, 1985

There is no truth to the old wives' tale that Ray Arcel worked Abel's corner on the night the world's first promoter, Honest Simon ben Yakuv, matched him with Cain in the real Canaan Arena. In the first place, if he had, Abel would have won. In the second, Abel obviously could not hook off the jab, a sure indication that he was never one of Dr. Arcel's pupils.

This weekend, The Doctor will be eighty-six years old going on twenty-four. He spent the last two weeks on a whirlwind vacation over in England. Confidants said what he really wanted to do was a little waterskiing in the south of France or perhaps swim the straits off Tierra del Fuego but he did not want to choose between the two because then he might have offended his fellow members of the Grand Canyon Free Fall Parachuting Club.

Meanwhile, word trickles out of Albany that on September 11, Governor Mario Cuomo is going to present a special citation to the man who trained the first fighter ever to win a Golden Gloves title and worked with a record twenty world champions from Charley Phil Rosenberg on up through Larry Holmes.

In short, after sixty-five years in the business, Dr. Arcel is about to become an overnight sensation in his own home state.

His own hometown is another matter, but as they say around the candy store, husbands and mayors are always the last to know.

In any event, this is a man who handled close to 2,000 professional fighters during his career. In recent years, he is best known for the care, feeding, and development of a gentle fellow named Roberto Duran, who at his peak would be roughly 7-5 to stop a mildly sedated Siberian tiger.

The reason Duran comes to mind here is that he was the focal point of Arcel's comeback, which began at age seventy-two after fifteen years away from the business. As every social worker knows, this is a time when we all must be tolerant of our senior citizens because their productive years are a thing of the past.

Arcel's were so far behind him at that stage that all he did was take a child of the Panama streets with an attitude that would have made Machine Gun Kelly look like Mary Poppins and turn him into a disciplined craftsman who became what most folks say was one of the two best lightweight champions who ever lived.

The other was named Benny Leonard.

Ray trained him, too.

Arcel is of, by, and from New York City. He was raised in Harlem and he learned his skills in the old Stillman's Gym and consequently there has always been a directness about him.

After watching Marvis Frazier's dissection at the hand of Larry Holmes, a television person once asked Ray if he would comment on the loser's mistakes. "What would you have done different," the guy demanded, "had you been in Marvis Frazier's corner last night?"

"I would have taken him to the movies."

"Be serious."

"I am. There is no reason to put your fighter into a mismatch like that. He trusts you. You are supposed to care what happens to him. It wasn't only Marvis who didn't belong. It was everyone who put him there."

"Trust" is a strange visitor to the syntax of professional boxing but Ray Arcel never betrayed it with his fighters and he never had a fighter who did not return it. It was never more evident than on the night of *"no más,"* when Roberto Duran turned his back on Ray Leonard and walked away in New Orleans five years ago.

At 3 o'clock that morning the Louisiana State Athletic Commission called a special meeting to withhold Duran's purse. A steady drizzle cut through the chill night air. Alone, Ray Arcel walked the slippery concourse from an adjacent hotel back to the Superdome to defend his fighter.

Tears began to form in his eyes as he spoke to the commission.

"Why did you go?" a friend asked in the predawn hours after Arcel had won his plea. "He broke your heart. His manager didn't go. The hangers-on didn't. Duran didn't even go."

"I went," he said, obviously overtired and very sad, "because he is still my fighter until tomorrow. It's my duty."

The gift of caring has always been with him. That's part of his city, too. Admittedly, it may be on a rather long lunch break these days, but cities—and city people—need it to survive. Ray never lost it.

At the start of World War II, Ray had a dandy fighter named Lenny Mancini (whose son later became the lightweight champion of the world). Lenny went off to Europe as an infantryman and was wounded. They sent him to France to recover.

In the hospital, he bumped into another Arcel fighter, a middleweight out of Brooklyn named Paul Klang. When the hospital finally gave them twenty-four-hour passes, they agreed to explore Paris together.

They ripped through Paris exactly the way soldiers rip through any city after months in the hospital. They put together a very wet night. The more bars they hit, the wetter it got. The wetter it got, the wilder they got.

They were diving for coins in a fountain when the MPs found them. As they led Mancini away, he turned to Klang and said, "Promise me one thing."

In his state, Klang would have promised Mancini Portugal if he'd asked for it. "Name it, buddy," he said, "just name it."

"Whatever you do, for God's sake don't tell Ray."

There is not a fighter Ray Arcel trained who wouldn't have said the same thing.

LA HIJA
ADOPTIVA

MAY 27, 1983

It was 1958 and this Little League All-Star team had come down to the island to play against the prepuberty sons of U.S. naval personnel stationed in San Juan and the base was making a very big deal of it. There was a crowd and a band and a big pregame ceremony.

Then the Navy kids went out into the field and this skinny pitcher started throwing bullets. The first three All-Stars went down on strikes.

When the Navy kids came in to the dugout, the pitcher's father called the pitcher aside and said, "Next inning, I want you to take your hat off after the second batter and turn with your back to home plate."

In the top of the second, the skinny pitcher walked the first hitter, then struck out the second on a pitch that got by so fast the batter couldn't have hit it with a canoe paddle. The pitcher turned, faced center field, and off came the blue baseball cap.

That's when the long ponytail came spilling down the center of her back.

All hell broke loose.

It was the first moment anyone on either team knew the pitcher wasn't a nine-year-old boy.

The crowd laughed.

The batter complained to the umpire.

The umpire looked up at the sky for help.

The more the batter complained and the more the umpire looked above for guidance, the more the crowd laughed.

Donna Terry won that game. But when it was over, a lot of young boys and old coaches on the island thought about it and said, "What the hell are we laughing at? She beat us all year."

Which, in what was then a socially retarded international Little

League structure, is how Donna Terry got barred from playing with the boys in Puerto Rico.

"I was an athlete," she explained over the telephone the other day from Berkeley, California, where she coaches a college team that current fashion dictates now must be called softball-persons, "and an athlete competes. So I did what I could. I played softball and I swam. I always felt a part of the island and when my dad was transferred, I stayed down there another year to compete for the Puerto Rican national swimming team."

The odyssey of Donna Terry, who remains one hell of a thrower of softballs, is a kind of yes-I-can testament. She has played softball in China, Mexico, Cuba, Canada, Puerto Rico, Venezuela, and all throughout the Continental United States. She took a comatose athletic program at Texas Women's University down in Denton, Texas, and won a national softball title.

So much for the routine side of the journey.

Next month, she is coming to Newark as a pitcher - coach with the Puerto Rican national women's team, which will be in New Jersey for the homestretch phase of its pre–Pan-Am Games training as a participant in the Bud Light–North Ward Center's International Women's Softball Series.

And when the first hitter steps to the plate for the Canadian national team, that batter will be facing the only woman in history who ever became a Puerto Rican by acclamation.

It is one hell of a story.

It did not come about because Donna Terry agreed to a part-time coaching job with the Puerto Rican team. It didn't even happen when she agreed to do a little pitching. It was, instead, the natural culmination of a love affair with the sun, the sand, the music, and the island itself.

It was no trick at all for Donna Terry to be allowed to compete for the island's national team. Under softball's international rules, you can compete for just about any country or national team. But once you declare yourself, you are bound to that affiliation for the rest of your competitive life.

Joining the team was easy. Being part of it was something else.

The club, which had its genesis in the planning of a man named Junior Cruz, who is the mayor of Guaynabo, is based in that town. To play for it is no small thing in Puerto Rico. Each year girls come from all over the island to try. There is more here than just the trips. There is the chance to be a part of a worldwide recognition of a people's rightful but rarely acknowledged identity.

Now here comes this daughter of two Anglo parents . . . this blue-eyed thrower of fastballs . . . wearing the national colors of Puerto Rico while darker-skinned candidates do not make the team.

"They always respected me for what I could do," Donna Terry will tell you, "but that was it. I love that island. It gave me my first chance in competitive sports. I always felt close to it. I felt I owed it a debt. But I understood how they felt. People wondered about my motives and they weren't always polite. I just had to live with it."

Then, in Cuba, Donna Terry pitched and won the game that clinched the Central American title. That night the team went off to celebrate. Donna Terry went to bed.

After midnight, she awakened to discover another pitcher named Ivellise Echeverria staring at her from the foot of the bed. If truth be told, they were hardly friends. They had had their differences for a long time over the obvious question— i.e., what was a blue-eyed Anglo named Donna Terry doing on the Puerto Rican national team?

For an instant, the silence was electric. "I love my country so much," Ivellise said.

"I do, too," Donna said.

"No, no. You don't understand. I am so proud to do it for my country. You cannot begin to know. How could you?"

The following week, there was a press conference in San Juan and the reporters were all shouting at once: "When you won the game . . . when you got the last out . . . when you brought the title home . . . . "

"No," Donna Terry shouted back. "You don't understand. It's not me . . . it's all of us . . . it's Puerto Rico." Then she saw Ivellise at the back of the room and called to her. Her teammates had to push Ivellise forward but suddenly the two of them were standing together and Donna was crying and Ivellise was crying and then they had their arms around each other.

In that emotional instant, Donna Terry finally became La Hija Adoptiva.

McGUIGAN FIGHTING FOR PEACE

JUNE 13, 1986

Six hundred yards from the Belfast home of Barry and Sandra McGuigan—down past the gaping pockmarks where once there had been a road before a car bomb blew it away—they came in the night to the entranceway of the last house on the block, rang the bell, and pumped twenty-seven bullets into the man who answered the door.

"They were IRA [Irish Republican Army]," says the man who will defend his WBA featherweight title against Stevie Cruz in Las Vegas on June 23. "But it doesn't matter. On another block, they would have been UDA [Ulster Defense Association]. Here they murdered a Protestant. On another block, they would have killed a Catholic.

"I hate them both . . . the IRA and the UDA," he says in a voice that conveys the idea that he has given all of this a great deal of thought. "I hate the old people who live in the past and poison our children's minds . . . who are even afraid to let them go to school together because kids have their own ways about them and they might one day be sayin' that 'Mom and Da are wrong. I don't understand why they won't let me go over on their block to play.' I've never understood them and I never will. I'm sick of it. All of us are sick of it."

Barry McGuigan is twenty-five years old and his growth to manhood coincided with the sudden rebirth of what the Irish refer to as "The Troubles." Growing up in the South in Clones, just a hair or two below the border with Northern Ireland, he has seen nothing but hate and violence. When he was fifteen and already an amateur boxer with a great future, he used to hop on his bicycle and wheel up toward Belfast because that's where the gyms were. On the way home one night, he saw two bodies in a ditch by the side of the road. One had been killed with a pitchfork. The other, shot.

He made the mistake of telling his mother about it. "You'll not be taking the cycle up there again," Katie McGuigan told him. "It's a poor bargain I'd be makin' if I risked tradin' a fine young boy for a corpse."

Now he is the champion of the world and he lives up in Belfast and he understands it even less.

"How could I?" he said over the telephone from Palm Springs, where he is training for the tripleheader at Caesar's in Vegas, where he shares top billing with Thomas Hearns and Roberto Duran. "How can anyone understand a world that's out of hand? The Brits and their army are here with guns . . . the RUC [Royal Ulster Constabulary] has guns . . . the IRA has guns . . . the UDA has guns.

"And there's the barricades. The Brits put 'em up, so does the RUC and the IRA and the UDA. Mother of Mercy, we have so many barricades you'd think we were in the business of making them. I'd like to slip around Belfast in the middle of the night and pull every last one of them down. How can I understand it when, as a Catholic, I am married to the same Protestant girl to whom I gave a toy ring when she was eight?"

There is more than rhetoric behind Barry McGuigan's hopes for Ireland. When they opened the first integrated (Catholic-Protestant) school in Belfast, Barry and Sandra dedicated it.

"Did they give you any trouble?" a guy asked.

"No, and if they did, I wouldn't stand for it and neither would Sandra. These are the children and they will be the future when this nightmare ends.

"It's wrong that I'm the only fellow who can walk through both The Falls and Shankill without having a problem. That's because I'm a champion. But if I can use that status this way, then that's what I'm going to keep on doin'."

The status of which he speaks stems from his role in a country with precious few current international heroes. He won the title in a spectacular match with Eusebio Pedrosa last year. He is 29-1. He is a rare athlete in a country that reveres boxing— an Irish-born, Irish-bred, Irish-managed champion who has campaigned primarily in Ireland.

In 1938, as European champion, Barry went off to England

to defend his title. It was there that he made a decision that will follow him later this month into the ring at Caesar's.

"You were born in the South and you live in the North," the promoter said. "Which [anthem] do you want us to play?"

"Neither," he said. "We have enough fist shakin' over songs already."

So this is the way it was on that night and every night since when Barry McGuigan came to fight. He enters the ring behind the United Nations Peace Flag. He wears a neutral-colored robe. He wears neither green nor orange and on his trunks is embroidered the dove of peace. The music that precedes him is the sound of his father singing "Danny Boy."

And it has been that way in Kings Hall, the 10,000-seat arena that almost geographically straddles the Belfast demarcation line between Catholics and Protestants. They come from each end to cheer him. On those nights, they are united. "It makes me feel tremendous. It reminds me that this is where I belong and this is where I'll live forever."

The Lord Mayor of Belfast wants to nominate him for the Nobel Peace Prize.

"Foolish," Barry says. "I don't deserve the prize and all I want is the peace."

DEBT TO
A TEACHER

JANUARY 21, 1982

PONTIAC—On Sunday, as they wait for the 49ers to break their offensive huddle in the heart of the only igloo to host a Super Bowl, Jim LeClair will look to the sidelines for the defensive call, pick up the sign, and holler the defensive signals into the wall of noise cascading down from the big storage tank they call the Silverdome.

When he does, the linebacker with the big 57 on his back will cock his head slightly to the left and stare straight ahead at LeClair's lips. Then Reggie Williams will wait for the snap and go out and do his job.

And you can take that to the bank. They call this thing the Super Bowl. They hang Roman numerals after it, charge enough for television commercials to fund the Venice canal system for a year, and trumpet the moments that form its countdown with all the restraint of eyewitness dispatches from the Second Punic War. They use words like *courage* and phrases like *playing hurt*.

But that's all they are—words and phrases.

This is the biggest single football game played and wagered on anywhere on the North American Land Mass.

But it's still just a game.

You want to know what a real Super Bowl is . . . you want to know what real heartbreak can be all about . . . you want to know about courage and survival and climbing a mountain no fifty-yard field goal can even approach?

Then think about that big #57 you are going to see on the tube Sunday, staring at Jim LeClair's lips in that Cincinnati defensive huddle. Think about Reggie Williams, a very important linebacker for the Bengals out of a very unlikely school (when it comes to pro football) called Dartmouth.

Never mind the cut lists and the waiver lists and the college drafts. The forces that shaped Reggie Williams's life go back long before he even knew about those things.

Forget the pros and the Super Bowl—they might never have happened. Forget Dartmouth—it might never have happened.

Reggie Williams could have been dumped on a human trash heap by an educational system where too few cared and even fewer knew what to do about it. Every member of the Cincinnati defense knows why Reggie stares so hard at LeClair when the defensive signals are barked.

Reggie Williams is no character out of *Dallas North Forty*, psyching himself up for the shock of contact. What he is doing is reading LeClair's lips. What he is doing—as he has done for nineteen of his twenty-seven years—is keeping alive the faith and love of an unforgettable third-grade teacher out of Scott Elementary School in nearby Flint. Long after a remarkable lady named Mrs. Chapman died, the new life she opened to him continues to grow and prosper.

He does not hesitate to tell the story. Yesterday, he looked a visitor dead in the eye and said it flat out: "In kindergarten . . . in first grade . . . in second grade . . . they questioned my intelligence. So did I. Then she came along."

If you ask Reggie Williams about his failing hearing, he will tell you that on his own private scale of ten, he rates it a six. He will tell you that to compound the problem, he developed a lisp—slight traces of which still remain.

And then he will tell you why.

He could not hear his early teachers. They would ask a question and he would answer a totally different one. And then the class would laugh and so he simply stopped answering and when he did that, he stopped hearing the sound of his own voice. The lisp followed.

"My mother worked very hard with me at home but she didn't know what was wrong. I still have my first- and second-grade report cards. Every grade was marked 'unsatisfactory.' "

They looked at Reggie Williams and all they saw was a little black kid who apparently couldn't reason and apparently couldn't speak and who might as well have been labeled "Do not fold, spindle, or mutilate. Just discard."

And then came the third grade and what nobody knew until then was the fact that maybe Reggie Williams didn't speak very clearly and maybe he couldn't follow what was going on, but one thing he sure as hell could do was read.

"I withdrew deeper into myself. When other kids played, I

read every book I could get my hands on. Mrs. Chapman noticed."

She could have done it the easy way. She could have simply scanned all those tests and notations his previous teachers sent along and said, "Well, that's just the way it is." But Mrs. Chapman was a teacher in the way that Vince Lombardi was a coach. She had his hearing tested. Reggie Williams does not even remember the name of the disease that almost robbed him of all the beautiful things that came afterward.

He can tell you that he remembers that with the aid of Mrs. Chapman and another teacher named Mrs. Bromm, he went through three years of medical treatment and speech therapy. He can tell you that through it all Mrs. Chapman kept telling him, "Read . . . read . . . you can be anything. You have the intelligence." He can tell you that he was graduated in the top five percent of his high-school class.

He can tell you that at Dartmouth he took a public-speaking class his first year and they laughed at him. "Well, they used to laugh at me when I was five and six years old, too. I worked like hell. At the end of the year nobody was laughing anymore."

Finally, he can tell you that before Mrs. Chapman died, he wrote her from Dartmouth, expressing his feelings. "That first diagnosis before she came along . . . it could have killed me . . . I could be nowhere today. I could be in that army of kids who just never . . . well . . . ."

Sunday will be time enough for the X's and the O's and the details of America's folk ritual. Today this space belongs to Reggie Williams and a lady named Chapman, who will not be here to see it.

It's a story at least as American as this whole damned super-hype week.

THE COACH, THE KIDS, AND THE MIRACLE

MARCH 14, 1980

This was back in 1963 and George Ireland was out at Oakton Park in Chicago on a warm afternoon shooting baskets. George had this nice little basketball team of his own at Loyola. Late in the year, they would beat Cincinnati in overtime for the NCAA title.

In any event, George was working out by himself, and off to the side of the court there was this young couple and their son sitting on a blanket. Each time the ball would roll away, the kid would toddle after it and try to pick it up. But there was something wrong with his coordination.

That's how George Ireland met Mike Frank, who was perhaps two years old and very clearly the victim of a physical and mental handicap. He spent much of his free time at the park after that, teaching Mike to try to use what is such a natural gift for most kids. From time to time in ensuing years, George would run into Mike's father around town.

Meanwhile, George Ireland finished up a twenty-five year coaching career in 1975. He had experienced two heart attacks near its conclusion but he will tell you quite candidly that his heart is the reason he left college basketball. The attacks were not.

Ireland differed with alumni and school authorities about the wooing of transfers and the winking at junior-college prospects.

So it was 1975 and George Ireland was through with basketball at age sixty-one, and then one day he ran into Mike Frank's dad in a store and Frank told him, "Mike is playing some basketball at the Center for Enriched Learning in Skokie and they could use some help with the team. Maybe you're interested."

92

There are forty men and women on the center's basketball team. There are those with Down's Syndrome (mongolism) and those with other forms of physical and mental disabilities. They run in age from sixteen to twenty-three and some of them attend school during the day, while others work in jobs for which they have been trained. But every night they make it to the center for what to them is the single most important highlight of the day.

The teams are coed. The center, which is run by the Young Men's Jewish Council, is nonsectarian and interracial. From the moment George Ireland first walked in the joint, he became knotted in a love affair that seems to have no dimensions.

"There are kids who play for us who never spoke," George said over the telephone yesterday from Skokie. "So I made a rule, I told them they couldn't pass the ball to anyone who wouldn't yell, 'I'm open.' Now sometimes you can't make out the words, and sometimes you can't be sure who said them, but those kids are speaking more and more.

"Mike, the kid I met in the park that day, well he's on the team and Mike has a thing about being touched. We'd have a huddle and I'd put my arms around the kids nearest me, and if one of them happened to be Mike, he'd run to the bench when I touched him.

"Then somebody explained the problem to me. Well, we have this rule that you can't play in the game unless your sneakers are tied. Some of our players can't do that by themselves and Mike was one of them. So I told him to put his foot on my knee and his arm on my shoulder and I would tie them. But he shook his head no, so I just said, 'Mike, you want to play, don't you? Well, we have to abide by the rules.'

"So he put his foot up but he wouldn't grab my shoulder. I twisted his ankle a little and he fell. Then he got up and put his foot up but he still wouldn't hold my shoulder, so I gave another little twist and he fell again. The third time he put his arm around me. I'm too old to cry, but . . ."

There is a basic beauty to the way George Ireland and his kids have entered into what surely is one of the purest coach-player relationships in the country. He has taught them a 2-1-2 zone and he has taught them to fast-break. This is how he teaches zone defense to these remarkable young people:

"Now each of you has a room. It's your room. Nobody with

the ball can come into your room. If somebody wants to do that, you keep him out."

"Can I slug him?" a youngster asks.

"No, I don't think you have to do that. Just take the ball away. That's good enough.

"Now the first two rooms we'll call tiger rooms and anyone I let play there can be a tiger. The big room in the middle, well, that belongs to the lion. Now what can we call the two rooms near the basket, because we need a really good name for that so the people in those rooms can really play tough?"

"Cougars are strong," a young girl volunteers. "They climb over cars on television."

"Okay," George says, "those rooms belong to the cougars. And you are going to be one of them."

Tigers, lions, and cougars—they are George's kids. This week there was no practice. This week, they came to the center and hung around and waited. Three weeks ago George Ireland checked into St. Francis Hospital in Evanston to check out an irregular heartbeat. They gave him an EKG and fifteen minutes later he was on the operating table. Yesterday, George came home with a pacemaker in the right side of his chest.

"So that's that?" a guy asked.

"That's what?" George Ireland said. "I have to get moving. I've got tigers and lions and cougars to coach."

Now go on . . . tell me . . . who's really Coach of the Year?

GRAMBLING'S GODFATHER

SEPTEMBER 6,1982

He is just two games short of 300 victories and that will establish him as an overnight sensation with all the gee-whiz producers in televisionland. But 300 is simply a number and not a very impressive one when you measure it against the life and times of Eddie Robinson, where his inolvement with people and not numbers long ago marked him as an extraordinary human being.

Since the guys who run to the videotape can also run to the record books, they can tell you that this places Robinson within that select Stagg-Bryant orbit of success—which misses the point by light years.

The truth is that you really had to be there to understand it. You had to walk the main drag of Grambling, Louisiana (then one of America's three all-black incorporated towns), and feel the electricity on game days during a time in space when the underemployed woodchoppers would come on down from places like nearby Hodge and sit in the stands along with the parents of red-clay country kids who all too often saw tangible evidence that college was supposed to be a place for somebody else's children.

You have to be able to picture a classroom on the campus at the University of Iowa in the early 1940s and watch the only black man in the room (a young coach named Eddie Robinson) reluctantly get to his feet at a national coaches' clinic to ask a question, and you had to see the fire in his face when they asked where he was from. He told them Grambling and somebody shouted, "Gambling . . . Gumbling . . . where the hell is that?"

Eddie Robinson smiled politely and explained out loud that it was "up near the Arkansas border" and finished the sentence silently to himself with the vow, "One day you suckers are gonna know exactly where it is."

You had to know that here was a guy out of a long-defunct

black school named Leland College, with a fistful of single-wing passing records and a diploma that in 1936 America qualified him only to load feed sacks at a Baton Rouge mill. By the end of that year, he was the head football coach at Grambling, commanding a staff comprised solely of himself and the night watchman and they lost every game.

A year later they won them all.

What you have to know about Eddie Robinson to understand the measure of his current 298 victories would fill a book. You'd need to know about the way he and Dr. Ralph Waldo Emerson Jones (then the school president) conspired together to drive an L.A. Rams scout named Eddie Kotel all over the Louisiana countryside while they argued over the salary he would authorize for Tank Younger, who would become the first pro out of an all-black school.

You'd have to know how they won that argument using Kotel's desperate and immediate need of a comfort-station stop, which they would not make until the deal was cut.

And you'd have to see Eddie Robinson escort Younger down to the boarded-up depot at Grambling, where the train never stopped unless you flagged it down, and listen to what he told him that day he sent him off into history.

"You got to make that team, Tank. You got to make it for yourself and you got to make it for all the young men who will be coming after you. They are going to judge them by you. If you can't cut it, then don't come back here."

"Coach," Younger told him, "I don't know nothing about no volleyball but if they're playing football, I'll make it."

He was the first. He was All-Pro offense. He was All-Pro defense. He became Eddie Robinson's consolation prize for being born too soon and born too small to go on up there himself.

He worked to get James Harris into the pros, which made him the force behind the first black professional quarterback of the modern era. He became the first black man to be elected head of the U.S. College Football Coaches Association.

He was all of this and so much more.

But most of all a man remembers a soft Louisiana twilight during a time before the media had discovered either Eddie or Grambling. It was the end of the final practice session before the annual homecoming game against Texas Southern.

"I can't complain," he told a friend. "It's been a good life.

But sometimes I do wonder. I wonder what it would be like to see 60,000 people up in those seats instead of 12,000. I wonder what it would be like to coach with the tools they give Woody and Bear.

"Hey, you got to wonder or you just ain't human."

Two years later, Grambling played in New York for the first time. Eddie drew a lot of attention. Sadly, everyone wanted to know where he was headed. They could have learned a lot more by trying to understand where he'd been.

BASEBALL'S
FOUNTAIN
OF YOUTH

AUGUST 7, 1986

Once, in another incarnation, there was a ballpark of ballparks with its late-inning shadows reproducing the image of the joint's spectacular façade against the infield and the sound of the P.A. announcer: "Your attention, please, now playing center field and batting fourth (except you knew he wouldn't get to hit) for the Yankees . . . #53 . . . Ross Moschitto."

They called him "Mickey Mantle's caddie." In games already won and lost or on days when Mantle's seven-inning legs began to ache going into the eighth, Ross Moschitto would grab his glove and head for the outfield. In a 110-game career, he got to swing the bat just thirty-six times. Once he even hit a home run.

The years were 1965 and 1966.

Twenty years later, Ross Moschitto is behind the wheel of his customized van on the Cross Bronx Expressway, weaving in and out of the angry rush-hour traffic on the New York side of the approach to the George Washington Bridge.

Behind him is an eight-hour montage of Long Island roads and clipboard estimates . . . eight hours of customizing security arrangements for clients—put the camera here, install the alarms there.

Now the traffic thins. The sight of a ballpark suddenly jumps out at him . . . no architectural façade to serve as a punctuation mark . . . no public-address system . . . no pinstripes in the locker room . . . in fact, no locker room at all.

But the tension inside him is the same. He will tell you he has been thinking about it all day long. It is twilight. Forty-one-year-old businessman Ross Moschitto pulls the curtains on the van.

98

It is the kind of ceremony you'd expect to take place in a telephone booth. One minute, he is mild-mannered businessman Ross Moschitto. The next, he emerges as Ross Moschitto, king of the Time Machine, in a blue suit with a red cape and a large S on the chest.

Well, not exactly. He is wearing the gray uniform and the red cap of the Emerson-Westwood Merchants of the Metropolitan Semi-Pro Baseball League. Who says you can't go home again?

It is eighteen years since he played out the string at what was then the Yankees' Triple-A farm club in Syracuse. Ironically, it was the same legs that qualified him as Mantle's late-inning clone that ultimately betrayed him. But here, when most men his age have to be pushed just to take out the garbage, he's doing the thing he always enjoyed most and by the very nature of the league's financial structure, paying to do it rather than receiving a salary.

Once he was a prospect who almost translated the wish into the deed. Despite what the major-league records say, he could hit. He hit so well at Johnson City in the all-rookie Appalachian League back in 1964 he was named Player of the Year.

But too many splinters on a major-league bench when he should have been in the minors learning and a set of weak Achilles tendons killed that dream. It wiped out the major-league prospect inside him but it never laid a glove on the ballplayer.

"I always wanted to try it again somewhere, just to do it," he says. "I've kept in pretty good shape and then I heard about this league. They told me I could come over and work out."

On July 4, the Emerson-Westwood Merchants were going to play the Wayne A's at Emerson High School and Ross Moschitto arrived in time to take batting practice. He had a couple of old brown bats with him. He was wearing blue jeans and a cutoff baseball shirt. When he stepped in to swing, the college kid throwing for him was only mildly interested.

"I looked at all those young kids," he says, "and I admit I felt a little strange." But when the ball started jumping off the bat, his sons, Ross Jr., thirteen, and Patrick, eleven, climbed on the outfield fence to watch. Except for the usual father-son softball games, they had never seen their father swing a bat.

Way to go, Dad.

Nine days later, when Ross Moschitto made his Metropolitan League debut—in the late innings against the Little Ferry Blue

Devils, ironically—he was used as a late-inning defensive replacement.

Two weeks later, the Merchants were down 1-0 in the fourth inning against the Clifton Baskingers. The bases were loaded. "Man, they haven't made those shoes in twenty years," the umpire told him. Back in the dugout somebody was saying, "You know, he hasn't had a hit in eighteen years."

Ross Moschitto fouled off a couple and took a couple, then slammed a double down the left-field line. When he steamed into second, he said to himself, "Well, that ends the longest batting slump in history."

Since that day, he's had two groin pulls and a sore Achilles tendon. But he's never had more fun.

"What does a guy need to turn back the clock, freeze time, and bend it to his will?" asked a fellow who couldn't do it if you put a gun to his head.

"Simple," Ross Moschitto replies. "I'd like to play until I'm fifty. All you need is the mind of a ten-year-old."

FOR THE
JOY OF IT

NOVEMBER 1981

For forty-five years, he would finish breakfast, walk into the living room, and look out at his office, which was just across the street. The proximity was of no small help because on Sundays, he could walk back across the street and finish the residue of the week's workload.

The place he finished it was in the school laundry room. On six days each week, Alex Yunevich was a coach. On the seventh, he did the team laundry.

Alfred University is a small (2,200 students), liberal arts college tucked away in the village of Alfred, New York, in the foothills of the Allegheny Mountains. It gives no athletic scholarships. If it ever strove to be Number One, it wasn't in the weekly football polls but rather in the field of ceramic engineering.

No, it does not play Notre Dame or Alabama or Penn State. But it plays football with players who play for the joy of it and who have no trouble relating to the coaching staff. This last was made easier by the fact that when you got by Alex Yunevich, you had just run through the entire list of paid coaches.

In forty-five years, he never had a player who failed to graduate in the required four years. In forty-five years, he never cut a player from the squad. Once there was a kid who ran like a web-footed ballet dancer. But for three years he was on the practice field every day. Alex gave him his letter. It speaks volumes about the way he looks at life.

The school has never owned a practice dummy or a blocking sled. The practice field is only seventy-five yards long. Once somebody suggested that Alex get an old automobile tire and hang it somewhere for the quarterback to throw footballs at.

"It's not a bad idea," he said. "When they start hanging tires on the field on Saturdays, I think I'll get us one for the rest of the week."

With all of this, in forty-five years of coaching, his teams won

177 games, lost eighty-five and tied twelve. Six times, they went the route undefeated. In 1971, they won the Lambert Bowl, emblematic of the East's small-college championship.

They were unpressured and unrecruited and don't think even though Alex has spent most of his sixty-seven years on this campus, that he doesn't know the way the other half lives.

In 1928 he went to Purdue on an athletic scholarship, where he played four years of Big Ten football in an era when the Big Ten football teams delayed for several years the return of many future coal miners to whence they had come. He even coached for a year there following graduation, took an assistant's job at Lehigh, and for three years was the head coach at Central Michigan.

Then the Alfred job opened up. Alex took it. Took it? Hell, he damned near retired the franchise. The more he won, the more the Big Brother schools started giving him the eye. He had no trouble resisting. He felt that this is the way a football program should be run and he had no desire to try it the other way.

So he stayed on at Alfred, playing teams like St. Lawrence, RPI, Ithaca, et al. He never felt the football program had to be upgraded, because in his words, "It's for the students and they seem to be getting what they want."

Although the school has a volunteer cameraman who films its games, the films were only for Alex. On Monday, he'd look at them and decide whom he needed to see privately. The squad never got to see them. His practice sessions were always relaxed. Sometimes, if he didn't like the way things were going, he would blow the whistle, call the players together, and begin by saying, "Did I tell you the one about these two traveling salesmen . . . . "

One suspects that this was what everybody had in mind back in the days when this game of football was taking root on the American campus. Do not think for a minute that the kids who played for Alex Yunevich were anybody's patsies. He always got the best out of them. This year, he took them up to St. Lawrence University in the rain and the mud and stole a game, 3-2. It gave him as much satisfaction as his unbeaten seasons.

He is finished now. At age sixty-seven he has decided to retire. Next year, he and his wife will go out to little Merrill Field (capacity 6,000) and sit in the bleachers on fall afternoons and continue to enjoy what to him has been a way of life.

He will watch somebody else's team play. The somebody else has yet to be selected. He has a tough act to follow. But let him be warned up front the way Alfred and the kids want it: This season, Alex Yunevich spent a grand total of $55.60 on recruiting. Mostly, the inflated figure was the fault of that new thirteen-cent stamp.

SUMMER SONG

JULY 5, 1984

So now we have passed July 4, the traditional moment for checking the major-league baseball standings and wondering if the old charm of "first on July 4, first at the end of the season" will work yet another time. How many summers as kids did we wonder the same thing? If that doesn't shake the memory, what will?

It is that time of the year again and what follows is a summer love song. In its way, some will interpret it as a mild commercial but that's all right because, after all, if the company hadn't made the ball, we wouldn't have had the game, and if we hadn't had the game, then a whole world of assorted dreams would never have had the forum for a special kind of reality.

After all, we were city kids in a world where nobody ever said, "Here, go wear the shirt with 'Mario's Pizza' written across the back and we'll build you a field with real dugouts and grass and water it by day so you can play on it by twilight."

The truth is nobody built us anything, which in that kind of world is not necessarily bad because then nobody ever made any serious federal, state, city, or neighborhood money off of our existence. When we played, we were the kids on our block against the kids on their block, and, shocking as it may be to what we have come to accept as 1984 reality, we were not numbers on an application for a subsidized hustle.

At its extreme, the only one who ever got paid was the summer playground director, who sure as hell earned it because he was the entire staff for blocks and blocks around. And you can take it to the bank that he never paid a mortgage off that kind of money.

The ball referred to earlier, of course, was The Spaldeen, which is still manufactured by the same company and which was the only piece of "bought" equipment for the stickball games. Gloves were illegal (assuming anybody had one), old broom handles were in plentiful supply, and all the grounds crew needed was a hunk of chalk to turn a slice of a city street into the Polo Grounds or Ebbets Field or (which was much closer to our hearts through geography) Ruppert Stadium, home of the old Newark Bears.

It was a game of improvisation . . . power was measured by the number of manhole covers within the scope of the ball's flight (three made you Mel Ott or Dixie Walker) . . . two fouls was an out . . . in its classic form, the pitcher had to bounce the ball six feet in front of the hitter.

But those rules were for the best of conditions. The best was rarely available. The park was two bus rides away and nobody had enough real baseball equipment to make the trip worthwhile. The emergence of the automobile as an American necessity crammed the macadam "playing fields" out of existence. The Spaldeen and the broom handle remained but a variant of the old rules emerged.

The best place to find it was in the schoolyards. Somebody painted a rectangle on the side of the playground wall at Avone Avenue School and a different form of the game was born. The pitcher no longer bounced the ball. He threw it as hard as he could and a Spaldeen could curve, jump and wind up spitting in a batter's eye. And if it struck anywhere within the rectangle, it was a strike. The manhole covers weren't there as benchmarks but a short left-field fence bordering on the back of a four-family home that faced Rose Terrace was. There was also a very irate man watching the occasional Homeric moment when a Spaldeen slammed against the rear of his home and the race was on—but that's a different story.

Stickball and its variations—in Alabama, where Willie Mays grew up, they cut the ball in half so it would last twice as long and called it "half ball." In Cincinnati, they played a form of it on small, empty lots and called it "funny ball."

Back in Newark, there were even other versions of the game—tailored to hot summer days when only two or three kids could come together. One of them, the batter, stood at the stone steps of a three-family house, facing the rear entrance to what was then the largest synagogue in the state of New Jersey.

The pitcher threw from across the narrow street. The steps of the house served as the catcher. The mythical base runners advanced by the height of the drive. The back of the synagogue was mentally calibrated: Singles were scored by driving the ball no higher than the door level and so on, until a home run had to strike no lower than the edge of the façade just below the roof.

On those rare occasions when the ball landed on the roof, somebody had to sneak into the synagogue, climb the stairs, and retrieve it. This created severe trauma to the players.

Half of them came from families whose parents were devout Catholics. The world was a lot different then. All of their upbringing, therefore, mitigated against their making the perilous journey. It fell, therefore, to the Jewish kids in the group.

For at least one of them, there was a peril even more unnameable. The area of the building to be traversed housed both the weekday after-school Hebrew classes and the pre–Bar Mitzvah class. The latter was presided over by a teacher named Mr. Ehrenkrantz and the retriever in question was a truant. He never worried about hitting the ball or catching it or even getting hit with it. What he worried about was having to go up and get it down off the roof at a time when he was not supposed to be playing any kind of stickball. He was supposed to be sitting at the side of Mr. Ehrenkrantz, learning to chant the Haftorah scheduled for his own Bar Mitzvah in September.

Feet from the entry door to the roof, Mr. Ehrenkrantz rose up in the dimly lit hallway. Although a tiny man, he seemed to stretch in the darkness until he became a kind of kosher Godzilla. Without a word, the retriever surrendered and went off to chant, placed forever on stickball's voluntarily retired list.

For all anyone knows, the dust of what was once that Spaldeen remains in the corner of that flat rooftop. The retriever-grown-older has no desire to look. A man does not seek to be reminded that nothing is forever.

FULL CIRCLE

JANUARY 10, 1985

There were four of them in the car. There was Ted Benson, who is now a dentist. There were a couple of ex-LaSalle players named Al Lewis and Joe Terry. And there was John Chaney, who was dozing in the back seat.

They were typical of the fifty-bucks-a-game weekend warriors who made up the Eastern Basketball League, and they were on their way to hard-rock country for another session of the kind of basketball that was as hard and tough as the anthracite that had shaped the whole region.

This was a world where the courts were small, the fans were violent, and the rosters were a blend of guys who kept the dream alive (people like Cal Ramsey and George Scott, who made it back to the NBA), solid ex-college players like Chaney, who needed a second job, and the crazies.

"The crazies were the guys who never grew up," Chaney recalled. "They were basketball addicts with borderline skills. They played every night as though the seventh game of the NBA championship had been dropped into Hazelton, Pennsylvania. They would put you up in the seats and keep on going."

This was about a quarter of a century ago, and Chaney, who had played well enough at a school called Bethune Cookman to become a low NBA draft choice, was teaching school down in Philly during the week.

His students didn't understand what he did on weekends. His wife, Jeanne, did understand, but, like most sane people, could not understand why he did it.

They were swinging around a curve on a three-lane highway just outside of a place called Liverpool on the other side of Harrisburg. There was enough ice on the road to play a Stanley Cup final.

Ted Benson tried to go left while his wheels went right. John Chaney jerked awake. He still remembers the view in every detail. The sight of another car trying to drive through your windshield will do that to you.

"It was the moment," he said, "when I officially retired."

The time lag between that night and today, when the Temple team John Chaney put together is one of the class basketball programs in the Atlantic 10, can be measured only in light years. The same must be said for the distance between where he is now and where he was on a lot of occasions.

For openers, there was the beginning in South Philly. It wasn't Rocky's South Philadelphia. The closest John Chaney ever came to that was when he saw the movie. South Philadelphia for John Chaney was a blend of violent ethnic neighborhoods and a brutal sea of despair where people thought of college as a place for somebody else's kids.

The basic dream John Chaney nurtured back in those days was the hope that one day he could negotiate the fifteen miles from his concrete island to the Temple campus. More than anything, he wanted to play basketball for a remarkable coach named Harry Litwack.

"But back in those days, the best a black kid could hope for at Temple was a partial scholarship, and I'm talking about people like Guy Rodgers," Chaney said. "So it was out for me; not only because I needed the full scholarship but because I knew in my situation I could not commute to a school and survive. I couldn't spend part of the day with a new life Temple offered and then go back to the old neighborhood at night. I wanted out.

"I wasn't thinking about my education. I had been the City Public School League MVP, and I was just thinking of a way to extend my basketball career. When they came up to see me from Bethune Cookman, I didn't even know where it was."

He played well, which was personal satisfaction, and he got a degree, which he will tell you he had far less to do with himself than a man named Hubert Hemsley, who was his roommate and against whom he had competed on the playgrounds of Philadelphia.

"Hubert is a successful doctor on the coast now. He knew why we needed our degrees. I didn't. He made me study. In the mornings when I would'nt get up to cram for a test, he'd go in the bathroom, get a glass of water, and throw it in my face. He kicked my butt for four years."

Now John Chaney is a winning coach with a winning program at the very school for which he had always wanted to play. The road to the job led him through the Philly school system as a teacher-coach, over those icy western Pennsylvania mountains as player in a nickel-and-dime pro league, and finally to a coaching job at Cheyney (Pennsylvania) State. At Cheyney he won an NCAA Division II title. He also washed the uniforms twice a week.

"The best part of coaching is off the court," Chaney said. "On the court it's work, and we treat it that way. We practice at 6:30 A.M. a lot. Nobody is going to miss an 8:30 class. My satisfaction comes off the court."

Last week, a former player named Albert Jones dropped by. "Sorry I never made it to the pros, coach," he said.

"What are you doing now?" Chaney asked.

Albert Jones smiled. "I'm a lawyer."

"The smile," John Chaney said, "was a statement for me. It said, keep on keeping on."

WATCHING
JUDY GROW

MAY 29, 1980

It was the springtime I will never forget . . . a blend of soft sunshine and golden twilights . . . and it was gone in the single blink of the calendar. But nothing will ever erase it from the well-spring of memory.

We never really know our kids. We think we do but we can't. Every day they change and every day we stay the same and the view from our vantage point is so overpowering that we substitute the wish for the deed by convincing ourselves that the weekly visits to the orthodontist will last forever and the stuffed animals will never wear out. And then one day we look up and the braces are gone and the boys who stop by the house drive cars and we wonder where it all went and why it happened so quickly.

So I really don't know what springtime 1980 meant to her beyond the first driver's license and the plans for college next fall. But I know what it meant to me. It turned me—for one brief, magnificent span—into a paternal inchworm, measuring for the first time the miracle of the marigold that marks a daughter's passage from childhood to young womanhood.

If the softball diamond was the backdrop, it is only because it provided me with a frame of reference to measure past against present and to open my eyes for the first time to the daily kaleidoscope of what it means to be a young woman at seventeen going on eighteen.

When she was ten she broke the high-jump record in her age group in Warren Township. A year later, in another town, she was averaging twenty-six points a game on the basketball court and the first time she ever jumped competitively she won the regional Junior Olympics long-jump title. Then another town and another move and she played field hockey and soccer and softball and then, three springs ago, her knee made a terrible cracking sound.

110

The operation is much the same as the ones I wrote about so many times when the Giants lost a linebacker or the Knicks a forward. They removed cartilage, they tightened the tendons, they put in a pin. She argued with her father, she reasoned with her orthopedist, and last year she finally got permission to try a little softball.

Nobody ever taught her how to pitch. They were cutting the squad and she couldn't run much anymore and she wanted to play, and, in the last preseason scrimmage, she claimed to be a pitcher and got by for an inning. But nobody really showed her anything about pitching that year. She pitched for the jayvees and the one varsity game she worked (which she won in relief with the bases loaded) held no more fun and no more significance for her than those long marathons that the girls who did not play varsity staged on makeshift fields.

But now it was the spring of 1980 and I never got used to what happened. She was starting and relieving and she was winning (5-2), but I never got used to it.

I would watch her walk slowly toward the mound with the blue-and-white cap pulled down low and the dark blue uniform with the white MOUNTIES and the number 13 across the front and I would ask myself, "Where is that kid who was three and who conquered the adults along the beach at St. Petersburg with her belly laugh and her wobbly strut and her bikini bottoms when I was off chasing the Mets most of the day?"

For an instant as she stood there—all five feet three inches of her—and stared at the catcher's target with her World Series "game-face," I would recall the way she was born with a defective neck muscle and the long nights when she lay on the bassinet and I twisted her head the way the therapist had taught me or the time she fell down the basement stairs and I held her in my arms while the pediatrician stitched her, and again I would ask myself, "Who is that person out there?"

And then she'd come in with that low outside strike and the umpire would give it his best major-league strike-three pump and she would grin and I would see the braces and suddenly the bubble gum would come to life and, reassured, I stopped asking questions.

At least *Those* questions.

And after the game, if it went too long, I would drive her to the movie house where she worked nights as a cashier and one night she wound up selling tickets in her softball uniform until I went home and brought her a change of clothes.

That night I asked myself other questions . . . questions tied so closely to the fact that graduation was closing in and the last season of what I—at half a century—would still have to call her childhood was coming to an end. Then I thought about the bad decisions in my life and what they cost her . . . I thought about the things I never told her and now both of us would be too embarrassed if I did.

And there was a moment, in a game that she did not win, when she dove back to third base and the third baseman's foot smashed into her braces and sliced the inside of her mouth. There was dirt on her face and she was spitting blood on the pitcher's mound and she refused to leave the game and I thought, "Do I know this person at all?"

And just when I figured that out, just when I understood what this one season of softball—with a coach who took her shattered confidence and put it back together and gave her that one moment that had seemed so preordained before the knee operation—must have meant to her, she turned into someone else.

She was modeling a pink prom gown for me.

A week later the braces came off her teeth.

And who is this new person who lives in my house? She's my daughter and I love her very much and this was the only way I could tell her.

. . . And The Ugly

THE ONLY SURE BET: MISERY

MAY 30, 1983

It was one of those Saturdays when the sweat would come oozing out of every pore in his body . . . a Saturday when the fear in his belly was hell's very own fire and the only way he could ease the heat was to drink a six-pack of beer in twenty minutes, the fear so great that he never once even tasted it. And when the beer was gone he couldn't go out for more because the terror wouldn't permit him to leave the television set unattended.

All he could do was to stare at the figures on the screen and as the ebb and flow of the game began to move in the wrong direction the sounds of his three small children at play would trigger the irrational response within him that they had so often seen before. The left tackle was holding? It was *Their* fault. The quarterback messed up the handoff? It was *Their* fault.

How could they do this to him . . . how could they break his intense concentration. He snapped at them. He spanked them—harder than he had a right to. It wasn't his fault that they didn't understand what Saturday meant to him.

On Saturday, the lie was a little easier to live—or so he thought. Saturday was easier because his wife was at her job as a bookkeeper. The kids could have turned on all the gas jets and thrown matches at them for all he cared. November Saturdays began for Peter with NCAA football and the rest of the day was catch-up time with telephoned action piling on telephoned action.

On a November Saturday in 1981, Peter socked it in on Ohio State and a quarterback named Art Schlichter. He had it all figured. It was going to bring him the stake that he would parlay into get-even money before Saturday night faded into history.

But the world was against him. The mysterious "they" who always seemed to be out there plotting his downfall were closing in on him and his shirt stuck to his clammy body. The beer was gone. The kids were monsters. And Art Schlichter was destroying him.

This kid with the golden arm was lucky to roll up a lousy forty-seven yards passing all day. The Michigan kicker got the field position. Peter went down the tubes, 9-6.

Who knows what Art Schlichter, himself, was thinking half a continent away that afternoon? Maybe there was another game to bet later in the day. Maybe there was the memory of the horses who walked when they should have run the week before . . . you could string together a thousand maybes and not be far wrong.

Peter, who had already crossed the fine line between embezzler and borrower to finance his habit, and Art Schlichter, who would stun America with gambling debts in the $750,000 range, didn't know it, but for years they were brothers under the skin.

Although Peter is eight years older, each lived a lie at the same time. Each flirted with suicide. Each was and, in truth, remains in the grip of a disease that can never be cured. With help, compulsive gambling can only be placed in remission. Each day brings to the recovering addict the biggest bet of all. The stakes are his very life.

Unlike Schlichter, Peter didn't have the NFL for help. All he had was a wife who wouldn't quit on him and a brother who blew the whistle to save him. After that came Gamblers Anonymous.

Now he is one of 9,500 members in thirty-nine states. His wife belongs to Gamanon, a corollary organization for the families of pathological bettors. He and Schlichter are battling the same disease, bound together forever by a shared agony.

Peter's story is better than most. While it contained the lies, the stealing, the personal hell, it did not contain the shylocks, who will be happy to teach you how to walk on your kneecaps if you miss the payments. Nor did his wife take the children and leave him. Most do. In point of fact, she worked hard enough in the face of disaster to save their house.

That part of the story, therefore, is not typical.

But for the rest, you could put a sheet of carbon paper between his story and those of his brother sufferers.

"I embezzled from my company and got fired. I got another job and embezzled again. I lied to my mother and took her money. I lied to my brother and my wife. Somebody would come to the house to visit and maybe leave a ten-dollar bill for one of the kids and I'd take that, too.

"I was a big shot. The biggest at the bar where I bet. I was drinking martinis and smoking cigars and living on fear and I couldn't even give my kid a dollar for a hot dog at a school affair. You remember every detail . . . Chester Marcol misses an extra point and I go down the drain against the Bears . . . Manny Soto goes fourteen shutout innings and we both lose in fifteen. You name it, I bet it. I bet on New Mexico University in basketball. I don't even know who's on the team. Hell, I don't even know where New Mexico is.

"It was my brother who saved me. He got me in the car and locked the doors and told me either I tell my wife or he does. Now I got the bonding company to pay back. But I'm alive. I didn't plow into that stone bridge near my house like I planned.

"I understand Schlichter. We're both trying to survive. In our league, there's only victims."

THE PRICE

SEPTEMBER 9, 1982

The word among the basketball people is that Bill Robinzine had money problems. His contract with the Utah Jazz expired at the end of last season. They did not enter into negotiations with him over a new one. Nobody around the league was interested. There had been talk that he might go to Italy, where the competition was good but the chances of a ticket back to the NBA for a twenty-nine-year-old free agent were not overly attractive. In any event, nothing was ever finalized.

On Wednesday, Bill Robinzine disappeared from his Kansas City home. On Thursday, they found him dead in the back seat of his car, an apparent suicide by carbon-monoxide poisoning.

People who knew him were stunned. One man, who was with him not long ago at an NBA Players Association meeting, said, "He had seemed in good spirits despite the fact that he was worried about his future. I knew he had some financial problems but there was absolutely no reason to expect this."

If, in fact, as seems the case from preliminary police reports, Bill Robinzine committed suicide, it opens a whole Pandora's box of thoughts about our social structure. Money problems aside, you could begin with the words of Eddie Donovan of the Knicks, who has given a great deal of thought to what happens to our superheroes when the cheering stops or even when it begins to die down.

"How can you envy them no matter how much money they make? So many of them are unprepared for what follows. They ride so high for so short a time and the crash is so hard when it comes.

"There should be a way to prepare them but to do it, you'd have to change a whole way of life."

Maybe it's time we did.

Of all the acts a man can commit anywhere on the face of the earth, the taking of his own life is the loneliest. There is, of course, a variety of ways in which to do it. Besides the obvious, there are slower ways . . . booze . . . pills . . . other drugs.

Since nobody who has been there can come back and tell us about it, we can only deal with the factors that can create that kind of loneliness rather than the feeling itself. What we do know is that something is horribly wrong with us if we can create a class of superstar mentalities that can deal with the most extreme physical pressures and cannot stand up to reentry into the real world when it's over.

Well, hell, the evidence is there. You can find it in junior high schools in parts of this country where high-school coaches begin hustling the kid to change districts at graduation.

You can find it in the guidance offices and in the administrations of more high schools than you think where it is far easier to change a transcript to ensure the athletic scholarship than to prepare the teenager for a life he can face.

You can find it on the college campuses where—well, you name it and they've already done it. And, Lord, can you find it in the pros.

Not so long ago, a former basketball player named Ray Scott, who had turned to coaching, sat in a Phoenix coffee shop and set his companion to thinking.

"You know I really think the NBA's divorce rate might be higher than the national average," he said. "And since I've been there, I know why. The hardest thing for a so-called star athlete to do in this country is to become a man.

"I know that sounds strange but you figure it out. All season long you don't have to buy a plane ticket, find a cab, or do most anything for yourself. All you have to do is pack your bag and leave it in the lobby and if you're good enough, then I think they'd probably do that for you.

"If you had a kid who was supposed to meet you somewhere and you missed connections and he called you in a panic, you'd tell him to hop on a bus and go wherever you are. But if a guy misses the team bus, he calls a cab and the trainer will meet him at the side entrance and he might even pay the fare, too.

"You do things like this long enough, you read about yourself long enough, and you really begin to believe you are something special.

"When the season ends and you go home, you go home to a wife who has been paying the mortgage, running the house, raising the kids, and handling everything. She wants to turn it over to you but you are too important to handle it. The truth is some of us who are heroes stay children a long, long time."

It was, of course, a generalization but it is probably the best capsulization you will ever hear on the subject.

Stealing a base is tough . . . running the fast break night after night is tough . . . going against an All-Pro defensive end is tough.

But living in the real world is the toughest thing a man or woman has to do.

If, indeed, the police report on Bill Robinzine is correct and, if either money or ego was really the problem, then it is neither the first nor the last time we will hear of things like this. There are former superheroes out there, in fact, who are dead men even though they still walk and talk and breathe.

The seeds from which they spring are planted long before they ever reach the major leagues in any sport. Something needs to be changed in our thinking so that we can save theirs long before they get there. Success without maturity kills you in any business. The only difference is that it happens faster in that group where legs go first.

THE LAST HURRAH

AUGUST 30, 1968

CHICAGO—On Wednesday afternoon the Illinois delegation held a caucus. It was a very democratic caucus, because Mayor Richard Daley didn't evade the issue. He told them exactly how he was going to cast their votes. He was going to cast them for Hubert Humphrey, whose boss has insisted on putting this convention in the middle of Mayor Daley's closed society.

Then the mayor went out to meet the cameras and when he read off the numbers some of the McCarthy kids in the hallway began to jeer and the mayor became very indignant. After all, this is his town and he knows what is good for it. Out by the amphitheatre, for example, he was horrified at all the garbage that had been nakedly dumped into empty lots for the past ten years while everyone in the mayor's administration was too busy to go out and cart it away.

Richard Daley knew what to do about that. What he did was to build no-see-through fences around each trash pile. The mayor is very thoughtful that way and so on Wednesday he really got sore at the McCarthy kids, who were all outsiders.

"This is Chicago!" he shouted at them. "This is America!"

Charitable people say that at best he was half right.

Chicago was a gas this week. It was a gas and it was a nightstick and it was kids sailing through plate-glass windows. It was registered guests in the lobby of the Conrad Hilton and Blackstone hotels choking under the impetus of tear gas. It was blue-helmeted policemen belting legally elected delegates on the convention floor where no police force from any city had ever set foot before. It was Richard Daley's town.

On Wednesday night a woman named Mrs. Esther Mallon was bitter and close to tears as she sat on a delegates' shuttle bus on the way home even before Hubert Humphrey had been nominated. Mrs. Mallon doesn't think much of Mayor Daley's law and order. But that's her fault. She was under the impression that the convention belonged to the delegates.

"I was pushed and shoved by Mayor Daley's police," she said. "I was trying to get across the floor on official business for the Rules Committee. A policeman shoved me back in my seat. He wouldn't let me get up. We didn't need the police. We have our own security people. But we had nothing to say about it."

Mrs. Mallon doesn't wear love beads and she doesn't sleep in parks—although the mayor would like to think that everyone who isn't on his payroll does. She is a duly elected delegate from Des Moines, Iowa. Her husband is the president of two insurance companies. She was a member of the Rules Committee—when she was still under the delusion that this convention had any rules except those Mayor Daley determined. It cost her $250 to come here to be treated the way the police in this town handle most women to whom they are bringing Richard Daley's law and order.

Mrs. Mallon has worked for the party for five years. Mrs. Mallon has had it. Richard Daley showed her a thing or two. Richard Daley showed the whole world a thing or two this week in Chicago.

He likes to think of himself as an old-school politician. School is running out on most of his fraternity brothers around the country but he still clings to his tight little island of Chicago. He runs it all just the way he ran Representative Carl Albert, the convention's permanent chairman, with hand signals. And because he runs it, what happened in this city this week both began and ended with him.

These are his police. You cannot tie their actions this week to any other police force this side of Prague. They could have kept those kids penned in Grant Park on Wednesday night while there was still time. They had the numbers and the military support to do it. They could have diverted the line of march. They had the numbers to do that, too. But the mayor didn't want that. He let them out of the park when there was nowhere to go and brought about the confrontation. When it came, the police reacted in the only way Richard Daley let them.

They clubbed the demonstrators for being in the streets and they clubbed them for not being in the streets. They chased them into the hotel lobbies and they clubbed them there. They clubbed them—and anyone else within swinging distance.

The police didn't belong on the convention floor. But Richard

Daley put them there. He turned his police loose among the delegations and in various parts of the hall all hell broke loose in the wake of their pushing and shoving.

On the second floor of the convention hall, the McGovern kids were calling Mayor Daley's police names. One of Mayor Daley's cops told a reporter, "What we need now is a can of Mace."

You can't blame the cops as a group. This is Richard Daley's town and everything in it—from the police to the jobs—belongs to him. Discipline is his bag. If he really wanted another behavior pattern from his police, he'd get it just the way he gets everything else in this town.

The Democrats could have avoided this disgraceful mess by not coming to this nightstick community. Richard Daley could have avoided most of it with a police policy geared toward containment instead of bloodshed. There were agitators here and they did, indeed, do their work. But they needed a climate of opinion to thrive and Richard Daley gave it to them.

A long time ago, Carl Sandburg looked at this town and wrote: "They tell me you are wicked . . . they tell me you are crooked . . . they tell me you are brutal . . . . "

It is August of 1968 in Richard Daley's town but Mr. Sandburg's lines still tell it like it is.

BROKEN DREAMS

MARCH 1977

Slowly but with all the inevitablility of a stream of sewage building up pressure behind a cracked manhole cover, the garbage that engulfed the televised U.S. Boxing Championships is straining to spew itself loose.

It is all heading for daylight . . . the depth of the phony records . . . the fighters who didn't get what they were told they were going to get . . . the collusion that turned this thing into a 100 percent solid-gold farce.

None of it means much to Johnny Copeland now. Nobody ever gave Johnny Copeland a damned thing he didn't have to fight for and that particular record remains intact. Well, that's not strictly correct. The U.S. Boxing Championships did give something to Johnny Copeland.

What it gave him was the cruelest gift of all.

What it gave him was the gift of hope.

And then it broke his heart.

You don't have to be a mystic to guess where Johnny Copeland has been these past seven years. All you have to do is look at his nose, which is long and which thickens at the middle into the unmistakable badge of a professional boxer.

In truth, that's what he always wanted to be. He grew up in a section of Joplin, Missouri, called East Town. East Town belongs to the poor. At Joplin Senior High he was never a threat to make valedictorian and he competed in few sports. By then he was already into amateur boxing. He got his picture in the paper. "For him," says his friend Roy DeMaris, the sports editor of the *Joplin Globe*, "it was a source of recognition. It was mostly all he began to think about."

Johnny Copeland turned pro on April 11, 1970, in Fort Worth, Texas, when he knocked out a guy named Bernabe Lopez in the fifth round. His manager is a guy named Doug Lord out of Dallas. For seven years, through places like Kalamazoo and Lake Charles and Des Moines and Topeka, they have been together.

After each fight, Johnny Copeland would go back home to Joplin and back to the construction business, where he helped put up the walls on new houses too expensive for him to buy, and wait for the phone to ring. He trained the best he could with the few options he had.

He was a lightweight but more times than he cares to remember he had to agree to go in with welters. It was either that or not fight at all.

"He can punch," Doug Lord says. "He's no world champion but he can punch." Of the thirty-three victories Johnny Copeland scored over the last seven years, twenty-eight of them came by knockout. "It's a damned shame this had to happen," Lord says. "He's thirty-one years old now and he knows it's almost over and he needs the money. One day he wakes up and he sees a chance to make some real money for the first time in his life.

"And it never happens."

When Don King announced the U.S. Boxing Championships, he launched into one of the better American Dream–type speeches. It was all there . . . the poor boys of all colors . . . bleeding . . . hoping for a miracle . . . lacking connections . . . now he (King) would give them that chance. The American Dream could come to anyone was the message.

And Johnny Copeland was fool enough to believe it.

When the tournament rules were announced, Roy DeMaris, who was sitting at his desk at the *Joplin Globe,* read the story on the wire and ran to the telephone to call Johnny.

"The guys in *Ring Magazine*'s U.S. rankings are automatics," he told him. "Johnny, they have you as number five. You're an automatic."

And over in Dallas, Doug Lord thought so, too.

That was last December. Doug Lord waited for the committee to send him the date. Meanwhile, Johnny Copeland put up walls by day and trained by the dawn's early light and in the cold Missouri night. A month earlier, in his last fight, he had knocked out a fellow named Dennis Haggerty in four at Joplin. A lot of things went through Johnny Copeland's mind. Mostly it was the money he had never earned (his largest previous purse had been less than two grand) and the one last run at glory he had been suddenly handed.

December melted into January and still no word. Lord began

calling Don King Productions. "I must have called three times," Lord says, "but all I ever got were secretaries. Then I wrote twice. I never got an answer."

"We couldn't understand it," Roy DeMaris says. "Johnny asked me to see what I could find out. When they learned I was a newspaperman they put me through to some guy. I don't know his name. He told me the contracts were going out in the mail that day. They never came. Two weeks later I saw the pairings on television. Johnny wasn't in."

The last two lightweights to gain admission were Greg Coverson of Seattle, whose manager admits he falsified the record of several of his fighters, and Jerry Kornelle, a Texan whose manager of record was the wife of another tournament fighter named Kenny Weldon. Weldon is the fighter who says he was booked by a Texas man for a flat thousand dollars and then handed a manager he never saw for $2,500 of his purse.

Doug Lord was never contacted. Johnny Copeland, who was ranked fifth in *Ring*'s January ratings, mysteriously slid completely out of them. The last contact Lord, DeMaris, or Copeland had with Don King Productions was the day they told DeMaris, "The contracts are in the mail."

Lord has been in boxing a long time. Once he managed a champion named Curtis Cokes. But mostly his fighters have been the honest workmen struggling for a buck like Johnny Copeland. When the tournament started, Copeland called Lord. It had been a cold Missouri winter. Construction work suffered from its assault by the thermometer. He needed money.

"We did what we had to do," Doug Lord explains. "We took three fights." On January 15 they went over to a place called Quapaw, Oklahoma, for 400 bucks and Johnny knocked out Bob Tigerina. A week later in Cincinnati he dropped a ten-rounder to a guy named Larry Stanton who is probably ten years younger. Two weeks later, in the same town, he outpointed Aunda Love in ten. The Cincinnati fights were worth about $1,500 each.

The tournament rolled on. King made American Dream speeches. Guys whose records were heavily larded with invisible opponents fought on television.

And every day, Johnny Copeland went back to building somebody else's house.

When the tournament got to San Antonio, Roy DeMaris gave up on King. He went down there to see James Farley, the New

York state athletic commissioner (at roughly $35,000 per year, who had become, at the very least, a foil in this thing). DeMaris says Farley told him that Copeland had belonged but that when he didn't reply to the invitation, it was assumed he wasn't interested.

"What invitation?" Johnny Copeland's friend asked.

"The one they sent."

"Anyone who says I was ever contacted by them or received a contract from them," Copeland told DeMaris, "is a liar."

Lord's affidavit is on file at ABC. ABC wanted to help Johnny Copeland but by then there was no helping anyone. By then, it was a question of stopping the damned farce.

Johnny Copeland is still in Joplin.

The American Dream is for someone else.

So, apparently, were the rules.

Why didn't he get in?

It will be worth examining some of those who did.

STOP THE
SLAUGHTER
IN THE RING

NOVEMBER 1979

DENVER—There is half a continent between the hotel room where this is being written and Bellevue Hospital, where Willie Classen fights for his life. But there is no distance and no time warp capable of dimming the memory of what I saw happen to him in the Felt Forum Friday night, and there are no answers to the questions that have haunted me since he came crashing through the ropes in front of me.

I cannot agree with the New York State Athletic Commission, which says the situation was "competently handled," and I cannot agree with its decision to close the inquiry. And this isn't hindsight. It is the same vision and the same set of facts that referee Lew Eskin viewed . . . that Dr. Richard Izquierdo viewed . . . that Marco Manuto, the manager of the fighter, viewed.

This fight could have been stopped in the ninth round, with no regrets, by the referee. That was basically a judgment call . . . a subjective one . . . and one which could have gone either way. But standing so close to both fighters, he could and did see what I saw. Willie Classen was pinned in a neutral corner and Wilfred Scypion beat hell out of him for damned near a minute. When they moved out of the corner the seeds were already sown for the explosion that followed and that brought about the standing eight count.

Classen survived at that stage primarily because of the inexperience of his opponent, who, in effect, held him up by pressing the assault instead of stepping back to finish it.

Still, Classen beat the bell. The decision not to halt there and then is, therefore, arguable. What followed is not. Willie Classen weaved on his feet and reeled back to his corner. The commission physician says he made his determination based on his conversation in the corner. I do not know or care what Willie Classen told him. I know what a desperately troubled fighter looks like. A referee should know. A doctor should know.

I know that when the bell rang, the stool was still in the ring (a cause for disqualification on its own), Willie was still on it, and there were people around him. I know that Eskin halted Scypion as he charged across the ring and I assumed he was also halting the fight. Instead, he waved everyone out of the ring. I know that when Willie Classen pulled himself off that stool he was helpless.

I know that Marco Manuto, the manager, sent him out. I know it because whatever he felt or said, he did not physically prevent him. I saw Eddie Futch wrestle Joe Frazier back to his stool in Manila on a day when Joe Frazier was fighting for the heavyweight championship of the world—as opposed to a Friday-night club match at the Felt Forum. I know I have seen a great many managers say, "That's enough." I saw Jerry Quarry stop his brother, Mike, from coming out.

All I saw Friday night was Marco Manuto failing to protect a hopelessly beaten fighter who was in his charge. I have to believe that when you are licensed to manage or train a fighter, there has to be some obligation involved beyond the monetary payment to the commission.

If there is not, then we had best look at the commission as well as the people it licenses. As long as I have been going to fights, I know there are two measuring sticks involved in the use of the technical knockout. The first is for a man in deep trouble. The second is for a man who at that moment—regardless of what has happened earlier—is hopelessly outclassed and cannot possibly hope to win without risking great danger.

Willie Classen filled both of those qualifications.

It is neither grotesque nor unnecessary to recall the four-inch geyser of blood that Willie Classen coughed up as he lay helpless in front of me. It is necessary because it was preceded by the sight of a damaged fighter unable to put his hands up to defend himself after the referee, the physician, and the manager had agreed to send him out for Round 10.

I do not know what is going to happen to Willie Classen. But should he miraculously pull his body together and beat the alleged brain damage and come out whole, I still in my heart cannot close the book on what happened and why it did.

We are going to have to make some decisions here. Boxing—for all its misuse and abuse—means a great many good things to a great many people. But boxing cannot be worth it if the kids who fight in clubs and on nonchampionship cards wind up with less protection than a migrant fruit-picker gets.

Referees and physicians are not timekeepers. Whether it was the tenth round or the third round coming up, the fight should not have been permitted to go on.

Managers have the greatest responsibility of all. No fighter's record . . . no one-in-a-million chance to win . . . nothing in the world can justify Marco Manuto permitting Willie Classen to get off that stool.

For too long the results of things like this have been seen in too many hospitals . . . too many mental wards . . . too many broken minds and bodies.

I stood by the open door to the Forum and watched them take Willie Classen to the ambulance Friday night. I will never forget the way he looked. I saw them take Benny Paret out in 1962, and he died. I knew a manager who sent a fighter named Georgie Flores out one time too often, and when Georgie Flores died, his manager had to admit to people at the hospital that he didn't even know where Georgie's family lived. There is more to being a manager, more to being a trainer, more to being an official charged with protecting people's lives than the payment of a license fee.

It is these memories and the memory of what I saw on Friday that make me cry out for somebody to use some sense and stop what went on there from ever happening again in the most sophisticated city in the world.

CELEBRATION GETS OUT OF CONTROL

OCTOBER 15, 1984

The best team in all of baseball finished light years ahead of its constituency on Sunday. Despite the artistry of the team for which it roots, which should have inspired joy rather than obscenity . . . despite the restraint of the city's police force, which was pushed to abandon reasonable sensitivity with legitimate cause but did not . . . despite the massive and, obviously, intuitive pregame pleading in the press, on the tube, and over the radio . . . the city of Detroit, Michigan, sank to the occasion.

Hours after the Tigers had clinched the World Series with a brilliant display of baseball ability, the two-legged garbage swirled around Tiger Stadium in disgusting waves. And for hours, the inmates were in control of the asylum.

The brief but strong rainstorm, which passed through the first postgame hour faster than an Aurelio Lopez fastball, did nothing to alter the size or temper of the mob outside of the ballpark. This is not surprising. Social retardates who find fulfillment in the vicious are not expected to have enough sense to come in out of the rain.

What happened in Detroit on Sunday evening moved Port Said up in class. There will, of course, be apologists, who will tell you that we are all overreacting, that this is 1984 and people think differently and so these things happen in the wake of the euphoria surrounding an historic occasion. It must be said, in fairness: So did the postgame celebration surrounding the French Revolution.

The day had begun under fog-shrouded skies but the mob—none of whom actually had tickets—began to gather more than two hours before the game. Boy, did they have fun. They got vomitously drunk.

130

You may quarrel with the syntax of that sentence but there is no other way to say it and still capture the magnificent scent of the moment when they completed the metamorphosis from crowd to mob.

Inside the stadium, when this thing ended, there was the usual nonsense of the exhibitionists coming over the railing, running around the field, and knocking each other down at a fast enough rate that, in the end, the police had to save them from themselves.

It was childish and served no intelligent purpose but the police were kind, the crowd grew tired, and it seemed as though nobody was seriously hurt.

Outside the joint, however, was something very different. Outside Tiger Stadium they were a panting, foaming, more-or-less living ad for mental-health month.

Again, there are those who will say, well, considering the crowd it wasn't all that bad. They did not stand on the roof at Tiger Stadium and look down on the senseless carnage. If truth be told, most of them weren't within miles of the joint. Anyone who was, and still condones or excuses what happened, ought to try catching a bottle with his skull and then see if he chooses to reevaluate his estimate of the situation.

It began with a tidal wave of those same bottles and cans, thrown with deadly intent at those police who had the temerity to suggest the crowd move back to the sidewalks so that automobiles filled with more rational people could proceed out of the area.

Quicker than it takes to write this, the crowd hurled itself at three police cars that had been parked next to the stadium. They dismembered them, smashing the windows with rocks and tearing loose the hoods.

They moved on to a fourth, turned it on its back, and set it afire. Desperately, as the flames soared high in the air and the smoke wafted across the stadium roof, a fire truck awkwardly tried to maneuver its way through an assinine crowd, which sought to impede its progress.

As the truck's siren split the air, the flames from the disabled police car shot higher. The real miracle of Detroit on October 14, 1984, was not fashioned by Kirk Gibson's bat. It was the result of the tenacious driver of that fire truck who got through. It took fifteen minutes to extinguish the fire. Gas was leaking all around the disabled vehicle. You do not even need the collective

IQ of that crowd to understand how close disaster was at that moment.

Shortly before 10:30 P.M., the idiots got out of control again. This time they trashed and burned a Checker taxi on Michigan Avenue right next to the ballpark, perhaps fifty yards from the street's intersection with Trumbull. Again, to one looking down from the roof, the flames and the mob were all too visible.

Within three blocks of the stadium, a disabled bus listed to its left in the center of the street like a beached whale . . . its sideview mirrors and its windshield wipers dangling from it like day-old spaghetti. From its radio you could hear the dispatcher at the other end somewhere in Detroit receiving calls from driver after driver who said, "We have a disabled bus here . . . streets impassable here . . . car on fire here . . . people are pounding on our door."

Hey, Detroit, do you know where your children are? Just look out in the street and see your younger generation at play. Just one baby step removed from Molotov cocktail time.

And then, mercifully one more time, the rain fell again and with it came the police in serious advance. As usual in such cases, the crowd broke and ran.

The last thing you could see from the roof was two of its numbers standing next to the burning taxi and urinating into the flames.

They were worthy standard-bearers for this army of the seriously distressed.

THE DEATH OF BOB VORHIES:

GRIEVING MOM SEEKS ANSWERS

AUGUST 18, 1980

The August sun drills football practice fields from one end of America to the other. In hundreds of college athletic offices, ticket managers sift through mounds of envelopes, sorting checks, allotting seats. Down the hall from them, sports publicity directors prepare multicolor mailings, extolling the All-America qualities of the player each has chosen to make the focal point of a campaign that hopefully will bring the school for which they work more attention, new football recruits, and the glamour-player necessary to secure a postseason bowl bid. In Mission, Kansas, at the headquarters of the National Collegiate Athletic Association, they are gearing up to reenter a world of big bucks and high television ratings.

And the sound of their collective shill—which will soon dominate both the sports pages and the airwaves—plays the same old question, "Who's Number 1?"

Meanwhile, in a tiny rustic corner of New Jersey, Delores Vorhies sits alone with her thoughts. Football is on her mind, too. She is a handsome woman who has seen such tragedy in the past three years that the lines of sorrow are etched in her face forever. She also has a question. It began to take shape in a second-floor room at the football dormitory on the Virginia Tech campus on November 21, 1977.

Nobody in the high-powered machinery of VPI football was willing to face the question—much less provide an answer.

Nobody in the university administration—despite all the flowery correspondence—could provide one.

A grand jury, operating under the strangest of circumstances, claimed it knew what *did not* happen but could not even hazard a guess at what *did*.

Who or what, Delores Vorhies is still determined to find out, killed her eighteen-year-old son Bob?

The big, 230-pound freshman running back died in his room alone, just hours after undergoing a set of punishment drills ordered by an assistant coach and supervised by a graduate assistant. From the moment Bob Vorhies's naked body was found by a teammate, the search for the answer to that question has produced a series of ludicrous theories, amended replies, and, one suspects, flat falsehoods.

The search for that answer killed Jerome Vorhies (Bob's father) just as sure as if the entire college football establishment had fired a shotgun at him. It bankrupted the father. Then it killed him. Some time this year—after a tangled trail of pettifogging by the university, its strange athletic establishment, and its former coaches—Delores Vorhies will finally try to fix responsibility in a Morris County (New Jersey) courtroom during her suit against the school and its athletic arm.

But there are facts that would not die long before the university tried to crawl away from this suit by seeking a change of venue to Virginia—where, as a state institution, it was unlikely to be sued in the first place.

Despite a puzzling death certificate that reads, "etiology undetermined" . . . despite a grand jury, which according to the late Jerome Vorhies had at least one employee of the university sitting in judgment . . . despite the constantly amended description of the punishment drills that Vorhies was forced to undergo the day after his role in a dormitory party . . . we do know the exact nature of those drills.

Consider a teenaged football player, having just finished a practice session (however light the university claims it was), forced under orders of former assistant coach Wayne Hall and the direct supervision of former assistant Marvin Baker and with the standing authority of former head coach Jimmy Sharpe to back it up, to complete the following in a blazing hot indoor fieldhouse:

- Ten fifty-yard sprints;
- Ten 100-yard sprints (each sprint and return to start to be done in thirty seconds or redone);
- Fifty push-ups;
- Fifty sit-ups;

- Two 100-yard bear crawls (running on hands and knees without feet touching the ground);
- Four additional 100-yard exercises of different kinds.

Consider the quote of Dr. Richard Bullock, the team physician: "I've said as much about this as I intend to. I think the best thing people could do is leave this thing alone."

Now consider, midnight on the night they found Bob Vorhies's body. The telephone rings in the Vorhieses' New Jersey home. It is an assistant coach calling. "It's Bob . . . what happened? . . . is he hurt?" Delores Vorhies pleads to know.

"Bob's dead," she is told.

Jerry Vorhies grabs the phone the instant his wife screams. He is told that his son has died of a heart attack. Two coaches who accompany the body home stick to that story and never mention the punishment drills.

It was two weeks after the funeral that a Virginia newspaper received an anonymous telephone call from a VPI football player telling it about the punishment drills.

Stories began to appear citing what VPI sources said were "penalty laps."

Within a week the penalty laps grew into more strenuous drills. Within ten days Jerry Vorhies knew exactly what hell his son had been put through in the Tech fieldhouse.

What follows here in the next few days is the story of that hell, Jerry Vorhies's search for answers, the NCAA's lack of interest and its incredible justification for that lack, and the tortured but well-reasoned thoughts of Delores Vorhies.

Some things Delores Vorhies does know. Nobody from VPI attended the funeral. The university consistently hides behind every ploy, from lack of responsibility for its coaches to hopeful immunity.

And she does know something else, too. She buried first a son and then a brokenhearted husband at Hollywood Cemetery in Union, New Jersey. The quest for truth has bankrupted her. The grave markers are both homemade.

"Time heals nothing," she says. "People who say that simply do not know. The last three months of my husband's life he told me he didn't want to go on. He said, 'I want to be where Bob is but I have to see this through.' "

Now Delores Vorhies will see it through for all of them.

THE DEATH OF BOB VORHIES:

A FATHER'S ANGUISH

AUGUST 19, 1980

Lane Stadium, home of the Virginia Polytechnic Institute football team, has a seating capacity twice the size of Blacksburg, the town in which it's located. The Hokies, as the football team is known, are supported by a booster club that includes some of the most influential names in the state of Virginia. The school makes no secret of the role a successful sports season can play as a money-generator among wealthy alumni.

When Bob Vorhies, a football running back and track-and-field shot-putter, was recruited for the fall of 1977, the coaching staff had good reason to look forward to his arrival. More than forty schools—both Ivy League and football factory-type—had tried to land him. He was a four-year honor student, first at Irvington (New Jersey) High and finally at Our Lady of the Valley (Orange, New Jersey).

When the VPI staff signed young Vorhies, they considered his father, Jerry, whose major interest in life was his son's athletic future, one hell of a man.

Three months later, after Bob Vorhies was buried (with no member of the VPI football staff, faculty, or administration present), Jerry Vorhies became something very different to them.

He went from grieving father to gadfly to open threat. Today, even after his death last spring, Jerry Vorhies remains an accusing finger pointed at the very heart of a system that refused to take responsibility for its acts.

When VPI dismissed most of the staff that subscribed to the punishment drills that allegedly killed Bob Vorhies—various sprints and calisthenics in a sweltering gym—it went to great pains to separate the firings from the death. The staff was fired, in effect, for losing. Yet the university president remains, the athletic association remains, and so do the unanswered questions about Bob Vorhies's death.

Even before the funeral in November of 1977, Jerry Vorhies, the father, began to ask questions. He was frustrated by the school and by the State of Virginia. He had to fight to obtain an autopsy report. The football team nearly revolted over attempts by the coaches to call the drills "routine." It was, in fact, an anonymous member of the team who revealed their existence to Jerry Vorhies.

The death certificate was changed from "cause of death: pending" to "probable sudden cardiac arrhythmia with acute congestive heart failure." But on the next line, which starts, "Due to . . . " there is the single typewritten phrase: "etiology undetermined."

It was more than Jerry Vorhies could bear. He pleaded with the university president, he pleaded with the governor of the state. He began to write poems about his son's death and placed them as paid ads in Virginia newspapers. He petitioned the National Collegiate Athletic Association, which told him, above the signature of David Berst, its director of enforcement, "NCAA legislation does not regulate the on-field procedures of an intercollegiate coaching staff and, to date, no specific standards have been adopted by the NCAA membership to be administered on a national basis."

In short, you can run a death camp disguised as a football practice field and the NCAA won't take a look—unless, of course, another school turns you in for stealing one of its prospects. As Jerry Vorhies grew more and more desperate, his efforts became open to ridicule by those who would benefit most from his categorization as a "grieving eccentric."

But he had been lied to by the school. It first reported heart failure as the cause of death with no mention of the horrendous punishment drills the boy had been forced to undergo for "dormitory misbehavior" (drinking).

"Nobody ever asks about disciplinary hearings and the simple courtesy of hearing the athlete's side," Jerry Vorhies told me before he died, "at least not if the coaching staff wants to mete out any punishment it chooses. My boy died and the man who supervised those drills now works with high-school kids. Let him sue me for that. What the hell do I have left to lose? They took my son away."

Jerry worked in Union, New Jersey, and every day at lunchtime he would visit his son's grave. In desperation, his wife, Delores, suggested they move in with their other son, Tim, and his family in Marcella, New Jersey.

"He would come home each night at 5 o'clock and go to his room and lock the door," Delores said. "He would write letters, clip newspapers, write poetry, petition people for answers. He stopped eating. He lost sixty pounds. He would look at his grandson and although he was only fifty, he'd say, 'I'll never see him grown. I don't want to live—except to change things for kids of every age. To make some sense of their athletic careers. To change the rules that could kill them.' "

On a bitter cold day this past spring, Jerry Vorhies went to the cemetery to visit his son's grave. An hour later, he was dead.

"This suit," Delores Vorhies said, speaking of the civil action she is bringing against VPI and its athletic association, "is not for the money. It's for the mothers of boys and girls who are still ten and eleven . . . it's to make somebody listen to us. I have been lied to and I have been frustrated. I have lost a son and a husband and if I win this suit, then you just watch . . . .

"If I win, then doors will finally open and people will not be afraid to listen. I want a law to protect these kids. For the rest of my—whatever life I could possibly have now—that is all I will work for."

THE DEATH OF BOB VORHIES:

SORROW TURNS TO ANGER

AUGUST 20, 1980

It was the spring of 1979 and it was the day Delores Vorhies realized that the tragedy that had taken her son, Bob, from her after a series of inhumane punishment drills on the Virginia Polytechnic Institute football field two years earlier had also taken the last bit of hope from her husband.

Jerry Vorhies knew track-and-field. He had taught their son the shot put. Now, as a last desperate effort to give his life some meaning again, Delores had convinced him to go over to Morris (New Jersey) Catholic High School to volunteer as an assistant track coach.

As the car nosed into the parking lot, Jerry Vorhies looked at all the young faces, turned to his wife, and said, "Turn around . . . I can't . . . I keep seeing Bob."

A year later, he was dead.

Delores and Jerry Vorhies had another son, a former Wagner College football star named Tim. It was Tim who sat with his father and brother and watched the color promotional film a VPI recruiter showed Bob when he was a high-school senior. And it was Tim who spoke with two assistant coaches who accompanied his brother's body home.

"They never said a word about those punishment drills," he says, and the bitterness is obvious. "One of them said it seemed to be something unexplainable, like a virus. They lied. The school protected the coach who ran those drills—right down the line. It was money . . . the money they put into their program. They just wanted business as usual. I don't understand people like that. They wanted to forget about Bob . . . maybe name a trophy after him . . . then go on with business as usual.

139

"The grand jury down there was a joke. Everybody in the whole town [Blacksburg, Virginia] is tied in with the school one way or another. You'd think somebody would listen. A factory worker dies and they have laws to go into the factory and find out why. There has to be a law . . . not only for college kids but for high-school kids, too. That's what my father should have lived to see.

"How do I feel about those people? My brother is dead. My father is dead. The score is 2-0."

Delores Vorhies sits at the dining-room table and sorts through the mountains of documents her husband obtained during his incredible crusade of grief and pain. She pulls out a copy of a page from her deceased son's freshman English composition book.

"I think if he had survived all that—no, I know if he had survived all that—he would have left to go someplace else. Read this," she says.

It stands as an indictment for which there is no answer:

> One thing that has really been bothering me is the dormitory restrictions. I live in the athletic dorm called Hillcrest. We have no visitations ever. I can't figure out why not. I know they, the coaches, can't really believe that this will stop us from having sex or whatever. They treat us like animals. They put us— the athletes, that is—on the outskirts of the campus, away from everyone else. Then we have our own cafeteria, which I hear serves much better food than what the other students get, but the point is that the jocks are cut off from the rest of the student body. It is as if we are lepers and they don't want to infect the rest of the students. But the worst is that we have no visitation. Many people disregard this rule whenever it is possible. Since we have no resident assistants, there is usually only one, say two coaches that live in the dorm, so many players risk punishment and sneak girls in. Many are successful and only a small minority are ever caught. Yet they make these ridiculous rules that they know are being broken and will continue to be broken.

The Vorhies family has gone through hell to get its hands on the documentation it believes is needed to prove that Bob

Vorhies was the victim of a sadistic and unforgivable coaching practice. Now it is bringing a civil suit against VPI and its athletic association.

While VPI never once attacked the kind of punishment drills its former football staff was running, it covered its tracks neatly with letters like this one from Lee B. Liggett, its legal counsel, when Jerry Vorhies asked for information about others who had undergone the drills:

> While our (VPI's—not the police) security investigators remember learning of such a record—at least in passing during these investigations—so far they are unable to turn up any notation copy thereof or the original. However, they will continue to search the files.

And then there is the cavalier attitude of the grand jury, which said of drills that included fifty-yard sprints (ten of them, from start to return in thirty seconds each or to be repeated), fifty push-ups, fifty sit-ups, two 100-yard bear crawls, and four additional 100-yard exercises—all following a team practice session: "We found the drill to be the usual amount of required exercise with no unusual features."

"That's why I'm going through with this suit. Somebody has to listen. Somebody has to care," Delores Vorhies says without passion. She has lived through the ultimate bitterness and now she puts it in perspective.

"He lived eighteen years. He was a student. He tutored other kids when he was in the third grade. He was a high-school honor student in Spanish. He was an athlete. I can't just let all of that go by. I can't just put him in the ground over there and say too bad it happened. He had to have a reason to die.

"Then maybe—if I can get people to listen . . . if I can get things to change for other youngsters—then maybe I can live some kind of life in the time I have left.

"I want someone to listen and I want someone to care. Why couldn't those creeps have gone by the rule? I want the world to hear the answer in court."

THE DEATH OF BOB VORHIES:

BLAME FEAR, MONEY, INDIFFERENCE

AUGUST 21, 1980

Shortly after the death of Bob Vorhies on November 21, 1977, members of the Virginia Polytechnic Institute football team were told by their coaching staff: "The VPI security people are investigating this case. We don't want to see them hampered from getting at the truth so you are not to discuss it with anyone."

Which may in part account for the fact that it took two full weeks before an anonymous caller tipped a Virginia newspaper to the fact that Bob Vorhies had run a series of inhuman punishment drills between the end of the regular day's practice session and his mysterious death that night. But from the moment Vorhies died—even as his parents up in New Jersey were being curtly told a story that studiously avoided any mention of "punishment drills"—the forces that fashioned the strange death of Bob Vorhies were following no inevitable pattern.

The local prosecutor did not want the case. He was, after all, in a no-win situation. He was more than eager to dump the matter in the hands of a special grand jury.

To understand that, you have to understand VPI and Blacksburg, Virginia. In its isolated corner of the state, Virginia Tech takes on a special meaning to its neighbors. It will even tell you when to plant your tomatoes. In more sophisticated parts of the state they tell "Tech jokes"—local versions of the traditional ethnic ones. "How does a VPI grad identify himself?" they ask in the intellectual environs of Charlottesville, home of the University of Virginia. "Why, by the chicken waste in his wallet," they laugh in reply.

"They are," a lawyer from another part of the state explained, "fiercely defensive down there."

The football and basketball programs are seen by many as a means of equality and prestige and a way to attract both alumni contributions and all that goes with them. But Tech has never been able to manage consistency in those programs despite moments of glory.

"The psychology of all that helped kill my brother," Tim Vorhies says. "They pumped so much money into football and it took on so much meaning that they looked away when the conditions that killed Bob were being enacted by the coaching staff long before that day in the fieldhouse. After he died they looked away again because they had put so many dollars into football that they couldn't see it go down the drain."

How far away did the school look? Far enough to keep any sensitivity—even to the feelings of Vorhies' parents—out of the picture. When the father requested his son's transcript he received a computerized report card that noted that all grades were incomplete and added the sentence: "Withdrew from VPI, November 21, 1977."

When the punishment drills came to light, the president of the university did not do what morality dictated should have been done. He did not say, "This situation is intolerable, it's over now forever, we will not permit it to happen again." In short, the school never took responsibility. Even now, as the Vorhies family prepares to go into court in Morris County (New Jersey) with a civil action, VPI still plays the role it chose for itself.

It tried to have the case thrown out on the grounds that as a state school it has sovereign immunity. VPI now seeks to have the case tried in New Jersey under Virginia law—which would separate the school from the case forever and force its athletic association to remain as sole defendant.

But then, nobody would take responsibility from the start. When the prosecutor opted not to shoulder the burden, he asked for a special grand jury to study the case. In Virginia, seven people serve on a grand jury. In the Vorhies case a man named T.M. Hepler of Blacksburg, Virginia, was one of them. T.M. Hepler is employed by Virginia Tech as a "county extension agent." He was also a contributor to the school's athletic fund.

If the State of Virginia and Montgomery County wanted the

inquiry to settle all doubts forever . . . if the school—which constantly withheld information from the family—felt the same way, they had a strange way of showing it. If the NCAA, that bastion of selective truth, cared at all about the death of one of the young men it so desperately claims it is trying to protect, it had a strange way of showing it. Had Bob Vorhies been caught accepting eleven bucks under the table, the NCAA and its cheesecake commandos would have been there in force.

Instead, it simply wrote the father that it was too busy to take an interest in the "day-to-day, on-the-field running of a college football team."

VPI covered itself with shame in the Vorhies case. So did the State of Virginia. And both are still at it. College football as practiced in Blacksburg, however, and as silently watched by the NCAA (when it isn't busy counting profits or TV ratings) is hardly an isolated case.

What killed Bob Vorhies?

Fear . . . fear of losing alumni support . . . fear of a coach losing his job for not winning . . . fear that unless some kind of macho Parris Island Marines atmosphere were developed, football would come crashing down . . . fear of a college president who defended the system through pettifogging.

Money . . . money spent on a program that had to justify itself . . . money spent because of the tangential effects an athletic program can have on the rest of the school when it wins.

Indifference . . . the indifference that occurs every year . . . the indifference that is occuring even now.

ALL THE PEOPLE, ALL THE TIME

DECEMBER 1969

In the spring of 1936, the late Alben W. Barkley spelled out the meaning of this country's constitution in one terse, all-encompassing sentence. For the benefit of a small but select coterie of sportswriters whose depth apparently cannot transcend the distance between the left- and right-field foul lines, it should be noted here that Alben Barkley was a lot closer to the mainstream of what America is supposed to be about than all the cliché-makers at the College Football Hall of Fame dinner the other night.

For the benefit of other people who think that patriotism is a popularity contest, it should also be said that Alben Barkley never grew a beard, bathed regularly, and was once the vice president of this country. On the night in question: "The Constitution cannot be preserved by assigning it to a shelf in some museum where it may be looked at but never used."

This is the way it's supposed to have been since March 4, 1791, when this country formally began to function under its new Constitution, and Bill of Rights, Amendment V of which guarantees due process of law to all of its citizenry. It is the reason why Muhammad Ali or Cassius Clay or whatever you choose to call him could not be thrown into the can by the simple act of refusing to be drafted. The same Constitution that guarantees its rights to you and to me and to Florida's Governor Kirk guarantees them to Muhammad Ali.

The Great American Dream—and it is a great one—is inextricably interwoven within the fabric of that Constitution. Ever since Muhammad Ali took his case to court—a case so complex that the Supreme Court sent it back to a lower court once and now still has an additional appeal pending before it—there has been an enormous amount of rhetoric from the boxing commissions, an anachronistic group of sportswriters, and a great many politicians.

The boxing commissions can be quickly dismissed. They still live in an age when the whole world was divided into good guys and bad guys, where some of the good guys are still patronizingly called a credit to their race and where every achievement from Wellington's victory at Waterloo to the discovery of penicillin is somehow linked to "the good of the game."

Much the same can be said about a segment of sportswriters who think the right of appeal is a letter you send to the commissioner when the umpire blew the infield fly rule.

But the politicians are something else. They are elected officials and there is not a place in this entire country where a governor or a senator or a congressman is not required to swear that he will uphold and defend this country's Constitution. The Constitution may be pushing two centuries. It may have been written in another world, where mores and attitudes and penmanship were different. But it is the only constitution we have. It is what stands between us and anarchy. Anarchy doesn't always wear an untrimmed beard and carry a red flag. Anarchy—like fascism—has a lot of uniforms. Anarchy is what you have when someone arbitrarily says there are laws for the good guys and laws for the bad guys. When that happens, then somebody must take the responsibility of identifying the two groups. When that happens a great many people will volunteer to do the identifying. Almost three decades ago, a lot of people who happened to have had Japanese parents blew their equal rights to the identifiers.

It is a fact that until the United States government turns the key and tells Muhammad that he starts right now serving his "three-to-five," he is entitled to the benefits and rights of citizenship. It is a fact that he is not getting them. If a promoter chooses not to promote Ali's fights he is within his rights. If people decide to picket Ali's fights, they are within theirs. But, until the day he goes to jail, nobody—but absolutely nobody—has the right to prevent a man from working if someone chooses to employ him.

It is not a question of degree. It is not a case of saying this charge is so reprehensible that we will suspend the Constitution for this man. It is not a case of patriotism. Because a patriot is a man who believes in this country and believes in its Constitution and holds any violation of any citizen's rights under that Constitution as an obscene mockery of what we are supposed to stand for.

The record is very clear on Muhammad Ali, a.k.a. Cassius Clay. It shows that he still has a legal option open to him. It shows that his case is still before the courts. It shows that he has the right to work. Sportswriters, for the most part, are record-book worshipers. It is impossible for them to grasp that it simply will not matter years from now whether the record books show that Muhammad Ali knocked out Joe Frazier or whether the rust of three years' inactivity made it possible for Joe Frazier to knock out Muhammad Ali.

Boxing commissioners are, in the main, political hacks. Their personal achievements are so minuscule that nobody will ever remember them, unless it concerns a night when their ignorance permitted a man of minimal skills to wind up as a cripple or a corpse because the promoter in whose pocket they were lodged demanded the fight be approved.

And politicians, well, when Madison Avenue can sell us our officeholders the same way they sell us our breakfast foods, politicians are like the wise bamboo—they bend in the direction of each wind and thus ensure they will retain their own grubby little foothold when the storm is over.

But what will matter a year from now . . . ten years from now . . . fifty years from now . . . is whether there was one politician in this country who dared to reaffirm his belief in the Constitution of this country. It is not an easy thing to defend a man's rights when the weight of public pressure is on the other side.

But if convenience were the yardstick, we would have blown it all a long, long time ago.

Hustlers, Rustlers, And Lovable Rogues

MY MAN FLIP

APRIL 17, 1983

Just a hustler's skip and a slide away from one of the refreshment stands at the University of New Mexico's basketball arena earlier this month, My Man Flip was holding court on the law of supply and demand. Down below him, on the arena floor, the University of Georgia's basketball team was going through its pregame drills preceding the NCAA semifinals and from one side of the arena the mating cry of the Georgia Bulldogs rose in passionate defiance from a couple of thousand allegedly adult throats: "How 'bout them dogs . . . how 'bout them dogs . . . woof . . . woof . . . woof."

"They got spirit, all right. You got to give 'em that," said the man whose business cards—if he ever had any business cards, which he obviously doesn't—ought to be embossed with the legend "America's Guest." "What they ain't got is money."

Then he scooped a mountain of cheese dip onto the end of a nacho from the take-out cup of genuine Southwest home cookin' he was holding, expertly rolled it around his tongue, swallowed gamely, and added, "Well, hell, it ain't them. It's the whole nation. In times like these you just got to git what you can."

My Man Flip was obviously speaking of the enormous impact of Ronald Reagan's Brave New World of Economic Quicksand. At an age that can only be described as roughly midseventies going on eighteen, he has seen the wheels of his own private gross national product make the complete cycle more than a few times.

The best way to explain My Man Flip is tell you that he is a type of nomadic public servant without portfolio. "I performs a needed service," he will tell you without hesitation. "I introduces peoples who need tickets to tickets who don't have peoples."

In the matter of this type of public service—people who lack social insight refer to such businessmen as scalpers—My Man Flip covers more ground in more cities and countries than anyone else in the field. If you, therefore, need an opinion on the economics of any sporting event, you simply seek out the outline of his broad-brimmed hat or listen for the clank of his gold chains.

Moments away from the first of the NCAA's two basketball cards in Albuquerque, it was Flip's considered opinion that the week was going to be an economic disaster.

Not for him, of course. He reads the signs, makes his calculations, sprinkles them with realism, and never gets struck.

"Well," a guy told him, "I heard a guy asking $300 out at the airport last night."

"Young 'un, huh?"

"College kid."

"He better stay in school. He sure needs some education," My Man Flip replied. "Askin' 300 is one thing. Talkin' 300 is one thing. Gettin' 300 is somethin' very different. I bet he's still out there. Still, the young has to learn. The experience will build some character on him."

As usual, Flip was right. Never argue with a man who has been there and back and lived several times over to tell the story. By game time on the night of the final, tickets could be purchased from those who had been the most greedy for less than face value.

This comes to mind this morning because the State of New Jersey, which only has two professional football teams, one hockey and one basketball, more fights in Atlantic City than any other city on the earth, racetracks both huge and small, and a collective scream of rock concerts that could reduce all the stained glass in the Vatican to chopped liver if it ever decided to move on the side of evil, has just enacted its first antiscalping law.

This is a selective slice of legislation in that it only sets rules for public facilities. In the words of the governor, "This will keep the thugs out of the ticket lines." It is, therefore, a relief to know that the legislation is not aimed at My Man, who never stood in a ticket line in his life.

The truth is that there are people out there whose actions are giving My Man Flip and the few remaining national institutions like him a very bad name. They send ill-dressed young folk into the streets around Madison Square Garden, carefully seeing to it that each has no more than a bare minimum of tickets in case of confiscation by the fuzz. They are the heads of highly mobile armies of soldiers known as "diggers" or "runners" (depending on their roles).

A few of them are not even above selling last year's unused play-off tickets on a dark street corner and passing them off as current. Others among them have even been known to deal in counterfeit goods, thereby creating major traffic jams within the confines of a single seat.

Clearly, they are something very different from My Man and the few survivors out there he deems worthy of the name colleague.

If they tell you a seat is at midcourt, then it's at midcourt. If they tell you that you will be sharing a ring stool with Marvelous Marvin Hagler, then Marvelous better slide over. They have paid their dues and they know the rules. They grow indignant only when amateurs break them.

Consider Freddie from Detroit.

Freddie has made the circuit. Yet when the baseball All-Star Game came to Detroit some years ago, they put a hurtin' on Freddie, which justifiably raised his indignation.

"Can't get nothin', man," he said. "The big automobile companies and the breweries and the ad people just swooped in and picked every ticket clean. It is not right to have to say no to people who expect yes. Folks comin' in from around the country and what can I tell 'em? Man, they embarrassed me in my own hometown. I wouldn't even mind that except for Mother."

"Your mother?"

"Yeah, she had her heart set on seeing Willie Mays play just once before she dies. Listen, man, I wouldn't ask you this but you know you only get one mother. Do you suppose you could . . . ?"

If My Man were there to hear it, he would have applauded.

SAY IT AIN'T SO

FEBRUARY 1986

There was this bar down in sun-kissed Miami Beach. Well, not really sun-kissed. If truth be told, Halley's Comet could have crashed through the roof and there still wouldn't have been enough light in the joint to tell whether or not it really had a floor. Consequently, when a guy accidentally knocked a dime off the bar and said, "Leave it for the sweeper," everyone kept waiting for a guy to show up at closing time with a broom and a scuba tank.

It was a watering spa that created a lot of transient history on a number of occasions. It was the command post of a free spirit and passionate defender of the free-enterprise system known to regular visitors to this space as Bernie the Bartender.

Bernie, of course, was the fellow who once scalped Super Bowl tickets for his rabbi ("only because the profits went to the temple sisterhood") and who gained another measure of fame by transporting customers from his bar to Dolphins games and back to his bar at no charge in a converted hearse called the Bernie-mobile ("they'll drink in some other joint after the game only over my dead body").

He is, what my late mother would call in her native Japanese, "a sports maven." What she would call his bar is something else, but that's another story.

This was the place where sports tickets moved back and forth across the bar at such a brisk rate before Orange Bowls that by kickoff everyone went out to the game, forgetting they had sold their tickets three times. It was a place where you could bet on the Dolphins or against the Dolphins or, if you happened to sit between the right people, you could even bet both ways, catch a middle, and collect on both ends.

It was the place where Bernie the Bartender introduced Bernard the Hairstylist to American football. Bernie was out of South Jersey and Bernard was out of South England, so they had a great deal in common. One Sunday, they were sitting in the bar looking out at a hurricane. The reason they suspected it was raining was because they could see through the window.

"I will take you to your first Dolphins game," Bernie told him. Bernie was sitting on about twenty-five tickets on a day when South Florida was blowing out toward Cuba. Since Fidel never called, Bernie sold his ticket to Bernard.

When they got to the ballpark there were 76,000 empty seats.

"Come," Bernie said, "I'll get you a better view. I have connections." They moved to midfield. Shortly after that the Dolphins tried to kick a field goal. Bernie told Bernard to be very quiet because this was a very important moment. It was doubly important to Bernie because it represented the three points he had given away when he made the bet.

Just then a lone apparition sloshed toward them and tapped Bernie on the shoulder.

"Go away," Bernie mumbled, noting the gale blowing into the Miami kicker's face. "Do not disturb me when I'm praying."

"I'm sorry," the apparition gurgled, "but . . . . "

"Go away," Bernard added as one of only perhaps eleven other people in the Orange Bowl. "The man told you he was at prayer."

"But he's in my seat."

"Seventy-six thousand seats and eleven people," Bernie later recounted, "and I have to deal with that lunacy."

Bernie was, after all, a fellow whose truth managed to supersede the legend.

There was the night before a Miami Super Bowl between Dallas and Baltimore. Bernie was at half-mast. "I would have thought," a seeker-after-history suggested, "that this would be your night."

"Some night . . . some Super Bowl . . . some payday," he said. "The Baltimore people got here late last night, tried to make up for what they missed, got drunk, threw up all over my bar, and I haven't seen them since."

"But there's still Dallas."

"Dallas. Dallas I really need. Dallas flies up here to Fort Lauderdale and lives on yachts. You can keep Dallas. Of course, you'll have to give me points."

At Bernie's, it was always sports . . . the talk . . . the betting . . . the ticket action . . . even the women's bowling team, which one night at 4 A.M. tried to hold a raffle with one of the customers as first, second, and third prize—until the guy passed out.

And then, just a couple of months ago—after twenty-eight unbroken but highly battered years—it ended.

"Now I go to sleep when regular people go to sleep," Bernie explained over the telephone last night. "I get up when the sun shines. It's disgusting.

"A guy walks into the bar and offers to buy my license. The next day I go down to the lawyer's office to humor everybody and he hands me a certified check. It was an offer I couldn't refuse. So now I tell him I got to round up my regulars and tell them when I'm closing."

"You just closed," the lawyer told him. "You can't sell any more booze."

Bernie thought about that. Then he thought some more. He thought about the people who used to ride the Bernie-mobile.

"Screw it," I said to myself. "I'll give it away." For three nights (until the last bottle was empty), Bernie held a party. "You would have been proud of me," he explained. "Every bum in the state of Florida was there . . . even guys who owed me money . . . no, make that especially guys who owed me money, now that they knew it was all free."

And so it ended. But as always it ended in Bernie's own fashion. The week before he made the deal he went out and bought a fish tank for 800 bucks. He put twelve fish into it and named each one after a steady customer.

The last night, a rival bar owner bought the tank for $1,400.

"He figured it was worth it. He figured the twelve guys I named the fish after would become his regular customers. It was a nice deal. How was I to know the fish would eat each other overnight?"

"They what?"

"Don't get me wrong," Bernie said. "I played it straight. Was it my fault the guy showed up after I had laid everyone two-to-one they wouldn't make it through the night?"

THE FIRST
SEVENTY
YEARS

FEBRUARY 1976

This was during a time in space before New York's St. Nick's
Arena wound up as a boob tube think factory . . . before Newark's
Laurel Garden was asked to beautify the city by disappearing
beneath a black-topped parking lot . . . before they stuck the
supermarket or whatever it is they stuck over the bones of
Ridgewood Grove—in short, it was back before people who
thought prizefights were violent things lost their argument in
today's few remaining fight clubs where the combatants display
all the aggression of recruiters for the Gandhi Salt March.

A man named Paulie Martin had become the manager of record
for a fighter named Babe Risko, who also happened to be the
middleweight champion of the world. Mr. Martin subsequently
became known as Frankie Carbo, a fellow who was responsible
for some great matchmaking because most of the fights he
brought about were honest. The reason they were honest is that
(a) Frankie loved a good fight and (b) the winner always wound
up belonging to him. Together, they formed a dandy combination
of factors.

In any event, it was 1929 and Mr. Martin, according to the
police blotter in Elizabeth, had been in a furious debate with
a couple of fellows who were selling whiskey, which Mr. Martin
thought either belonged to him or should have belonged to him.
It was a pretty even argument but it ended abruptly when Mr.
Martin was suddenly the only one left standing and the other
two were just a little bit dead.

Which is how the manager of Babe Risko, middleweight
champion of the universe, came to be spending a long weekend
in the Elizabeth jail. Meanwhile, in the heart of beautiful

downtown Newark, a man named Willie Gilzenberg was studying the possibilities.

The possibilities were very important to Mr. G., who was both a fight manager and a fight promoter. He is remembered for many reasons—all of them fascinating—including the fact that he once matched Tony Galento against the Octopus in a wrestling match in Seattle. Galento figured it was a billing like the Masked Marvel or the Swedish Angel or the Killer Knish. It was only when Gilzenberg handed him the swimming trunks that he became suspicious.

It was also Mr. Gilzenberg who steered a fighter of great courage and modest talents named Red Cochrane to the world championship and who once fortuitously managed to open a bank and get forty grand deposited after banking hours for a client of his, a welterweight named Joe Dundee.

This was important because that night Mr. Dundee took the short way out of the fight by hitting his opponent in the protective cup so hard that they heard the "Bells of St. Mary's" all the way in the back row and the governor of the state of Michigan was screaming, "Hold the purse . . . hold the purse," which of course Mr. Gilzenberg had already shipped off to Maryland.

When asked how he was able to get the bank open after closing time, Mr. Gilzenberg will tell you modestly, "The teller was only making forty clams a week."

You may draw your own conclusions.

In any event, Mr. Gilzenberg noted that unless Babe Risko defended his title within a few days he was going to lose it for nonfeasance of office. Willie Gilzenberg knew of a game middleweight named Tony Fisher, who would fight but who was no mortal danger to either Mr. Risko or Mr. Martin-Carbo.

Which is how Mr. Gilzenberg wound up in the jail where a policeman who then moonlighted as a referee tenderly led him into Mr. Carbo's motel room.

"I don't care to discuss no Babe Risko at the moment," Frankie Carbo told him. "As you can see I have a few other small matters to think about. If you want your guy to fight my guy then you go on over to Brooklyn and you discuss the terms with Joey A. You tell him I sent you. Now please go away and let me think."

The joint was located (honest) on Pineapple Street. It was a three-step walk-down speakeasy and when Mr. Gilzenberg rapped on the door, he was greeted by a very large eye. The eye was looking at him through a sliding panel.

"Go away," the eye said.

"I gotta see Joey Adonis."

"He don't live here," the eye said.

"Let me in. Paulie Martin sent me."

Which is how Mr. G. discovered that the eye was attached to a large, muscular body that had biceps larger than Mr. Gilzenberg's thighs. It led him past the sweepers and the tables with the chairs piled on them and the broad on the piano who was practicing to be a sort of six-round Helen Morgan and into the back room where Mr. Adonis was hard at work.

The work he was doing was counting stacks of hundred-dollar bills. He was very neat and since there was apparently some great religious significance to making sure each of five piles was of equal size, he never looked up.

"Paulie says Tony Fisher can fight your guy at our place," Mr. G. said.

"So," Mr. Adonis said, his fingers still moving back and forth across the five piles, "you got it."

"Just like that?"

"Yeah, you meet the conditions . . . the conditions is that if your fighter wins we own 90 percent of him."

"When do I get him back?"

"When he loses."

Risko won a tough fight. Mr. Gilzenberg will tell you that had Fisher been able to put him away, Joey and Frankie could have stuck the conditions in their ear. But it never came to that. Today, Frankie is in the federal storage bin in Atlanta and Joey Adonis died the other day and Willie Gilzenberg just turned seventy.

He promotes an occasional fight and manages an occasional fighter but most of his time is taken up with the wrestlers, whom he helps mastermind up and down the East Coast.

"I would like a heavyweight fighter," he will tell you. "Not for the money but for the hell of it. He could lick streetcar conductors and washroom attendants until he was ready and then we would all have a lot of fun because we would win the world championship . . . I guarantee it.

"But what's the sense in talking?" he sighed. "You tell a kid to hit the heavybag today and the first thing he says is, 'But will I ever play the guitar again?' "

CASEY'S DAY

MARCH 1966

ST. PETERSBURG—They had worked frantically yesterday to keep Casey Stengel from learning prematurely of his election to Baseball's Hall of Fame. He is seventy-five years old and there is this metal pin in his hip and he walks with the aid of a jagged walking stick.

They had to break all the rules to get him in now and since this is the last big thing that is ever going to happen to him, they cast about desperately to find a way to keep this moment as fresh and as green for as long as possible.

They had told him that Mrs. Charles Shipman Payson, the mother of the Mets, had wanted him to make a special award to George Weiss, the club president, because this would be Weiss's final spring training. He would make the award out at Huggins-Stengel Field, where the Mets are preparing this year's version of eternal optimism. It must remain, they warned, a dandy secret.

George Weiss is not much for receiving trophies and Casey is not much for giving them and he must have pondered this a great deal the night before when he sat at a corner table in the bar at the Colonial Inn. There were three of them—Casey, his wife Edna, and Yogi Berra—and then a man from Cleveland, Ohio, walked over and wanted to buy a drink.

"Well, that's very nice of you," Casey said, "but I am an old man with a bad leg and I have to use this cane to walk and tomorrow they are going to take all the amazin' Mets out to Morrison's Cafeteria and I have to get up at 6:30 so they can give us coffee and a donut, which you have to pay fifteen cents for, and that's very nice."

A few moments after Cleveland, Ohio, retreated with a very large case of audial hemorrhage, Casey got up and walked to the lobby and requested a 6:30 A.M. call. Then he went to bed and thought some more about George's trophy.

He was up at 5:30 A.M., and Edna stirred in the adjoining room and as soon as Casey knew she was awake, he charged in there and said, "Dammit, Edna, if this is for me today I want to know about it."

"I don't know what you are talking about," Edna Stengel said in all honesty.

"Now listen, Edna, don't fool around with me."

"Good night, Casey," Edna Stengel yawned.

At 7:30, he stood in the lobby and waited for Lou Niss, the club's traveling secretary, who was going to drive him to this annual breakfast for the Mets and the Cards and then to the downtown theater where the Chamber of Commerce had scheduled a sort of salute to baseball.

He wore a brown suit and a gold tie and a big, yellow, snap-brimmed hat with a doll-sized baseball player stuck into the hat band. On the way to breakfast, Niss avoided further discussion about the presentation by saying, "I see that Pittsburgh says Jesse Gonder is a new man over in their camp . . . all slim and in shape."

"I been hearing about that new fellow for seven years," Casey grunted, now thoroughly distracted, "and nobody's ever seen him yet."

When they left the cafeteria, they rode the team bus a block and a half to Loew's Theater and then Casey, trying very hard to use the big, black cane as little as possible, strode into the lobby, where he was immediately blinded by Miss St. Petersburg's teeth.

People were wandering around the deeply carpeted foyer, eating Danish pastry, and drinking coffee from paper cups, and Miss St. Petersburg stood straight and tall with the burden of the city on her shoulders.

She wore a brown checked dress and a little silver crown and she smiled furiously in a mighty effort to see how far the human face muscles can stretch laterally without shattering.

The theater was about one-quarter filled with Chamber of Commerce types, who were polite through the early ceremony and who came abruptly to life as Stengel moved to the microphone.

"Now I been comin' to this here beautiful city for a long time," Casey began, pausing briefly to gather steam, "and it is a little early in the day for me because this is the hour I generally go to bed but I do enjoy these breakfasts each year and once I got up real early and took a fine tour with the sun comin' up and I saw all your beautiful office buildings and yachts and I was a little surprised to also see some of my players at that hour.

"I come here with four ballclubs and we used to have to get on the ferry to go down to Sarasota where the circus was but if we took that ferry we never got there. Well, now you have lost the circus but you have gained the Mets and some people would say this is very much like a circus by itself.

"But I will tell you, I seen the way those players come chargin' up here a little while ago to be introduced and they come faster and closer than my whole infield played all last year and so I think the world is going to be amazed and thank you very much."

In the lobby, Casey paused to sign an autograph for Miss St. Petersburg, lost his hat in the confusion, and went back to the hotel where Niss warned him once again of absolute secrecy.

Over at Huggins-Stengel Field, the joint was lousy with television cameras and still photographers from all over the Free World. Back in Niss's blue Rambler, Casey and Edna and Harold Weissman, the club publicity man, were on their way to the park and Casey was saying, "Well, if I got to make a speech for Weiss I better think of something very clever to say. I better rehearse it, so how is this? I've known Mr. Weiss forty-five years and he went to Yale and had the higher education but I got to make all the speeches," Casey began. He was still rehearsing when Niss eased the car into the parking lot.

"You look very well," a man said as Stengel got out of the car and brandished his cane.

"I got a windblown sunburn," Casey explained. "I feel very good because the breakfast was amazing. Why you could have juice and eggs and bacon or ham and one or two teeny biscuits. The menu was most satisfactory but now I got to make a speech. Now wait a minute," Casey said, shrugging off a volunteer helper, "I can't coach because it's ninety feet but I can sure walk thirty feet to give this big award to Mr. Weiss."

A battery of microphones was set up in front of the clubhouse and Ford Frick, who used to be the commissioner of baseball, made the announcement. When he did, Stengel blinked three times very hard, said, "I'll be damned," and a huge smile smothered the violent crisscross marks that ran casually across his face in all directions.

"I guess we should say thank you 1,000 times," Stengel said, and then proceeded to do it. "It's an honor to be picked with that other man [Ted Williams] and he'll probably give me five minutes to speak when we get to Cooperstown because I hear he ain't much on talkin'. Once I couldn't get him out for four years and if I see him I will hook this cane around his neck."

The photographers hollered for Casey to kiss Edna once again but he cautioned, "Be careful. I only got strength for four of these a day." Then Weissman suggested a walk to the grandstand and a wave to the people.

"Well, you better run ahead and tell them what this is all about because if you don't they are liable to throw things at us."

This is the Mets' town. More than that, it is Stengel's town—a place where the senior citizens come with blankets and sunshades and rest their canes at their feet because this team took Stengel when he was supposed to be too old. He is one with them and they are one with him.

As he approached them he made a low bow. A woman in a babushka and a checked shirt hollered, "Throw away your cane, Casey," and Stengel smiled, put his arm around Edna, and said, "Before we go any further this lady is really Mrs. Stengel so let's don't make any remarks you shouldn't. By the way, I am in the banking business but I'm not on the loan committee so I hope this welcome is for real. I appreciate it."

He bowed and waved his cane and they waved their canes back at him and they stood and applauded. Then the Mets began their first squad game of the season. It took just two plays for Roy McMillan, the shortstop, to throw the ball ten feet over the first baseman's head.

THE HUSTLER

AUGUST 1985

When Bobby Riggs was seven years old he was playing in front of the house back in Los Angeles when his older brother came over to him and said, "You see that kid over there? He's a year older than you but I want you to race him to the corner and if you win I will take you to see a Tom Mix movie this afternoon."

"That was my first lesson in the incentive system," he explains. "Then I asked him what would happen if I lost and he said he would kick my can.

"That was my first lesson in the motivation system."

He says he does not necessarily list the pair in order of significance.

Somewhere in this world there may be two people who know nothing of the life and times of Robert Randall Riggs. One of them is an Indian fakir, who cuddles up on a bed of hot coals roughly thirty-seven kilometers southeast of the Punjab. The smart money is laying 6-5 that before the decade is out, Bobby Riggs will challenge him to a footrace across an open-hearth furnace. It further says that Riggs is 8-5 to win the race and 6-5 to sell the guy a case of dry ice when it's over.

Man does not live by bread alone but Bobby says it will do until something better comes along.

"Would you say," a fellow who should have known better asked him yesterday, "that you are the best hustler your age in the world today?"

"Absolutely not," Robert Randall Riggs replied archly. "I am the best hustler in the world at any age—period. You wanna bet?"

A long time ago a wise man laid down a set of three serious rules that can keep you going for a long time if you don't try to bend them . . . never play poker with a man named Doc . . . never eat at a café named Mom's . . . never ask a bald-headed barber why you are losing your hair. To which, he obviously should have added a fourth: "One day a man named Robert Randall Riggs is going to come up to you and ask whether you'd like to play him tennis while he is chained to a donkey, golf while he is sitting on a camel, or cards while he is blindfolded. Then he is going to ask if you want to play for money. Run like hell."

This is, of course, the same Bobby Riggs who made a fortune off the climate of opinion set by the women's movement when he went down to the Astrodome and let Billie Jean King prove that the best female tennis player of that time could beat a fifty-five-year-old man. For that event he fashioned a phantom society as a marketing device that he called Riggs (male chauvinist) Pigs.

"I lived off that for a dozen years," he recalled yesterday. "I got movie roles and TV spots and endorsements. We drew 40,000 to the Astrodome and sixty million saw it on television and after she won I cried all the way to the bank."

On Friday, Bobby Riggs returns to the sport of the crime, teaming with Vitas Gerulaitis to face Martina Navratilova and Pam Shriver (a doubles team that hasn't lost in two years) at Atlantic City's Convention Hall. The match will be shown on pay-per-play cable television; the winners will get $300,000 and the losers $200,000. Bobby Riggs is now sixty-seven years old and quite obviously the more things change the more they stay the same.

This is the Bobby Riggs who played doubles for money while leading first an elephant and then a donkey on a leash as his partner. Asked to comment on the play of the donkey that night, one of the defeated women remarked, "There were two asses on the other side of the net tonight."

But sing no sad songs for the opposition. They received fair warning forty-six years ago and if they didn't learn something from that lesson then it is too late now.

In 1939 Bobby Riggs went to Wimbledon to win the biggest tennis tournament in the world. The day before, he wandered into a local bookmaker's shop with a former tennis player and British sportswriter named John Olaf. His return passage was paid and so was his hotel bill. He took whatever money he had left, laid it on the counter, noted the odds were 3-1 and told the man, "Put it all on me."

"Uh, Robert, old man," John Olaf said, "don't you think that . . . . "

"Stop thinking," Riggs replied. "You're hurting the team. By the way," he said, turning back to the bookie, "after I win, if I let it ride what will you give me on my winning the doubles, too?"

He got 6-1 on that.

"Now after I win the doubles . . . ," he continued.

"Robert," John Olaf interrupted, "you must be mad. For heaven's sake let's get out of here."

"Twelve-to-one on the mixed doubles," the bookie interjected.

"Done," Robert Randall Riggs replied as he led John Olaf toward the door.

It cost the bookmaker well over $100,000 to learn his lesson. Riggs and partners went 3-for-3.

"Of course you could buy a lot more with the money back in those days," he hastens to add, "but I still manage to get by. I have a golf match slated against an Australian pro over there in which I will be permitted to substitute a throw for a shot once every hole. I want to suck Lee Trevino into the same kind of deal. Meanwhile, next year, thousands of women bowlers will be in a tournament to see who gets to bowl against me."

"For a purse?"

"Really, now, is it necessary to ask? And after that I will . . . . "

"How do you keep this up? You are sixty-seven years old and you act as though sleep is overrated."

"I wouldn't know about that," Riggs replied. "I never bother to get any—but if you care to bet a little money and you want to see who can sleep the longest or snore the loudest . . . . "

"Call me around 2023 A.D."

"I'm putting it in my datebook now, " Riggs said.

THE EASY WAY

All over America, the head-knocking reaches monumental proportions these weekends as the best college football players and the best college athletic publicists on the continent battle to attain the role of best college team in American for alma mater.

But that distant rumble you hear isn't thunder. It's the sound of Morris Newburger, laughing himself silly from the front row of that Great Press Box in the Sky as he thinks, "What a waste of time. What a waste of effort."

He's entitled. He made a hell of a run at it forty-one years ago this month without the benefit of a school song, a single player, or, for that matter, a school.

One thing hasn't changed since then. Autumn Saturdays are frantic in the sports departments of America's newspapers because half of the nation's adolescents are out kicking and catching footballs while the other half are up in the grandstands watching. Somebody has to record all this activity for Sunday's Rosetta Stones.

On an October Saturday in 1941, the sports department of a newspaper called the *Herald-Tribune* was running true to form. The telephones were playing "The Bells of St. Mary's" in a nonstop symphony. For the 456th time a man named Harold Rosenthal reached for the phone.

"Hello," said a soft, dignified voice. "I would like to report a football score."

"Collij or hi?" Rosenthal replied in a voice that barely concealed a snore.

"College."

"Shoot."

"Plainfield Teachers 37, Winona 0."

"Thanks."

And so it began.

The next day, Mr. Morris Newburger, a successful New York

stockbroker, damned near broke his neck rushing out the door to grab the Sunday papers. There, nestled among Penn, Penn State, and Pittsburgh, stood the name of Plainfield Teachers. It was in the *Trib*. It was in the *Times*. It was in Morris Newburger's mind. The one place it wasn't was in Plainfield, New Jersey. Mr. N. had kicked New York journalism right in the funny bone.

It began on the previous Friday night in a plush Westchester restaurant where Morris and a few friends were having dinner. He was what newspaper copydesks refer to as a "line-scoreholic." Some folks read league standings. Some people read stories. But Morris was positively crackers over that column that is headed "Yesterday's College Football."

He was particularly hung up on a school called Slippery Rock. Where was Slippery Rock? Who cared about Slippery Rock? How did Slippery Rock get its name in the paper? Morris simply had to know.

So he invented Plainfield Teachers, and Harold Rosenthal, who would later become one of the best sportswriters the town ever had, kept Mr. N.'s date with destiny by simply picking up the phone.

The next week, Morris went down to Philly to see Penn play Maryland and while waiting for his train in Philadelphia's 30th Street Station, he excused himself from his friends, dashed into the nearest phone booth, and placed calls to the *Times* and the *Trib*.

"We just licked Randolph Tech 35-0," Morris said after identifying himself as the Plainfield P.R. man.

"Where is that?"

"Where is what?" Morris said in something of a sweat.

"Where is Randolph Tech?"

"It's, well, it's, you know, right outside of Wilmington."

"Oh, yeah," the voice said. "That's right."

Round two for Morris.

What happened after that was more fun than watching a city editor fill out his expense account. In rapid-fire succession, Mr. Newburger created a school nickname (the Dons), a head coach (Ralph "Hurry Up" Hoblitzel), an offense (the "W" Formation), and a Chinese-American fullback named Johnny Chung.

He also created a publicist (himself) named Jerry Croyden and a letterhead on which he began sending stats and feature material to New York sportswriters. He mailed them all. The big draw was Johnny Chung, who ate bowls of rice at halftime and who, in victories over Winona, Randolph Tech, St. Joseph's, Scott, and Ingersall, scored sixty points.

"Hey," one of the familiar telephone voices said to Jerry Croyden-Newburger after Ingersall fell to the mighty Chung by two touchdowns, "better give me lineups. After all, you guys are unbeaten."

"Oh, yes," Morris said, "the lineups. Yes, of course. Well, at left end . . . ," and he proceeded to reel off the names of every distant relative he owned both here and in Europe. "Sorry about the subs. I'm new at this. I'll have them next week."

But there wasn't any next week. By then all of Wall Street was laughing at New York's giants of journalism and word finally drifted up to *Time* magazine. It also reached a man named Cas Adams, one of the town's best sportswriters. The game was up.

It was a pity. Newburger had planned to beat Appalachian Tech 20-2, injure Chung, have him limp off the bench the following week to beat Harmony Teachers, and invite Plainfield to play in the nonexistent Blackboard Bowl.

While it lasted, however, it was the greatest hoax ever perpetrated on New York City's sports departments. With great glee the *Tribune* blew the whistle on itself in a midweek story.

The New York Times, which took itself more seriously than Mother's Day, did not acknowledge what Morris had done to it.

There is no truth to the report, however, that some day it will award Plainfield Teachers a retroactive national title.

SUPER FLEX

JUNE 1976

The last time we left Jack Walsh, the honest strongman, it was like 3 A.M. in Philadelphia, Pennsylvania, on the sidewalk in front of the Zu Zu Club. Mr. Walsh had been a guest seminarian on a radio show called "Jack McKinney's Night Talk," which was a very class operation as evidenced by the fact that a taped replay of it was then in progress over the radio in the Zu Zu Club's men's room. As you can see, it was a highly emotional evening.

Mr. Walsh is the last of the red-hot professional strongmen. He moves railroad cars with his middle finger, bends iron bars, shatters chains, and lifts a platform filled with twenty—count 'em twenty—beautiful dancing girls above his head while the house orchestra plays "The Strain from Hernia."

Sometimes he tries to pull tugboats but the tugboats as of this writing still hold undisputed possession of Jack Walsh. This is another thing you have to like about the honest strongman. His victories may be monumental but his defeats are supercalifragilistic dandies.

At any rate, the last time we saw Mr. Walsh he was walking away from the Zu Zu Club, muttering that his real ambition in life was to sneak into somebody's basement and lift up their house. As he spoke, he puffed away on what he insisted was the world's strongest two-cent cigar. It looked like a mushroom cloud in search of Los Alamos and it smelled like the "during" portion of a before-and-after deodorant ad.

"It wouldn't be too hard," he said from inside his private cloud. "It would be my crowning achievement." Since Independence Hall was still intact the following morning, one must assume that Mr. Walsh's patriotism overcame his aesthetic instincts and that he had simply wandered back to Trenton, New Jersey, to park his cigar.

That was two years ago and despite periodic communiqués from Mr. Walsh's social set, there had been no direct contact until yesterday, when the telephone rang.

"Hello, hello," the voice said. "I just lifted a 670-pound motorcycle with my middle finger. What do you think of that?"

"I think you ought to sign yourself into the emergency ward and sleep it off."

"No, no, this is Jack Walsh, remember? Now what do you think of it?"

"I think you better put it down before you develop what nice Jewish mothers call 'a killer.' "

Jack Walsh was calling from somewhere in Pennsylvania where he had just broken the listed world record for lifting motorcycles filled with lead weights. Exactly where this record is listed isn't quite clear, but Mr. Walsh is very explicit about the previous recordholder.

"It breaks the mark of 635 pounds previously held by Jack Walsh, who broke the mark of 615 pounds set by Jack Walsh, who broke the record of 607 pounds set by Jack Walsh, who broke the record of 570 pounds set by . . . . "

"Jack Walsh."

"Don't be ridiculous. It was set in 1920 by Warren Lincoln Travis."

"Who's he?"

"Who's who?"

"Warren Lincoln Travis."

"Forget it. He's not important."

In any event, if you wish to challenge Mr. Walsh you must bring your own motorcycle, your own truss, and your own money. They are not listed in the order of importance. "I am the strongest man in the world," Mr. Walsh reminded his listener, "particularly if somebody wants to bet a little bread on it."

Things have been going pretty well for Mr. Walsh since that night in Philadelphia. He is working steadily in clubs and on television. He has rejected all challenges from tugboats and, best of all, he has given up bullfighting. This last is particularly encouraging since Mr. Walsh never really started.

For the benefit of strict continuity—to say nothing of sanity— the next voice you hear will be that of the honest strongman: "I really needed a gig. I was flat and I was stuck on the coast and I ran into this guy who runs the bullring in Tijuana and I told him I'd fight a bull bare-handed so he put me on.

"Well, I get down there and it is just a beautiful setup . . . I mean it was like where has this been all my life? I am a celebrity and they got me in this plush hotel and I am signing the mayor's name to all the tabs and in the afternoon I sit around and tell all the reporters how I will bust this ugly bull in half with one karate chop to the neck. It was all so beautiful that after three days I figured something had to be wrong, so I went down to look at the bull.

"Well, he's in this pen and there is fire coming out of his nose and I say, baby, if I go in there with you one of us has to come out dead and you are the one with the horns. I figured I'd better psych him.

"So I go back to the hotel and I get this big iron bar and I go back down there and I start to shout at him and then I really show him who's boss because I bend the bar in half.

"But he was a very stupid bull. He didn't know that he met his master. I mean he never realized the odds against him. The idiot just put his head down and charged the fence and there were splinters flying everywhere so I said forget it. Then I pick up the paper and I read that the bull is 1-20. I don't mean to beat me. He's 1-20 to kill me."

"So naturally," a listener suggested, "you rose to the challenge."

"I rose the hell across the border, that's where I rose," the honest strongman replied. "They said I was passing up a great honor."

"But the mayor was paying the bills."

"Like I said," the honest strongman replied with great dignity, "I'm not greedy. If it's such an honor, let the mayor fight him."

OLD DUTCH

JUNE 1968

On Saturday, he came shambling into the locker room at Baltusrol with his shirt hanging out over the back of his pants and a golf cap in one hand and a soggy hand towel in the other. He walked over to Ben Hogan's locker where Hogan was sipping a can of beer, looked him up and down, and made his pronouncement for the day.

"Ben," he said, very much like a coconspirator on the interfraternity council (And why not? He is fifty-seven and Ben is fifty-four and they are still something to reckon with in a business that is supposed to belong to kids who weren't born when they started.), "Ben, it is hot out there. I mean it . . . is . . . hotter . . . than . . . hell."

"Well, thanks, Dutch," Ben Hogan said. "I've got to go out there again tomorrow and I knew I could count on you for comfort."

A few hours later, old E. J. ("Dutch") Harrison, who was hustling for a living playing fifty-cent syndicate golf before Jack Nicklaus was born, went out and shot just two over par in the U.S. Open. The next day he played it at even par. When it was over, Old Dutch, the oldest man in the field, had tied for sixteenth among the 150 who had started this four-day treadmill, picked himself up $1,650, and said, "See you next year, fellows," which he will at age fifty-eight.

Old Dutch comes to mind here because you can't walk five feet at a major golf tournament without tripping over some young crew cut with the college diploma and forearms grown powerful through isometrics and the deep, rich tan that comes along with playing the golf tour and getting to meet the right people at the right clubs.

When Old Dutch was their age, he was sunburned, too, but the shading was lobster red because the roadster he and another guy shared in 1930 had no roof and no back window. He was a country boy out of Arkansas and while there probably wasn't any money where he was heading in those days, there sure as hell wasn't any where he had come from.

The story comes to mind every time a man sees Old Dutch because he is a living bridge between the days when country-club members used to warn other more liberal members, "Would you want your daughter to marry a golf pro?" and the glorious popcorn-and-marshmallow world in which professional golfers live today.

He has played in more tournaments than any other golfer in the world today, which will come as something of a shock to those people who think the game was invented by and for the benefit of Samuel Jackson Snead.

A couple of years ago on a rainy March afternoon in Fort Lauderdale, Old Dutch was sitting around at a kind of family reunion. He had gone down to Florida to play in the PGA Seniors' Tournament and the round had been washed out and now Dutch and Snead and Denny Shute and Gene Sarazen and Tony Manero and perhaps twenty more graduates of a very tough school were having class night on the rocks: "Easy on the water and who the hell has the cards?"

Dutch remembered that old roadster that had taken him away from Arkansas thirty-seven years ago. He remembered the way he and his partner had set out to find a golf tournament here and a hustle there and the way they were driving through Herkelelum, Missouri, with their extra underwear and their golf clubs in the back seat when suddenly Dutch suggested they stop because there was the chance they just might be a little bit dead if they didn't. Somebody was shooting at them.

The somebody was the Herkelelum, Missouri, police force. Dutch and his buddy had been winging along at forty miles an hour in a thirty-mile-an-hour zone and the Herkelelum fuzz, which hadn't had anything to do since Jesse James hung it up, knew its duty when it saw it.

"We were lucky. If they had been any more out of practice they'd have killed us," Dutch recalled. "I'll tell you those days were surely something. You traveled light and you traveled far and you ate when and what you could."

Dutch weaves a powerful web and once he nails you in it, there is no way in the world you are going to get away alive without hearing the story about the big double-hustle at Pinehurst. You could hear it a hundred times but, when he tells it, you have to concede that there really is no way you want to get away without hearing it again.

Dutch and a fellow named Bob Hamilton were scrapping for what-to-eat back in 1934 and they had a couple of vacationing schoolteachers on the hook down at Pinehurst in a thing called syndicate golf. Whenever a man won a hole by himself, he picked up half a buck from each of the other players.

"So we came up to the first tee and here is this guy sitting there with a long-sleeved shirt and a tie and knickers and I look at Bob and he looks at me and Bob says, 'See if he's got any money.' " The tourist allowed that he did and Old Dutch smiled and said, "Shucks, you can't lose more than $9 in this thing."

Just as the mark stepped up to the first tee, he turned and said, "Any side bets allowed?" and right then and there Dutch Harrison knew he was in one hell of a mess. The guy won twelve clear syndicates, took everybody's money, and Dutch called him aside and explained that Pinehurst was a very large course and maybe the guy ought to work his own side of it.

"That was the first time I ever met Sam Snead," Dutch Harrison will tell you. "He took us for twenty-four bucks, which was our bankroll back then and you can go ask him. He can tell you the names of the other guys. He can probably even tell you the serial numbers on the bills. I know Old Sam ain't spent them yet."

Magic Moments Remembered

IT'S BYE-BYE, BAD OL' DAYS

JANUARY 26, 1987

PASADENA—Get out the old crop duster and write it in large, vapor-tinted letters across the sky above the ancient Rose Bowl. Let them drift eastward from the San Gabriel Mountains all the way to the Jersey Meadowlands and beyond. Here on the same day when they honored America's old folk hero, Mickey Mouse, and its newest one, Phil Simms, the Giants finally became a team with no ghosts in the attic.

They buried them all by osmosis last night in one magnificent Roman Numeral Super Bowl performance—all of them, from the memories of Ken Strong and Ward Cuff and Mel Hein through the legends of Charley Conerly and Y.A. Tittle, from the leather-helmeted ghosts of the old Polo Grounds to the faint echo of "Huff . . . Huff . . . Huff" and the visions of long-gone tunes of glory it conjures up of crisp autumn afternoons in a stadium on the New York side of the Hudson, where nobody plays football anymore.

They buried those ghosts and they did not forget to send those other demons, the ones of failure and ineptitude, back to limbo along with them.

It wasn't a football game at all. What it was was a full-fledged exorcism performed before a small, intimate congregation of 101,063, while half the world watched on home television, which is just as well. Past history being past history, the Giants being the Giants, nobody would dare take what happened here last night on faith alone.

The Ghost of Giants' Football Past is dead. This is a team of flesh and blood, and the way it hammered reality home to the Broncos in the second half, it emerges today as a shining measuring stick for all the lineal descendants yet to come in Mara Tech's future.

And towering above the proceedings was #11 on your program and #1 in the Super Bowl MVP voting.

For all those who said he could never take a team this far, let alone win it all, the name is Phil Simms and last night he dominated these proceedings as few players have before him. He completed twenty-two of twenty-five. He threw for 268 yards. He threw touchdowns to Zeke Mowatt, Mark Bavaro, and Phil McConkey.

But he was even more than that. In the airborne portion of this battle, which was supposed to belong to the here-he-comes-again magic of John Elway, it was Simms who stood in the pocket behind an offensive line that gave him rocking-chair ease and turned the Denver secondary into chopped liver.

For a half, this team of killers walked a tightrope that made a liar of the scoreboard. Yes, it left the field trailing 10-9 at intermission. And yes, it had some help from Denver's barefoot-boy-with-cheeks-of-red, Rich Karlis, who missed two medium-range field goals.

But once the elder statesman of the Giants' rush line put the punctuation mark to the message he and his colleagues were delivering in the trenches, the Broncos knew a lot more about the way their chances were slipping away than the huge crowd watching from their seats in the bowl even began to suspect.

With the Denvers leading 10-7 late in the second quarter and Elway attempting to pass out of the shotgun from his own 13, George Martin came straight at him from his defensive end position. Ken Lanier, the Denver lineman between them, couldn't stop him. Neither could a second anonymous jersey that joined the effort. It was strength against strength.

Martin ran right over them. He nailed Elway in the end zone for a safety to cut the margin to 10-9. But the play did more than that. It told the Giant defense where the money was and it warned the Denver offensive line that it was about to be mugged for it.

There are days when the guy across the table is going to laugh in your face and draw an inside straight, days when you leave home twenty minutes late for work and find every traffic light along the way is a delightful green. That's the way it was for pro football's new King of Super Bowl Mountain last night.

Sean Landeta is the best punter in football. The Giants are trailing 10-9 early in the third quarter. It is time to punt and pin the Broncos down. But the up (blocking) back is Jeff Rutledge—he who holds for place kicks, he who spent a week imitating Elway in practice, he who never gets to do much of anything. The one thing you know he isn't in there to do is block.

The Denvers are trapped. Rutledge sneaks up behind the center, Denver powerless to substitute. Rutledge sneaks up the middle for the first down. The Giants, with the best punter in the league, don't need to pin Denver down with a punt. Rutledge has done it with a silver stake.

Well, we told you this was an exorcism. The Giants go on to score five plays later.

In the very same quarter, Raul Allegre kicks a field goal, the Giants reach back into the P.S. 47 playbook for a forty-four-yard flea-flicker pass to set up Joe Morris and his happy feet for a one-yard scoring run. Denver is reeling.

It is trailing 26-10, and for the third quarter, the Broncos manage to gain two, whole, entire yards. But the Broncos don't need the stat sheet to get the message. They had been clinging to the side of a sandpaper mountain for the previous half. They see the inevitable fall coming, and as they tumble, they will not even be left with fingerprints.

The final score of 39-20 is simply a number.

The Giants can open the attic again. No self-respecting ghost would even dare try them today.

JUST COLOR DOUG'S DAY BEAUTIFUL

JANUARY 1988

SAN DIEGO—You can draw any sociological implication you want out of what Doug Williams did here yesterday if you feel you must, but please do the rest of us a favor and find yourself a closet somewhere for that kind of nonsensical monologue.

If you think anything else besides the fate of the Redskins was riding on his throwing arm yesterday, that's your problem. He didn't come in here having to throw the ball any farther or better because of who he is.

"It's my belief," Joe Gibbs went out of his way to point out after Williams' magnificent performance—340 yards and four touchdown passes—"that America is long past that."

Doug Williams came to San Diego for one reason and one reason only. He came to try to win a football game. And he won it with the kind of day few quarterbacks have ever had anywhere, anytime, any place.

Make no mistake about it. Williams was a quarterback long before he got here and long before the week-long barrage of inane questions generated by a plantation mentality that insisted on linking his job and his skin color.

Despite an early ten-point deficit . . . despite a script that seemed to dictate in the very first quarter that John Elway was destined to rise above San Diego as though he were part Houdini, part Prince Valiant, and straight out of Central Casting . . . despite a sickening moment near the end of that period when Williams went down on the Jack Murphy Stadium grass, his legs spread-eagled like a pair of scissors, and had to leave the game for one series of downs . . . despite it all, once the Redskin offensive line began to assert itself, Williams steadily emerged as the quarterback he knew in his heart he was long before he ever came here.

On Wednesday, Richie Petitbon, a Redskins assistant coach, watched Williams work on the practice field at Cal–San Diego, shook his head and kept his thoughts to himself.

"It was almost too good to be true. I have never seen a quarterback look as good in a practice session as Doug did," Petitbon finally confided to Gibbs.

On Friday, Eddie Robinson, who had never had a quarterback in the Super Bowl before and who coached Williams for four seasons at Grambling, arrived as his former player's guest.

"Don't worry about him." Robinson said. "There's nothing this game is going to ask for that he already doesn't have."

Nor were they worried down in Zachary, Louisiana. At B.J.'s Seafood on Highway 19, they had a forty-five-inch TV screen in the back room, a $5.99 catfish-fillet special on the grill, and what must have seemed like half the population of Williams's hometown crowded into the joint, waiting to see the guy they knew was a quarterback as far back as the nights when they would cram into the sardine can of a stadium where Chaneyville High played its home games.

Nobody had to tell any of them Doug Williams was a quarterback. The annual Zachary Sausage Festival each May may be the town's hot event, but it's an outside bet that there will be a Doug Williams Day on the horizon to give the festival a run for its money.

But, for all that, a lot of people knew there was a lot that a lot of other people didn't want to know. They took some convincing, and in the span of fifteen minutes of some of the finest football any quarterback has ever played, Doug Williams put the exclamation mark on his statement.

When he went down and limped off the field, there were those who felt he would not be back. The Redskins had a horrible field position, they couldn't get started (he was 3-for-8 at the time), and a lot of second-guessers expected his replacement, Jay Schroeder, to be in to stay.

Such people know nothing of Williams, and Joe Gibbs is not among them. They are people who do not understand the real tests of toughness. Doug Williams does.

In the spring of 1984, Williams, his wife, Janice, and their new baby visited her folks. Janice was standing by the refrigerator when, without warning, she collapsed. She died a month later of a brain tumor.

Nobody will ever quite understand the pain Doug Williams survived. People who know him best will tell you there were times when he, himself, couldn't measure it. But survive he did. And nobody bothered to ask whether a black quarterback could make it through that.

Yesterday's injury was a hyperextension of his left knee. By the second half, he was wearing a brace and extra tape. But, on the first possession of the second period, there was no time for that. And, as if that weren't bad enough, he had spent three hours in a dentist's chair the night before, undergoing root-canal surgery. But he sucked it up and went back to war.

Unless you spent yesterday in a cave interviewing troglodytes, you are aware of what Doug Williams did in that brief fifteen-minute span: touchdown passes of eighty, twenty-seven, fifty, and eight yards—thirty-five points in five minutes, forty-seven seconds of possession.

Yesterday, Doug Williams was more than a quarterback—he was an artist, standing tall behind an offensive line that wrapped him in cotton candy, coated him with Teflon sweat, and surrounded him after every scoring pass with the kind of emotion shared only by warriors trying to climb the same mountain.

There were 73,302 people in Jack Murphy Stadium, and not one cared a damn about the sociology of the winning quarterback. They knew what they were seeing—and it wasn't pigmentation; it was brilliance.

"I didn't come here as a black quarterback," Williams said after he was through dominating Super Bowl XXII, reaffirming what a lot of people who do not deal in folk myths knew all along.

"I came here," he said, "as the quarterback of the Washington Redskins."

He left as the MVP of the Super Bowl.

STING LIKE A BEE

OCTOBER 1974

KINSHASA, Zaire—All month long there had been a clue, and the ones who couldn't see it simply didn't want to see. For the first time in years, Muhammad Ali had gone back to the heavybag. He had promised a puncher's fight and he delivered. The floating butterfly never materialized.

Sting like a bee?

Hell, he stung like a full-blown tarantula. They had chanted. The thousands and thousands of them who poured into Stade du 20 Mai on a steaming African night thundered the chant over and over: "Ali . . . boom-ah-yay."

It means "kill him" in Lingala, and he damned near did.

The end came at 2:58 of the eighth round. It had begun to take shape two rounds before. At least those were the visible signs. But from the very start, the man who had said all along that he would win back the title and win it easily had fought the perfect fight.

Joe Frazier had been a sitting duck for George Foreman in Jamaica. Ken Norton was a petrified rabbit, moving on wooden legs and staying within the killing arc of George's hammers in Caracas. Each had tried to run.

Muhammad did not. From the very start, he fought a calculated positioned fight. To George's astonishment, he gave him the ropes. He pinioned himself against the red-and-white strands and he let George take his shots. But he covered up and he pumped the jab at the ponderous Foreman with rapidity and from beginning to end he reached back to the oldest of prizefighting techniques.

It is a ploy that wins Golden Gloves titles and silver-plated watches for AAU hopefuls but it is a sucker punch . . . as old as Cain and Abel . . . as embarrassing when it works as it is self-defeating when it doesn't.

It is called the right-hand lead.

It was his lance and his armor all at the same time. Combined with the jabs on other occasions, it first took position away from Foreman and then backed him up, reduced his eyes to bleary crimson slits, and then drove him to the canvas in the one and inevitable knockdown necessary to close it out.

It began the way it always does with George. He was there. He cut off the ring and, as he closed to hammer the ribs, a man recalled what Joe Frazier had said to him just seconds before the bout: "George will cut him off. You can be sure and he'll do it early. If he [Ali] can fight off the ropes then he'll win."

Ali not only could but did so willingly. He conceded Round 1 to George as a kind of second movement of the theme he had begun to play shortly after both of them were in the ring waiting for the gloves. The theme was contempt. Surrounded by the flags of Zaire and the United States, crushed by flower girls, and already sweating in the pressure cooker of an African night, Ali walked in a huge circle, screaming his battle plan at Foreman, who sat quietly on his stool.

"I'm going to pop you to death," he shrieked. "You can warn all the suckers . . . you're through, sucker."

And he went out and gave away Round 1 but delivered the message all the same. He fought entirely off the ropes. He let George dig in time and time again and then he laughed and he jabbed and he threw the first of the right-hand leads.

In Round 2 George held, he bombed with three straight lefts, he shoved, and then from Ali's corner came the cry with one minute left: "Pop . . . pop . . . pop." Ali moved. He hammered home a straight overhand right and George looked puzzled. He jabbed. He threw a combination. All punches went straight for the head. With the partisan crowd chanting as one, he stole the round.

On this scorecard, George never took another one. It began to turn for good in Round 4. George's rushes now had become more stagger than terror. His belly heaved like a beached whale. Ali stunned him with the same straight overhand right to the forehead. With Ali pinned against the ropes, George drew back his hands and pumped to the body. It meant nothing.

A round later there came a left hook and a right cross as Foreman again moved toward Ali, who was on the ropes. George's eyes were puffy and suddenly he wobbled as Ali exploded a right and a left against his face. Two rounds later, the whole fight lay against the night in a single frozen tableau.

Ali was pinned in George's corner. Beneath them Archie Moore and Dick Sadler gestured hysterically for George to move in and chop him down, as he had all others before him. But George couldn't move. He had never been hit so many times in his life. He had never been so confused. He had always been the giant wrecking ball, and each time he had swung he had been instant urban renewal.

It took two more rounds to get it all done. Two thunderous rights . . . devoid of finesse because none was required . . . sent George groping for an invisible handle. He never found it. A third right nailed him again. And then Ali backed off, to the horror of his corner.

"Don't stand there," Drew Brown hollered. "Jeez, go on in and do it," Angelo Dundee screamed.

With the round winding down and George tottering helplessly on flat and weary feet, Ali caught him flush with yet a final straight right-hand lead. George stiffened and Ali stepped forward in a final, cutting gesture. Right hook . . . left cross . . . close to the chin.

George spun slowly to his left, made a half-circle, and fell virtually in sections. Zack Clayton, who had pretty much let the fighters work out their own things in their own way, stepped in then. At the count of ten, George was almost up. It is just as well he didn't make it.

He was savagely beaten. Totally outclassed and totally outfought. Further carnage would have proved absolutely nothing. It would have evoked more taunts from Ali. "Show me something, sucker, show me something." And no more curses from Foreman.

"Why, Joe Frazier is far more dangerous than Foreman," Ali said afterward as visions of "guess what" loomed on the horizon in the back of his head.

"I really thought I was winning the fight," Foreman said, in an incredible burst of confusion in his dressing room. "I still don't feel as though I lost it." Which is a fair indication of how much Muhammad took out of George this evening.

There had been native dances and drums . . . pomp and ceremony . . . but in the deep swelter of complex emotions, an ironic fact was lost. Exactly fourteen years ago this night, in Louisville, Kentucky, a kid named Cassius Marcellus Clay stepped into the ring for a fight he had personally arranged with Tunney Hunsaker.

It was his first night as a pro and he earned exactly $2,000. It is a lot further between then and now than the distance between there and Kinshasa.

SEPTEMBER SONG

OCTOBER 1975

MANILA—It was a huge gold monument, roughly the size of the center of a Filipino basketball team. And the hot ring lights danced off its surface. It was supposed to add incentive to what happened here this morning (Manila time). Giving added incentive to Muhammad Ali and Joe Frazier is like telling the Mississippi River to roll.

They did not fight for the championship of the world, Manila, Paraguay, or anywhere else.

What they fought for was the championship of each other.

It ended when Eddie Futch, the challenger's manager, refused to permit him to answer the bell for the fifteenth round. Ali was the winner on a burst of sheer courage and a deeper reserve in his gas tank. But you cannot ever say it is ended.

It will never end with these two. Despite the fact that each one's days in the sun dwindled down to a precious few even before this match, what happened here in the climax of their September Song will link their lives forever.

Yes, they are older. Yes, they are not the men who coauthored Super Fight I, but still they move into the twilight together and the basic difference between them seems to be the anatomy that God bestowed on the man who retained the heavyweight championship last night. They were both hurt. They were both exhausted. But when it counted, Muhammad Ali had what was needed from him—stamina.

Joe Frazier displayed what was required of him—guts. And Eddie Futch, the graying sixty-four-year-old trainer, who has been with him day after day for several years now, waiting for this night, played his role, too. He contributed compassion when he summoned the referee to end it with Frazier on his stool.

The final scene in this morality play really began in the thirteenth round. By then, both fighters were shells of what they had been but they stayed eye to eye and gut to gut. At the start of the round, Ali, calling upon memory more than plan, stung the challenger, who was moving in. He caught him with two consecutive combinations, all to the head. Now Frazier was hurt for the first time since the early going.

Muhammad drove a straight right hand and Joseph staggered backward. For what seemed a frozen hour, they were caught in this tableau. Frazier, knees wobbling . . . body reeling . . . fighting the pull of gravity. Perhaps eight feet away, Ali watched . . . his legs like twin pillars caught in quicksand. He did not have the strength to move forward. They embraced again. Frazier survived the round. But the fight was really over.

What can you say about the fourteenth? Ali was the consummate pro, knowing his job, reaching somewhere back inside his bronzed wet body and firing nine—count 'em, nine—straight bull's-eyes at Frazier at the start of the round. Blood hung in a loose, damp rope from Frazier's mouth. His eyes glassed. His legs trembled. Incredibly he came . . . he came on to hold and to survive. But when the bell rang, it was apparent that Joe Frazier had fought his last fight. And his most courageous fight.

The referee, a policeman named Carlos Padilla, moved toward Frazier's corner. It was an unnecessary gesture. On one side, George Benton, assistant trainer, bent over Frazier. On the other side, Futch was moving toward Padilla. When Padilla did not quite understand what Futch wanted, the sad and weary trainer spread both his hands out, palms up.

The referee immediately signaled the end across the ring to Ali's corner.

It was the most incredible of nights. They came into the ring—Muhammad the champion attired in a white silk robe . . . Frazier in denim. It was straight from Central Casting, and the crowd responded. For the first time in his long career, Muhammad was soundly booed.

This is Frazier's town. Modesty goes big in this city but when it ended the city belonged to both of them. Ali for his magnificent finish, Frazier for his magnificent attempt.

Early on, Muhammad took charge . . . on the scorecard but not in his intestines, which were being soundly pounded by Frazier. Moreover, it was a new Frazier in one way. He was making Ali miss. In all the fights in all the cities to which Muhammad has taken his road show, he has never experienced so much difficulty landing punches in the early rounds.

By Round 9, Muhammad looked sore and bruised and weary. He had clowned to the crowd between Rounds 2 and 3, but he wasn't clowning now. The Philadelphia Hook—that cobra that has a will and life of its own and only seems to borrow Frazier's body to live—had thundered home in Frazier's buried corner again and again. There was no conversation. There was pain on Ali's face. There was, therefore, a hell of a war in the making.

Even in the eleventh, Frazier pumped home as Ali was pinned in Joe's corner. There was no panic. But there was enormous concern in Ali's corner. At that point, this fight was virtually even. Then, in the twelfth, in a very subtle way, it began to turn . . . not with an explosion . . . not with a roar . . . but with the faintest trickle of blood that was to follow. It was in this round, for the first time during the weary, gut-wrenching session that Ali was able to win a round fighting his way out of a corner in which Frazier had him pinned.

The pattern had been set.

It was a time for heroics. Even the referee contributed his share. He jerked Ali's glove from behind Frazier's neck on several occasions. He warned Ali about hitting and holding. He cautioned Joe Frazier after a low blow. In short, he made them both better fighters—particularly Ali.

In the end, it was Ali's night and it was so because there were moments during those furious assaults in the corners when Muhammad could have fallen. He won it going away at the finish. He won it with honor.

And Frazier . . . well, his story is obvious. In battered and painful seclusion with the dressing-room door closed behind him, he said to nobody in particular, "I was there, wasn't I?"

"The reach . . . that's something you can't do nothin' about." For once, Muhammad's hackneyed publicity bleeps were true. It was, indeed, a Thrilla in Manila.

THE HARDEST THING HOLMES EVER HAD TO DO

OCTOBER 4, 1980

LAS VEGAS—It was over. The crushing irony had frozen the customers in their seats. Muhammad Ali, whose first great moment in this strange business had begun with a beaten fighter slumped on the stool, went out as a part of that very same tableau. In 1964, the fighter had been Sonny Liston. Thursday night, he was named Muhammad Ali.

In the first rush of confusion that filled the ring, Larry Holmes had rushed to embrace the battered Ali, and then as body shoved against body, and as myriad small fights broke out around ringside, Rich Giachetti, Holmes's manager-trainer, fought his way across the ring to where Ali sat battered and immobile.

Giachetti crouched in front of him and put his arms around him. "You will always be a champion," Giachetti said. And then Muhammad Ali, ever the realist, looked back through swollen eyes and croaked through battered lips: "I underestimated the mother, Richie. They told me . . . they said . . . hell, he is so good."

It is worth repeating because it is of so little import that you will hear it so rarely elsewhere. This one comes from the only source. Remember it when they tell you that Larry Holmes beat an old man . . . that Larry Holmes is lucky. Remember it. It comes from the man who knows best.

Later, after Holmes had met the press, he went directly back to Caesar's Palace, took the elevator to Room 301, and spoke privately with Ali.

"I was standing in the hall when he came down," explains Leroy Diggs, a key Holmes sparring partner who contributed heavily during the long prefight training period. "I saw the man's eyes. He was crying. He is somebody few people really appreciate.

"I know in my heart if anything had happened to Ali . . . if they had let that fight go on any longer . . . then right now you would be sitting in another press conference because Larry Holmes would have retired then and there."

Earlier Holmes had said a poignant thing, the kind of thing that speaks volumes about the sensitivity of the man whom most people now will acknowledge as the heavyweight champion of the world.

"When you fight a friend—and to me, he's a brother—you do what you got to do but you don't get happiness."

"Each round after he came back," Giachetti said in the wee small hours of the morning after, "I looked at his [Holmes's] eyes. There was no joy in them. People will never understand that what he had to do was the hardest thing of his life—not the training, not the fight plan, but WHO he fought and what he had to do to him.

"He [Holmes] proved his greatness on a night against the wrong man. He won't get credit, at least not the credit he deserves. Like the man said, it was something he had to do."

"The best way to explain it," said Leroy Diggs, "is that he don't make you feel like he's the boss. I sparred for Norton and Shavers and Frazier and Spinks. Leon could offer me a million dollars and I wouldn't ever work for him again. Larry, hell, the money was great but it ain't the money. What it is is that he makes you feel you are a part of it all. Man, as far as I'm concerned, he made me feel that I got a piece of the heavyweight title, too."

It is worth remembering. It is also worth remembering that when the moment of raw, naked truth came down on Muhammad Ali, his manager, Herbert Muhammad, signaled to Ali's chief of security, Pat Patterson, to tell Angelo Dundee to stop it. It is worth remembering that when Dundee, who had thought about stopping it on his own a round earlier, tried to get the referee's attention, both Rahman Ali, the former champ's brother, and Drew (Bundini) Brown, a corner man of much hysteria, each tried to restrain Dundee.

In that, there is a great sadness. Ali sat on his stool with a face that had become a caricature of itself, a fighter who would have been stopped three or four rounds earlier had he been someone else. Loyalty can be a strange sword. Dundee was trying to save Ali's dignity and perhaps his life; one wonders how those who profess love for the fighter could try to prevent him.

Finally, it should be noted that despite all the rhetoric and all the noise and all the Ali chants (even in the ninth round when anyone who felt compelled to yell anything should have been screaming to stop it), it was a fight for the professionals.

They bet it that way . . . they figured it that way . . . the suckers poured in the money on Ali and the pros waited. An hour before fight time, a guy walked into a Vegas bookie shop and laid down $100,000 in cash on Larry Holmes.

It spoke louder than all the chants of "Ali . . . Ali . . . Ali . . . . "

THE END OF A LONG JOURNEY

NOVEMBER 27, 1980

NEW ORLEANS—It was over. Roberto Duran, who publicly defrocked himself, had left the room for a postfight press conference, surrounded by an army of supernumeraries dressed in softball suits with the Panamanian flag emblazoned across the back. Carlos Eleta, the manager, had left with him. The cameras were gone. The freeloaders were gone.

Now there was only the crude residue of a night gone sour . . . the discraded tape gleaming oddly yellow under the fluorescent lighting . . . an old newspaper . . . a trail of debris left by the sycophants who had jammed the joint. Now there was only the silence and the two of them sat there on rickety folding chairs . . . talking softly . . . the sound of their long pauses speaking volumes.

They have come a long way, these two . . . down through the decades when Ray Arcel walked fifteen miles from Queens to Stillman's Gym with a nickel in his pocket for lunch and Freddie Brown first began to bandage fighters' hands in arenas that the weight of time has transformed into parking lots and supermarket sites today.

Later, in the hotel coffee shop across from the Superdome, Freddie would look down at his coffee mug, look up, and say, very much like a man whose love for his fighter precluded naming the unnameable possibility: "He didn't have no viciousness . . . I mean that ain't Duran . . . I've known this kid a long time. It was like he was off somewhere else."

But now, the old cardigan sweater was crammed into the little gym bag. He wore a blue-checkered sport jacket and a blue tie.

Across from him, Arcel still wore the long-sleeved tropical sport shirt that is his working uniform.

"What happened, Freddie . . . what happened?"

"Who the hell knows?" Brown said softly. "How do you figure something like this . . . a kid like that . . . . Come on, Ray, get dressed. Let's get out of here."

"I want to walk back, Freddie. I need fresh air."

"So come on, let's get out of this place."

Then the door opened and Emile Bruneau, the head of the Louisiana State Athletic Commission, was standing there with clear anger in his voice. Bruneau and Arcel and Brown are graduates of the Great Depression School of Boxing. Nobody can begin to assess the ties that bound them together from a hundred shared ringsides. "I want to know what happened in that ring," Bruneau said.

"I wish I could tell you," Arcel replied. Cramps? "I don't know. I know in the fifth round he said his arm hurt. Then he spoke to the Spanish trainer [Nestor Quinones]. I don't speak Spanish. I don't know what he said. I told him if the arm hurts, he should try using it. I told him there was still time to win the fight. I don't know what else to say . . . what to do."

"Well, I do," Bruneau said. "You find King and Eleta and tell them to get over here right away. I'm going to hold up the purse."

So Ray Arcel, age eighty-one, and Freddie Brown, age seventy-six, walked slowly off along the rain-soaked pavement to the Hyatt Regency, where Arcel found Eleta. Together they sat and talked with Colonel Reuben Parades, the second highest-ranking Panamanian military official. As they spoke, Sandra Eleta, the manager's daughter, was talking on the telephone with General Omar Torrijos, trying to discuss a trauma neither of them understood.

Then Eleta and Arcel walked back to the Dome to meet with Bruneau and the commissioners. Meanwhile, from Duran's eighteenth-floor room there came the sound of music and singing and Duran's voice. It was a strange moment within its frame of reference, but the next morning Saoul Mamby, the junior welterweight champion, would think it rational.

"I sat up with them. I got drunk with them. What else can you do at a time like that?"

Back at the Dome, Bruneau was telling the other commissioners that "I know Ray Arcel for years. I know Freddie Brown. Neither of them would ever do anything in this business that was wrong but I have been in boxing since 1923 and I have never seen anything like tonight. I want to tell you what he thinks happened."

Arcel repeated what he had told Bruneau earlier and then Bruneau made a motion to suspend Duran and hold his purse (although how much of that money is in Louisiana is highly conjectural), and then Arcel held up his hand and looked Bruneau in the eye and he said with a great sadness in his voice, "Please, before you act, let me plead his case."

They were the words of a man whose whole life has been steeped in honor and duty and now in this moment when he had no explanation for the bizarre scene that had happened a few hours earlier . . . at this moment when heartbreak clearly cut deeply within him in the wake of his last fighter's last fight, he would not resign from a role that has been part of his life for more than sixty years.

It was the reason he never wanted to manage fighters and never did. It was the tie that forever binds trainer and fighter together and now he was performing what he said later would be his last official act in that role.

"I don't know what happened in that ring tonight. I know Roberto Duran is one of the great fighters of this era. I know everything he has ever done until now has brought honor to this business and to himself. This morning if anyone would tell me that Roberto Duran would quit in the ring, I would throw a punch at him. If he felt he could fight no more, then remember he is no intellect. He is a human being who believed what he felt. Thank you."

An hour later, Ray Arcel sat wearily in a straight-backed chair in Room 1818 of the Hyatt Regency. The tie was still in place. The vest beneath the dark business suit was still buttoned. The sadness hung in the room like a mushroom cloud. His wife, Stevie, was sprawled across the bed . . . her eyes were red but never wavering from her husband. Two close friends from Panama were there, too.

"Have you ever seen anything like this with any fighter you ever trained?" a guy asked.

"Never."

"Do you know what happened?"

"No, this is one of the greatest disappointments of my life. I feel so badly for Carlos [Eleta] . . . so badly for Colonel

Parades . . . so badly for the people back in Panama. Yes, we had troubles with his weight. He would leave the gym at 150 and come back the next day at 154 and I pleaded with the people around him not to sneak him food and then I would talk to him and he would say, 'No worry, Ray, I knock him out.' But tonight he was listless. He would come back to the corner and I would ask him how he felt and he would mumble he was okay. And the way it ended . . . .

"I saw him turn away and there was so much noise I assumed the bell had rung and then Leonard hit him a body shot and I called to Freddie that fellow is hitting him after the bell. And then there was the confusion."

All night long Ray Arcel fielded phone calls. Now it was 2 A.M. and then it was 3 A.M. but he could not sleep. Burned into his memory was the sight of the fighter he and Freddie Brown had taken wild and untutored virtually off the streets of Panama City and turned first into the lightweight champion and then into the welterweight champion and with Arcel it had never been the money . . . he has a well-paying job . . . he had a lifetime of professional brilliance . . . but at the finish there was the memory of the frozen tableau which would not leave him.

Roberto Duran in the middle of the crowded dressing room, surrounded by the Latin press . . . the noise . . . the shouting . . . and the one moment when Arcel's eyes met those of Freddie Brown. Each shook his head. Even the sight of Duran crying in his room the next afternoon cannot erase that painful moment.

ROYALS GRAB THE GLORY

OCTOBER 28, 1985

KANSAS CITY—Eleven to nothing and it doesn't even begin to tell it.

Now they have become the patron saints of every high-school baseball coach whose team is losing a sectional final 23-4 in the eighth inning and who will call his players off to one side and invoke their name.

They are the Little Engine That Could—and did . . . they are Team Cinderella, and ask not for whom the clock in the city square tolled last night because you already know and it wasn't them. You look at their uniforms and you say, "Freeze. Nobody leave the room until we identify these people."

You get the feeling that the name on the front shouldn't say "Royals." It should read "St. Jude's Tigers" or "Lourdes Senators."

Last night, under a full moon, just a hop, skip, and a tiny piece of freeway away from the border of the very spot where Dorothy and Toto made aeronautical history, the only team ever to lose the first two games at home, and then win it all, took off their masks and revealed themselves as the Kansas City Royals.

And to all the slick intelligentsia on the East Coast and all the laid-back Californians, who insisted that playing an entire World Series in the state of Missouri was like putting the Hope Diamond into a corn-silk setting, let it be said that the people who played the game and the people who sat in the two parks to watch it got along very nicely without them.

They saw a dandy series. They saw history in the Royals comeback, and last night, with twenty-one-year-old Bret Saberhagen, who looks like he ought to be signing high-school yearbooks, throwing for the home side, they saw the ascendancy of their patchwork heroes to glory.

They saw something else, too. They saw the total disintegration of the St. Louis Cardinals, which culminated in the fifth inning when the Royals scored six times on seven hits, two walks, and a wild pitch.

They saw a moment of abject stupidity that swung into focus that same inning when Joaquin Andujar was brought in from the bull pen to retire the Royals, who were in midexplosion.

Joaquin, who bristles when you mention that he hasn't won since August, thereby making him the strangest of twenty-one-game winners, has not been very effective in the post-season.

Earlier in the series, his complaints were enough to make you think that the umpires possibly had conspired to embarrass him.

Most folks think Joaquin was doing a good enough job of that all by himself—but that's another story.

In any event, when home-plate umpire Don Denkinger called a ball instead of what Joaquin thought was a strike, he came off the mound toward him, shouting all the while. It did not appear as though he were screaming, "I am sorry, old chap, but it appears to me as though you may want to reconsider that particular hasty decision."

It took three players to restrain him. At the same time, Whitey Herzog, the Cardinals' manager who has been a real charmer this series, rushed at Denkinger and managed to get himself thrown out of the game, thereby proving himself to be no dummy. Would you want to continue sitting there in his position?

After a similar pitch, and a similar exchange, Joaquin, who had to be wrestled under control again, was kicked out.

Actually, he escaped more easily than starter John Tudor, who punctuated his removal from the game by pounding on a metal fan in the locker room.

The fan won, and Tudor was taken to a nearby hospital for stitches.

In any event, the fifth inning obviously settled it, but on such a night it would be a shame to overlook the hero who actually provided enough runs for Saberhagen before the ultimate carnage broke loose.

The runs came in the second inning against John Tudor with Steve Balboni on base.

Out in Portland, Oregon, Darryl Motley was known for several years as the Grant High basketball player who once held Danny Ainge of North Eugene High to just eight points in the state high school basketball final.

Sorry, Grant High. Darryl has a new distinction now.

He tied into Tudor and slammed a tremendous foul into the left-field seats, breaking the bat in the process. A new bat . . . a new pitch . . . a rocket that nestled into the seats in fair ground near the foul pole for all the runs Saberhagen would need.

The rest was so one-sided, so easy, and so definitive that you had to wonder what took this team seven games to get the job done.

Saberhagen, the MVP, was marvelous. This is the same young man who only three years ago stood on a pitcher's mound in California with a grandstand full of kids behind him and pitched a no-hitter to win the L.A. city championship for Cleveland High.

When you consider that in the past ten days he won two World Series games, became a father, and now could probably be elected mayor of Kansas City, you could do worse than recall the words of his mother, Linda.

She was asked yesterday what she thought of all of this.

"When he was a kid, he used to say he was going to do this some day, but, of course, I never believed it. Then I think of the way he was hit by that ball during the play-offs in Toronto and how dangerous it was and I say to myself that I'm sure glad he didn't pick football."

That thunderous noise in the background, Momma Saberhagen, is an *a cappella* chorus of all of Greater Kansas City shouting a collective "Amen."

GAME SIX TAKES PLACE IN BASEBALL HISTORY

OCTOBER 16, 1986

HOUSTON—How are you going to describe it?

Where do you even begin?

You start by placing it alongside all the measuring sticks ever assembled for the kind of events that reaffirm the shining truth that professionals at work need neither paintbrush nor sculptor's chisel to fashion a work of art.

Yesterday in Houston was Johnny Unitas in the gloom of a December Sunday while the wind and the cold bounced off the concrete façade of Yankee Stadium and he took the Colts down the field against the Giants and through the Valley of the Shadow of Sudden Death.

It was Muhammad Ali and Joe Frazier slamming into each other in the teeth of a blazing Manila pressure cooker. It was the miracle of a dead heat with two tons of horseflesh straining for the wire flank to flank and heart to heart.

What the Mets and Astros put together under glass for sixteen innings, four hours, and forty-two minutes was the greatest baseball game ever played.

For the Mets, it was as basic as blood and sand . . . the blood they poured into an incredible comeback that used up every pinch-hitter but one and drained every possible emotion . . . the sand they believe with their collective heart is as much a part of a Houston pitcher named Mike Scott as his toenails.

For a week they had lived a nightmare that echoed from one end of their dugout to the other like the screech of a fingernail on #5 sandpaper. For a week the players ranted and the general manager litigated and the entire franchise trembled. And yesterday, for four hours and forty-two minutes they reached down inside and played with the desperation of men determined to take tonight off their calendars and Mike Scott out of their lives.

And so they won it and this October week will forever be reckoned in Houston, Texas, as one afternoon too long and one day too short.

You cannot begin to describe how many times the Mets staggered and clawed their way back during this study in gut-wrenching endurance . . . how many times Hal Lanier, the Astro manager, could see Mike Scott in his mind's eye, reaching for the ball on a Thursday night that will never come . . . how many minidramas were played out against an overall backdrop that down the road is going to stand alone as the measuring stick for the limits to which two baseball teams can push themselves.

Think about Ray Knight . . . who was a teammate of many of these same Astros for two and a half years . . . who almost didn't make the Mets in the spring.

It was Knight who delivered the sacrifice fly that produced the tying run in the Mets' three-run ninth and whose single in the sixteenth broke that tie. And when it came down to that moment in this time capsule, with Darryl Strawberry nestled in at second base after a leadoff double, Knight walked down to his manager, Davey Johnson, and asked if he wanted him to bunt.

"Hell, no," Johnson told him. "Drive the ball to right field and get him home."

"I can do that," Knight said. And he did.

There was Jesse Orosco, who won three games in relief in this series and took a one-run lead into the fourteenth and watched in frustration when Billy Hatcher, who hit six whole, entire home runs this year, drove a fastball up the left-field foul pole to tie it again. It was Jesse who kept on struggling after he took a three-run lead into the bottom of the sixteenth.

And it was Jesse who faced down Kevin Bass, the best Astro hitter in 1986 at the finish, on a 3-2 pitch with the potential tying and winning runs on base. The pitching chart says he did it with six straight sliders. But the tightness in Jesse's chest will tell you that his heart was as much a part of it as his pitching arm.

There were Len Dykstra and Wally Backman, coming off the bench and making things happen, each driving in a run and scoring a run . . . Dykstra, who bristles when they call him "too small" and who is not supposed to be able to play center field, but does . . . Backman, who had a major-league bat in the minors but who crouched in the blazing Florida sunshine hour after hour, fielding ground ball after ground ball from a former Mets coach named Bobby Valentine.

You can run down this roster from end to end and all the stories fall neatly into place.

There is a bravado that comes in the wake of a championship. The Mets may forget the drama of the night they took off the calendar, and the pitcher, Scott, from whom they took the ball in Houston.

But not Davey Johnson: "I just got a pardon."

But he wasn't given one. The Mets took it.

SMART MOVE

APRIL 1987

NEW ORLEANS—It was a Final Two for everyone . . . for the sons and daughters of the Indiana cornfields . . . for the mid-America balladeers of the Legend of Bobby Knight . . . for the take-the-three-points bettors of America . . . for all the second-second-guessers from Syracuse, New York, where spring may not come at all this year, to California . . . and for the army of self-appointed cousins by the dozen of Keith Smart, who will claim kinship this morning in numbers far outstripping the entire population of his native Baton Rouge.

Indiana did not win as much as it used what it had to magnificently endure.

Syracuse did not lose as much as it succumbed to the sin it fatally decided to ignore.

And nobody had the slightest idea of who was going to do what to whom until the final thirty ticks of the clock. The final score of 74-73 doesn't tell it. The real margin was about the width of a gnat's eyelash.

A single play?

Well, it had that.

A single coaching decision?

It had that.

A hero straight out of Central Casting?

It had that, too.

And like a single illusion seen through a fixed telescope, it all happened in the final thirty seconds. At that point, utilizing four changing defenses, Syracuse had played Steve Alford about as well as anyone could hope to play him. It had outrebounded Indiana. It had muscled its way through the Shadow of the Valley of Indiana's rolling screens and it had led much of the way.

Now with Indiana trailing by a point and Syracuse inbounding from its own end of the floor, it took Indiana just two seconds to foul Derrick Coleman.

Now it was Peril City for the Orange. They are a terrible foul-shooting ballclub. "I didn't think anything when they [Indiana] did that," the Syracuse coach, Jim Boeheim, would say afterward. "I can't worry about things I can't control."

So now it was a time of decision . . . a freshman at the foul line with a slender one-point lead, shooting a one-and-one . . . Indiana guaranteed at least one more trip down the floor. On Saturday, against Providence, Syracuse had knocked in missed foul shots for two-pointers over and over again. Last night, it was outrebounding Indiana.

The choice Jim Boeheim faced with this: Play it straight and remain in position for an offensive rebound or concede the rebound (should the shot be missed) and bring the big men back down court to avoid an offensive foul on the rebound and protect against the transition basket that could lose it for him.

He opted for the latter.

The argument over the decision will be around for a long time. Boeheim said, "We had enough points to win the game. We had the lead. We wanted to protect it." Knight said, "I think he did the right thing. What would you say if his kid picks up an offensive foul going over someone's back for the rebound?"

It is arguable either way.

What followed is not.

Coleman's try never had a chance. It skittered off the rim and away to the right, where Daryl Thomas swooped in to grab it with twenty-seven seconds remaining. Twenty-two seconds later, Joe Hillman, who had come off the bench, set a screen.

Enter The Mouse that Grew.

Keith Smart is the hero only Central Casting could produce. He is the Prodigal Son from up the road in Baton Rouge that nobody recruited. He is the overreacher who had, as a five-foot three-inch sophomore, had no chance to crack the starting lineup of the best high-school basketball team in Louisiana.

He is the pest who grew to five feet six inches and then five feet nine inches and then finished second in a tug-of-war with a motorcycle and blew almost all his high-school career.

In a world of McDonald's High School All-Americans, he is the guy who didn't make that team but who made another one after school behind the counter at the Golden Arches, which sponsors it.

He is the orphan of the half-court storm who couldn't stay away from what he loved, who played the game night after night at a Police Athletic League gymnasium and found his way to junior college.

He is the lonely jump-shooter far from home in Garden City, Kansas, who got a letter from Bobby Knight asking him if he wanted to come to Indiana after his junior-college career—and who threw it in the garbage because of all the horror stories he had heard. He is the junior-college transfer on a one-man crusade to dispel the image of all the nation's juco kids as dysfunctional illiterates who march only to the beat of a bouncing basketball.

To prove that point, he carried and passed courses adding up to eighteen credits his first semester to make himself eligible.

And now, home from the cultural way-stops of Garden City, Kansas, and Bloomington, Indiana, Keith Smart, a six-foot one-inch guard, towered above all the giants on the Superdome floor.

It was a fifteen-foot jumper as he let it go as the clock showed just five ticks left.

"I just took what they gave me," he said, sitting calmly afterward in the eye of the postgame hurricane. Syracuse was sagging inside to cover Stevie [Alford] tight so he [Thomas] was looking for me and it worked."

He let it go and as it arched toward the net, the promise of overdue springtime died up in Syracuse, New York.

With the game and the title on the line, he made it. "Pickup games is the only time I ever made a shot to win a game like that," he said.

Well, what did you expect from Central Casting's man of the hour?

Just like Jimmy Stewart, he knows when to get on and off a stage.

DREAM TEAM'S FAITH PAYS OFF

MAY 9, 1983

LOUISVILLE—In the quiet chill of a Churchill Downs morning the other day, a groom named John Sears, Jr.—*nom de turf:* Top Cat—called the roll loud and clear during an impromptu forum outside Barn 41. "For a long time now, it's been him [Sunny's Halo] and Dave and me. I rub him and Dave walks him."

He did not add that Sunny's Halo does the running, but the performance he fashioned Saturday in between the clap of thunder that marked the gloomy post parade and the sight of Top Cat leaping into trainer David Cross's arms was enough to make a believer out of Pegasus.

The Dream Team won the Kentucky Derby, and if faith is the measure of devotion, then it is clear that rarely in the history of this mile-and-a-quarter cavalry charge has an army marched off to "Weep-no-more-my-lady time" with as unshakable a conviction that it held Absolute Truth firmly riveted beneath its saddlecloth.

There were 134,444 rain-soaked pilgrims huddled together under the closest thing you will ever see to an Armageddon sky. And they will tell you that you had to see how easily this lightly raced colt put away a Panzer division of challengers to believe it.

As for the members of the Dream Team, well, they believed it a hell of a long time before they got to see it. Each, in a special way, paid his own dues.

Consider David Cross . . . born in the shadow of a racetrack

205

that no longer exists in Vancouver . . . a rider of third-rate thoroughbreds and quarter horses . . . five years a saddle-soaper and racing-silks custodian in the jocks' room . . . twenty-five years a trainer on a hard-knock circuit . . . and finally faced with a choice between convictions and groceries.

When Dave Cross took over Sunny's Halo, he had thirty-five horses in his public stable. The truth is that he, his wife, Patti, and Top Cat *were* the stable. And because of that and because of the time involved in bringing a horse up to the Derby, other owners grumbled. There were ultimatums. Long before he got to Churchill Downs, the stable had dwindled to just three horses— and one of those was for sale.

But Saturday, after the ultimate vindication, as David Cross stood before enough television cameras and enough pencils to record the merger of West and East Germanys, somebody remarked that life was going to be different now for him.

"Yeah," David said, touching the brim of his rain-soaked cowboy hat, "no Green Mountain Park or Missoula, Montana, straight ahead. We'll be going to Baltimore for the Preakness."

And now things will be different for Patti Cross as well.

"Usually," she will tell you, "he gets so nervous that we have to run down to the stall and spend the night there with a bucket of fried chicken."

Patti Cross had $200 going in a Vegas winter book at odds of 100-to-1. That's a twenty-grand payoff. David Cross is not going to change his work habits, but who is to say that Sunny's Halo won't have the only horse-sitters in the world who share a bucket of caviar?

Then there is David J. Foster, who bred and owns this animal. When David, who had owned thoroughbreds with modest success, decided to breed his own, he had two brood mares. The first, Mostly Sunny, began the venture by giving birth to a colt, which broke a shoulder and never raced. The second, Dub Dub, followed by aborting twins and dying in the process. And then Mostly Sunny brought Sunny's Halo into the world.

David Foster had faith, too. He is sixty-seven years old and nobody is ever going to have to throw a benefit dinner for this Canadian stockbroker. Thursday, somebody offered him $6 million for a half interest in Sunny's Halo. He declined. That patience is going to be paid off geometrically when syndication time rolls around.

Finally, there is Eddie Delahoussaye, thirty-one-year-old down-home jockey from southwestern Louisiana, who equaled a serious bit of Kentucky Derby history when he became only the fourth jock in more than a century to win the race in two consecutive years. He was a winner down home and a winner during the less-glamorous meeting at Churchill Downs. In short, he was a highly skilled professional, but he never got the real national attention until 1979, when he moved to California.

He has simply gotten better and better. The first to tell you that would be Dave Cross.

"What did you tell him when you met in the paddock?" somebody asked the trainer.

"I asked him how the weather was in California. He knew what to do better than I did," Cross said.

And so the Dream Team went to work.

When they slammed out of the gate, Sunny's Halo loaned the lead to Total Departure. They came busting out of the gloom and past the stands for the first time with Sunny's Halo running easily. It was Delahoussaye's dance and he choreographed it masterfully. Into the backstretch, he went for it under a strong hold at the half-mile pole and captured the rail. Total Departure had run the good rabbit's race and he paid for it. He backed all the way up to dead last.

The only honest challenge came from Desert Wine, who hung on gamely and made a brief move in midstretch. It was here that Delahoussaye went to the whip and Sunny's Halo went into overdrive. He won it by two lengths.

For the record, Caveat was third. It was an interesting third because he came from dead last and at one point went ten horses wide to make up ten lengths. That may be worth remembering.

But so are the words of Top Cat: "If a horse runs up on him and hooks him, he'll pin his ears back and go."

Saturday, he went.

A NEW QUEEN

JULY 1984

She is not the kid next door in the same sense that the image-makers fashioned first Olga Korbut and then Nadia Comaneci. They were the little Olympic swans, bringing gymnastics to new heights on the one hand but keeping things in a safe and comfortable perspective for the male chauvinists among the congregation. After all, in their domination they nevertheless remained forever sugar and spice.

But, now, meet the Queen of the Games of Los Angeles.

Her name is Mary Lou Retton, and you know by now that on a single star-spangled night in UCLA's Pauley Pavilion, this sixteen-year-old kid from West Virginia by way of Texas changed the face of this sport in a way that doesn't square with what all those beauty-and-grace hucksters told us to expect.

She may be the lineal descendant of Olga and Nadia in terms of preeminence, but the ball game ends there. She is not the marriage of the balance beam with *Swan Lake*. She isn't out to tame it, she's out to housebreak it, leash it, and bring it home.

In the words of Bela Karolyi, the Romanian expatriate who has been her personal coach for two years, she has opened the field to a different kind of young lady and, look out, world, a hell of a lot of them will be coming your way from here on in.

She is neither pixie nor Kewpie doll. She is a real athlete and if this country was going to alter the balance of power in women's gymnastics, then it figured that the symbol around which it rallied was going to be someone who didn't tiptoe across the threshold. It was going to be somebody who kicked the damned door in.

So here comes Mary Lou. Watch her tackle the vault. See her stand at the edge of the runway, studying the task ahead. Nowhere else during the four stages of Friday night's performance could you see it so evident.

Mary Lou Retton, peering down the runway, was not looking

at the future. She *Was* the future. And when she began to run, it was a wonder the damned building didn't shake. She is so powerful, so aggressive. As she stood there she seemed to be the ghost of every little girl you ever knew who was told, "Don't play so rough . . . what have you done to your dress . . . ?" and who is finally told that she can be an athlete in her own right if that's what she chooses to be.

You know, of course, about the end result of that powerful burst down the runway the other night, the sail through the air and both parts of the exercise left you with the feeling that if she didn't run through the wall, she would soar through the ceiling.

You know, too, that it brought her the gold and will change her life. One man's life will not be changed all that much. His name is Bela Karolyi. The reason it won't change is that he has already carved out his time in space. How it would have changed would have been if Mary Lou had come up short. He was counting on the fact that it would not happen.

For more than two years, Retton's parents permitted her to live down in Houston with the Karolyi family because she had insisted it was the only way she believed she could make it to the Olympics and it was something she wanted more than anything else in the world.

After what Karolyi put her through, this last should be obvious. He is no pussycat, this very pushy Romanian with the bristling mustache and the ability to dominate an interview session no matter which of his pupils is supposed to be the interviewee.

If Mary Lou supplied the youthful drive and the marvelously powerful little body to do this, it was Karolyi who supplied the road map. He was the master architect who gave the world Nadia Comaneci. He is also the man who, on March 30, 1981, walked with his wife into her aunt's studio apartment in Manhattan and said he was going to defect.

There are conflicting accounts of what followed next. Karolyi's version is a tribute to the free-enterprise system, the faith of a Houston bank, which loaned him money to get his gym started, and the triumph of coaching ability in a country that was about to produce gymnasts whose time had come.

Other American coaches tell it a little differently. They do not like the way he recruits his students when they are enrolled with somebody else. When he explained about his first job at the University of Oklahoma, where he taught one class and worked after school in the gymnastic coach's private school, he said he had to take a newspaper route to supplement his income and his dedicated forced-savings program.

Another coach says, "That would make him the first $48,000 newspaper boy you ever saw."

But the truth is that either way he has done the job with Mary Lou Retton brilliantly. For two years he has pushed her, conned her, helped her, psyched her, and taught her. The desire to do this thing almost became an animate creature. When she tore up her knee and had surgery as recently as June 15, you had to wonder. But on June 16, she was back on the stationary bicycle . . . on June 23 she was working out, and by June 30 she was back with the team.

On Friday night, just before she went up there for the vault on which she needed a perfect score to get her gold, Karolyi yelled to her: "Run strong, then bang. Hit it, then high. Okay? Okay? Strong, bang, high. You can do it, Little Body," he said, using the nickname by which he has called her for two years.

"Well, I did it," she had said as Karolyi sat next to her late Friday night. "It was all worth it. Everything."

"You have to understand," Bela explained. "It is a miracle. She has been through the more difficult moments when everyone else falls apart. You cannot believe the pressure that is going through her head when she stands there tonight. Somebody isn't blind just because they are a kid. They know all that is developing around them and so it is with Mary Lou.

"In thirty-five years in gymnastics, I have never seen someone like her. There are no ways and no points in this judging system to grade her final vault tonight."

Unlike any similar moment most nongymnastic folks can remember, it wasn't magnificent.

It was awesome.

The Faces of Courage

ANOTHER MIRACLE FOR JEFF BLATNICK

MARCH 27, 1987

This was in Los Angeles in 1984 and you could have turned the U. S. Olympic team press guide inside out and still not found his name. You could have punched it into the all-wise, all-knowing official computer of the Olympic Games and after the lights stopped blinking and the bell stopped ringing, the best it could belch across the screen was the single line: "Blatnick, Jeff, U.S.A., unfound."

But Jeff Blatnick wasn't lost. Ask his parents, Carl and Angela, who were there the night he won the gold, waving the hometown flag of Niskayuna, New York, in salute. Ask the Swede he beat to win it . . . the Yugoslav, who was his first upset victim in the superheavyweight division of Greco-Roman wrestling . . . or the desperate Greek who bit him on the hand. When he showed the Yugoslavian referee the teeth marks, that arbiter of Greco-Roman law and order, who had a vested chauvinistic interest in Blatnick's defeat, told him he had done it with his own fingernails.

He won it all, but just being there was miracle enough. You couldn't have found a doctor or a radiologist who would even remotely concede the possibility.

They were wrong about him. It is the reason today he wages a second private battle against cancer, determined to prove them wrong again. But Jeff Blatnick doesn't see it as a "battle." He sees life as the gift it is. He is simply too busy living it to concede anything.

This past weekend, he was playing tennis in Indian Wells, California, in a tournament sponsored by Carillon Importers, which featured a brigade of 1984 Olympic gold-medal winners. It was staged for the benefit of Childhelp USA, a national organization dealing with the physical, emotional, and educational needs of abused children and their families.

"I have seen so much family love firsthand," he explained yesterday. "I had to be here to help a lot of people who haven't."

Two years before the 1984 Olympics, he was lifting weights when he noticed several lumps in his neck. Within a week, he was back home in the doctor's office in Schenectady, New York. The diagnosis was Hodgkin's disease. Within a month, they had removed his spleen and started him on radiation therapy.

"My parents had lost my brother, Dave, in the spring of 1977. Now I had to tell them," he says with great emotion, "that Number 2 was on the chopping block. It was then that I saw the kind of love and courage from them that is hard to imagine.

"I got them to let me move out to a friend's house. I couldn't watch them suffering along with me. I told them I would check in with them every day and I gave them the doctor's number. I love them and I thank them for having the courage to give me that gift of their own ultimate love. I understand how they hurt, but they helped me move."

Incredibly, he began to train again. The hardest part was facing his parents. "When you train, you get tired. They'd look at my eyes and see the fatigue there and it was impossible for them to tell whether it was from the training or the cancer."

But Jeff Blatnick made his miracle. The doctors told him there was every reason to think he had beaten it. All of America knew his story and his mail was staggering. He answered every letter. "If I thought a second letter was needed for the writer's family, I wrote that, too."

Then, in 1985, he noticed a lump below his beltline. They cut him again and they ordered chemotherapy. "At first I cried and then I raged and then I said, 'I can beat this thing again.' "

Incredibly, during both radiation and chemotherapy, he never lost his hair and he never got sick. "There were times when I wanted to get sick but I would not permit it. It was the same with my hair. You can't prove it, but I believe there is a link between attitude and performance. You don't have to be an Olympic champion to be one of the three million like me walking around. The hardest part was beating the loneliness of chemotherapy. But you can do it."

When Jeff Blatnick went back to St. Claire's in Schenectady for his final chemotherapy treatment, he wore a full-length raincoat. As he walked into the room, he let it fall open, revealing the tuxedo he had rented for the occasion. The staff roared its laughter.

"Every day they see people and have to assess them and share their heartache. I wanted to give them something different. I wanted to give each of them a smile. It was the only way I could try to pay them back."

Once again, the doctors shook their heads in wonder and announced the disease is in remission.

"You get hit like that and you're like a golfer facing a sand trap. You can figure there's a lot of sand between you and the green or you can say that there is a lot of green out there between the sand," he says.

"For me, it's a matter of fault versus attitude, and I'll take attitude. It's like that whether it's a final exam or a job or a game or even life and death. It's what you give back that counts . . . helping someone else when it's hardest to give. You have to work for your dreams—they're what keep you going.

"I believe you can do anything you damned well want."

He is twenty-nine years old and he plans to wrestle competitively again next month.

NO SAD SONG

JULY 29, 1983

This was in 1954 and they were headed down a two-lane highway through the April sunshine toward Pine Bluff, Arkansas, for a local high-school gym for an exhibition game. There were four of them in the car, including Boyd Bowie, who was doing the driving, and Junius Kellogg, whose long legs were pretzeled in under the dashboard. All of them were members of the Globetrotters and this was their two-week "vacation period." It seemed like a good idea to pick up a little walking-around money by scheduling some exhibitions in towns where the Globies didn't normally play.

Kellogg, who was supposed to head south with the Trotters' South American tour team the following week, was sound asleep when the right rear tire blew. As Bowie fought for control, the car spun dizzily on the soft shoulder, hurling chunks of earth into the air and never finding the traction it needed to remain upright. Later, they would tell Kellogg that it had flipped five times but the only memory he would carry away on his own was the wave of emptiness welling up behind his eyes and the sound of a distant voice framing a question that even Junius couldn't answer: "Is he alive?" the voice asked. "Does he have any chance at all?"

Junius Kellogg was the only person hurt in that wreck. For the first six weeks of the nightmare that followed, he drifted in and out of a coma. That very night, a doctor had telephoned down to Portsmouth, Virginia, to advise his family, "If you don't fly out right away, you are going to be too late."

Theodore and Lucy Kellogg had eleven kids. He worked as a laborer and she cleaned other people's homes. There was only money enough for one of them to fly to Pine Bluff so Lucy Kellogg went out there and for six weeks she sat beside her son's bed.

Even as he slipped in and out of consciousness, he had heard the doctor tell her that he would remain paralyzed from the

215

neck down for life. Deep from within the silent world that had enveloped him, he remembers that he kept trying to cry out, "No, man. You're wrong. I'm only twenty-three years old. This can't be."

What neither the doctor nor Junius knew at the time was that the swelling surrounding his spinal column had clouded the prognosis. Later, as it began to subside, Junius Kellogg suddenly discovered that he held a piece of his future in his own immobile hands.

Her name was Mrs. Inez Fowbush and she was a professional therapist and every day she went by the book. She knew he couldn't move a muscle but she exercised every movable joint and then she would say, "Move your thumb . . . move your pinkie . . . move your big toe."

"I would strain to do it," Junius Kellogg recalled yesterday. "I would strain so hard I would sweat."

One day Inez Fowbush, who, along with Junius never doubted that all things are possible, saw the thumb move. She raced for the doctor. "Impossible," the doctor said. "It's probably just a reflex spasm." Inez Fowbush went back down the hall to Kellogg's room and told him: "You saw it move. I saw it move. That's no spasm. You can do it."

He was moved first from Pine Bluff to Little Rock and ultimately to Kingsbridge Veterans Administration Hospital in the Bronx. When he was released, five years after the accident, Junius Kellogg could do everything but walk.

People still wondered about him back then. He was, after all, a celebrity long before the accident—not that he sought the role. He was the starting center on the Manhattan College basketball team and one day after practice a former Manhattan player knocked on his dorm door, walked into his room, and exchanged small talk for a few minutes. "You know," the guy had said, "you could make yourself some money. Just win by a little less and you could help your family. I know your folks could use the money."

"I threw him out," Junius recalls. "I wasn't looking to hurt the guy but I knew the rule. I knew if I didn't report it, I was in trouble. We went down to play St. Joe's in Philly that weekend and on the way back I told Kenny [Norton, head coach]. I didn't name the guy but Kenny knew. He had seen him at practice.

"Then the people from the D.A.'s office asked me to go along with them. I had two meetings with the fixers in a bar on Broadway. They asked me to set up the De Paul game in the Garden. The cops grabbed them. It was the start of the 1951 scandals."

Before those scandals ended, players from CCNY's national championship team, LIU, and NYU were among the local college kids arrested. Kellogg continued to play ball, but as an active reservist he was recalled to the army during the Korean War. When he was discharged, he came back, doubled up his studies, and was graduated with his class.

He is, of course, a remarkable man. But then he will be the first to tell you that he has remarkable roots in Lucy and the late Theodore Kellogg. Although his father left school in the third grade and his mother in the sixth, most of their eleven children went to college. All are successful in their own right. "They gave me something. It was something I reached back for during those long days of therapy. Without it, I would have quit. Without it and them, I wouldn't have made it out of Pine Bluff."

He worked in the accounting department at Pan Am, coached a world-championship wheelchair basketball team, owned and ran his own bar, and now for the past three municipal administrations, Junius Kellogg has served as first deputy commissioner of the New York City Community Development Agency, which monitors 300 educational housing and social-service groups.

Recently, at a thirtieth reunion, his classmates created an academic scholarship fund in his name. They raised $50,000.

"I can't bitch about my life," he told them. "Too many good things have happened to me."

A PARALYZED JOCKEY'S STRUGGLE TO RIDE

NOVEMBER 29, 1980

It was the kind of tableau jockeys do not have to see to understand and people who do not ride horses in parimutuel combat cannot really understand even if they see it.

On April 12, at Gulfstream Park, Mickey Solomone's mount snapped a leg without warning, crashed to the track, and catapulted the jockey into the path of a pair of trailing horses. He fractured his skull, broke six ribs, punctured a lung, and shattered his right thigh.

Through it all . . . through seven months of recuperation and doubt . . . Mickey Solomone vowed to ride again. They always say that. But on Wednesday, he rode at Calder Racecourse in Florida. Twice. Neither horse won. But the winning and losing, of course, did not matter.

What mattered was that at age thirty-seven he was back doing what he wants to do. It triggers memories of another Thanksgiving Day more than a decade ago . . . another jockey . . . another story far more incredible.

His name was Francisco Martinez. He was out of Puerto Rico. Now it was Thanksgiving Day at the Kessler Institute of Rehabilitative Medicine and there was a foot of snow on the ground and a dishwater-gray New Jersey wind was knifing along the hospital driveway from the wide-open golf course across the road.

A man had come to see Francisco Martinez as much out of admiration as out of journalism. This was surely no Arcaro . . . no

218

Shoemaker . . . no Triple Crown rider. He was nineteen years old and his body could not have endured more torture if you'd run a Panzer division across it.

He had been riding down at Atlantic City and there was a traffic jam and the heels of another rider's mount had clipped his mount's and suddenly there were three horses down and a wall of blackness was pressing down on Francisco Martinez's eyes.

Two hospitals later, he was alive—and still paralyzed. It was at that point that the Jockeys' Guild moved him from his South Jersey hospital bed to Kessler. The Jockeys' Guild has gone that route before with other men. For all the puffery of which the Derby and the Preakness and the Belmont provide the tracks, the owners, and the trainers, it remains a pure fact that when jockeys get hurt, it remains for the other jockeys to take care of their own.

Now on an ice-cold Thanksgiving morning, as the wind howled against the windows, Francisco Martinez—who spoke very little English—sat in his wheelchair, a nurse at his side, a crumpled letter in his hands . . . a stranger on a hellish journey through a foreign land.

"The letter is from his girlfriend," the nurse explained. "She told him she didn't think she'd be coming around any more. He got it yesterday. He really doesn't know anyone else up here."

Jockeys, for the most part, are not imposing physical figures despite their massive upper-body strength. Francisco Martinez, laboring under the burden of pain and personal heartbreak, looked more like a hospitalized child waiting for some home-study instructor to bring his algebra lesson.

A doctor was telling the visitor about the jockey's daily therapy . . . about the determination it took . . . and finally added, "He is remarkable. I see no reason that he will not walk again some day."

Then with his bilingual nurse as interpreter, Francisco Martinez retold the story of his first days around the track in the sun down at El Commandante, his journey to the mainland, his early career, and the agonizing chronology of the accident in Atlantic City.

He spoke of the joy that life on the racetrack held for him . . . a kind of joy that outsiders really do not understand and probably would never want to experience.

"Will you miss . . . I mean never being able to ride again?" the visitor asked. "They tell me the Jockeys' Guild is very good at placing injured riders in other jobs at the track."

And then Francisco Martinez did a thing that nobody in that room will ever forget. Slowly, with inch-by-inch effort etched into his young-grown-old-too-soon face, Francisco Martinez, clinging with all his might to the edge of the nearby bed, pulled himself erect. In halting English he said, "I will ride again. I will ride in the Kentucky Derby one day. You shall see."

Incredibly, a year later I saw his name in the race results. He never got to the Derby. It doesn't matter. Through him it is possible to share Mickey Solomone's newfound joy.

COACH OF
THE YEAR

MARCH 1985

It began and ended in much the same fashion, with the season opener and the conference-title clincher four months later standing side by side like a pair of overtuned violin strings.

In November, they had gone over to Southwest Louisiana to open both the season and the home team's new fieldhouse, and there was enough emotion boiling over from the little huddle alongside the Jacksonville bench to melt the brand-new paint.

Just before they went out to play, Bob Wenzel, the coach, stared up at each one of their faces from deep inside the circle. Even with where he'd been and what he'd returned from, he is not given to taking himself seriously. But in that single instant it all poured out of him within the framework of a simple declarative sentence: "I thank each one of you for being what you are."

Then he turned away and walked back to the bench.

"Did you cry?" a man asked the coach of Jacksonville University's NCAA-bound basketball team over the telephone yesterday.

"Yes."

"Did you let them see you crying?"

"No," he answered, and somehow you knew the question was almost unnecessary.

Thirty games later, Jacksonville (21-9) went over to Birmingham and won the Sunbelt title and the NCAA bid. A sea of kids in green and gold came pouring across the floor and the Jacksonville players were slapping palms and somehow they all came together in a wild circle and Wenzel, who was in the middle of it all, shouted, "Thank God, we did it."

And a big freshman center out of St. Petersburg, Florida, named Kittles shouted back into the group: "Thank God for giving us our coach back."

The wording on no Coach of the Year plaque even comes close.

They have come a long way together, this coach from out of Long Island who played his college basketball at Rutgers, and this team that learned its own perspective about what's really important when it saw him hang between life and death for six days.

A little more than a year ago, Jacksonville was playing Alabama at home and just before the half, Bob Wenzel felt the world go pop inside his skull. "It felt," he explained, "like some guy had just run up and hit me on the top of my head with a sledgehammer. Well, I knew that I'd had the flu and I just thought that maybe it was related to that."

At 2 A.M., his wife, Neva, asked a neighbor to sit with their six-month-old son, Alex, and rushed him down to Memorial Hospital, where the team doctor, Duane Bork, was waiting. The next day, peering through the haze of sedation, Wenzel saw a second doctor standing over him. They told him what he had was a leaking cerebral aneurysm. In language more familiar to basketball coaches (and the rest of us), he had ruptured a blood vessel in his brain.

There are two ways to deal with the problem: (a) Operate at once; (b) Sedate, let the blood filter out, and then operate. They chose this one. The surgeon, Dr. Walter Grande, explained it to him.

"What are the percentages of my coming out alive?" asked Wenzel, who is not a man to mess around with euphemisms.

"You said that?" a caller asked.

"Listen, I'm a coach. That's how I think. I heard he had a pretty good won-and-lost record.

"The night before the operation was pretty emotional for me. I think it was really the only time like that except for the game at Southwest Louisiana. I had a six-month-old son. I kept thinking about him. The next morning they gave me a shot and took me down the hall. I was drifting off to LaLa Land when the orderly started to shave my head. He hollered out, 'Hey, we got the basketball coach here. I'm gonna leave him a present.'

"He left a little tail of hair from the top of the neck down. Later on, when the rest of me was as bald as a billiard ball, my players loved it."

The operation took seven and a half hours and when it was

over, Bob Wenzel never looked back. A month or so later, he went over to the gym to see his team, which was about to leave for the Sunbelt Conference tournament.

"I could tell right away they didn't know what to say. It was like they expected me to drool or something. For a long time a lot of people who knew the story had the same reaction when they met me for the first time."

And now, a year later, Bob Wenzel takes this team to the NCAA Tournament—right through the front door as league champion. He has been at Jax since the 1981–82 season. "When I came down to interview for the job," he recalls, "there was no locker room and the gym still had four wooden backboards."

"What's your salary plan?" they asked.

"Hey, I've been an assistant coach at four schools. I don't have a salary plan. I just want the job."

Patrick Henry couldn't have been more convincing—or better priced.

There will not be many schools of Jacksonville's enrollment (2,400) going to the NCAA. You look at urban schools and you think about De Paul, for example. But De Paul has 13,000 students.

"We can get just about any player we want if you draw a circle around Greater Jacksonville," he says. "Of course, there's a lot of ocean inside that circle. That means we can sign the best fish in town."

This is a strange team, to say the least. Its first sub is six feet seven inches and he replaces a guard, moves to forward and another forward, Ron Murphy, moves to guard. Murphy plays three positions each game. Otis Smith, who has played more minutes than any other player in NCAA history and played high-school ball right in Jacksonville, is its version of a superstar.

But it wins.

"You have to understand," the coach says, "that I really didn't have brain surgery. What I had was a John Wooden implant."

"John hasn't been around that much lately," a guy cracked. "How do we know that you and he aren't really the same person?"

"Just watch the way my kids play," Wenzel said right back.

FOREVER FOUR

MARCH 1988

The call came Tuesday evening. As she listened to the voice on the other end of the telephone telling her that Eddie Roman was gone, Zelda Spoelstra kept reminding herself over and over again that the doctors had said there was only a 30 percent chance at best going in, but the three of them had argued that he was a fighter and it wouldn't be the first time the odds were so heavily weighted against him.

She sat alone with her thoughts for a while and then she reached out, picked up the telephone again, and dialed. As soon as she heard Floyd Lane's voice, all she could say was, "What we thought never could happen has happened."

There was an eternity of silence on the other end and then Floyd Lane said, "He tried to the end, didn't he? Somebody has to call Ed Warner now."

And suddenly, if the mind can will what the heart desires, there were four of them again.

Ed Roman died of leukemia and today the city's newspapers and television screens will be filled with the echoes of the college-basketball scandal that rocked the town nearly four decades ago. And in so many ways, they will miss the entire point.

The point is not the single collective mistake committed by man-children in a world for which they were not prepared by those who benefited most. The point is really the incredible triumph of the human spirit rising from the pain of its aftermath. Ed Roman, who fought the last fight of his life as hard as he could for as long as he could; Floyd Lane, who came back to coach basketball at City University; Ed Warner, who went to hell and back to beat drugs and who, with the help of the others, continues to fight yet another ferocious battle from his wheelchair; and Zelda Spoelstra, who is their friend and their Boswell, were never survivors. They were winners.

The bond, which is in no way lessened by Roman's death, is the product of who they were, what they struggled against, and what they became. To understand it, you have to forget everything you have come to accept in what major college sports so often is in 1988. You have to forget the legacy of yellowed newspaper clippings, written by men who never looked for answers but whose opinions were shaped by clichés, which they never questioned. You have to go back to the Jewish ghetto of the Bronx and the dead-end despair that marked a different kind of black ghetto.

Roman was a big, skinny kid who could put the ball in the basket for Taft High School. Lane was the glue that held the team together at Franklin. Warner was the one you had to stop when you played DeWitt Clinton. And Zelda Spoelstra was a cheerleader at James Monroe High.

At a community center called Bronx House, the three basketball players became family. On beautiful nights Lane's mother would put her arms around the other two boys and say, "These are my Eddies. These are my other sons." It didn't matter that she was black and her Eddies came in separate but equal colors. It was almost a foregone conclusion that all the relatives wanted the three to play together at what was then CCNY.

Nat Holman, the coach, wanted them, too. City was special. In the era of New York City college basketball's mountain of success, there was the bee sting of NYU freelance, the belly-to-belly muscle of Manhattan College, the storehouse of natural skills at LIU, and the let's-run-through-the-wall-for-Coach-Lapchick emotional fire of St. John's.

But at the top of the mountain there was CCNY. Because of the school's intellectually elite and economically free nature, it had the smartest players. They passed the ball and dribbled the ball and shot the ball by the book. And they were winners.

Zelda, a year younger than the trio, went to every CCNY game. She grew up with the three of them and as she will tell you, "I knew the NYU kids, too. But they were the kids from Brooklyn who had more money. Economics made me a CCNY fan and friendship kept the four of us together."

In March of 1950, despite an erratic season, CCNY did what no other college team will ever do. Through a calendar break that no longer exists, it won both the NCAA and the NIT championships. Within days, Holman was the city's resident genius and the players were overreachers who, with supreme coaching and spectacular determination, had emerged as superheroes.

By the following February, everyone knew why that season was so erratic. The first point-shaving scandal in the town's history exploded. Along with CCNY, players from LIU, NYU, and Manhattan were arrested. With the help of a very influential member of the clergy, St. John's beat the rap.

The plot was hatched by a thug named Salvatore Sollazo. The theme was always the same: "So you win by less. Who gets hurt? Not the school. Not you. Maybe a bookmaker or two."

There were no previous scandals to warn them. None of the head coaches, for all their postscandal self-piety, warned them. They were poor kids, with no big-figure pro contracts on the horizon, committing a crime for surprisingly little money and for which nobody they knew of had ever been charged.

Justice was hardly evenhanded. Some players were sent to jail as "examples." All were banned forever from playing in the NBA. In the aftermath, Roman joined the Army, Lane went into community work with kids, and Warner, who had no family support system, went back to the streets and ultimately into major problems with narcotics. Zelda Spoelstra cut clippings and wrote letters and tried to get people to put this into the perspective that the world of 1951 really should have had.

They stayed in touch. And they helped each other. They would not let themselves quit. Roman was a CCNY honor student and his triumph was as classic as it was unnoticed. He got his degree and went into teaching, then added a master's and a Ph.D. He became a respected psychologist.

The four formed a magnificent support system. They helped Warner bring himself back from the hell of drugs. When a car crash almost killed him, they took turns in the hospital feeding him. When Lane went back to City as coach, Roman became a familiar figure at practice. When leukemia struck Roman, Warner told him, "You got to fight. You were here for me. Now we are here for you."

They are good people and they will be together again tonight at the memorial service.

WILLIS

APRIL 1970

There are things that come to mind . . . Ken Venturi, staggering down the eighteenth fairway at the Congressional Club in Washington, D.C., playing the thirty-sixth hole of the long, long afternoon in a ninety-eight-degree oven . . . reeling with sunstroke so severe that during the lunch break they had to use medical help to get him through the simple body functions of nature.

There was Carmen Basilio, on, Lord, so many nights when the slender tissue-paper of his skin had been ripped to the bone and the blood was running off him but still he came. One night, a French fighter named Ray Ramechon split the area above his eye into a mass of streaming red tributaries. But still he kept coming. And he won.

There have been others, too. Sandy Koufax, with the elbow swollen like a pregnant grapefruit, never knowing when each pitch would be the last one . . . Jackie Kemp, taking a needle in his shoulder seconds before the kickoff and another in the same spot at halftime and coming back to do it each and every Sunday for an entire season.

You could throw in Joe DiMaggio with the bone spurs triggering little spears of pain from his swollen heel all the way through his nervous system, and Mantle and Namath with their knees.

And now there is Willis.

On Monday night, he lay helpless, twitching little spasms on the Garden floor, betrayed by a capricious vertical muscle that had taken too much over too long a time. On Tuesday night, he slumped painfully in his seat on the huge 747 jet bound for California, every normal movement like sitting and standing a private little hell. On Wednesday, they gave him steam and ice and ultrasound and then they, too, gave up. On Wednesday, he sat in agony on a stiff-backed folding chair and watched the Knicks die a little.

On late Wednesday night, there was the slow, painful five-hour flight home and the taxi ride to the Garden and more ultrasound and then, mercifully, sleep, but still he needed the pills to provide it. On Thursday, as the Knicks were just twenty-four hours away from Armageddon, West, there was more of the same and doubts and fear and uncertainty.

But Friday was magnificent. Everyone knows what happened Friday night. Friday was Willis Reed in the big, empty Garden at 6 P.M., bouncing the ball and shooting and trying to run slowly while Dr. James Parkes watched and waited. Friday was Willis heading back toward the dressing room, still limping, still not knowing, and then there was this brief tableau when Wilt Chamberlain, who was on his way to change, had spotted him on the runway and Wilt walked over and said, "How do you feel?"

"Well, I can tell you," Willis grinned, "I can't go to my right."

Friday night . . . Friday night when it counted it was Willis Reed, walking stiff-legged into the training room while inside the arena was already filling with the first noisy pilgrims and somebody was hanging a huge sign from the balcony that read, "REED, WE NEED YOU." He climbed up on the table and Dr. Parkes shot 200 milligrams of a drug called carbocaine into Reed's thigh.

They were all out on the floor by then, the Lakers in their purple-and-gold warm-up suits and you could see them sneaking little glances down toward the other end of the floor, waiting to see if he would be there. The noise tipped it first. The noise was an ocean of sound, smashing against the antiseptic concrete walls. It followed Reed all the way onto the floor.

Up at the other end, the Lakers suddenly began to shoot furiously. Dick Garrett was the first to give in. He turned slowly and looked back, following Willis Reed's movements as he sank a short jumper. Then West and then Baylor and then, finally, the big man turned, too.

Wilt Chamberlain put his hands on his hips and watched and watched and watched. He made it a point not to watch when the teams left the floor. And then there was Willis standing on the sidelines and Dr. Parkes was rubbing Reed's stomach gently and whispering in his ear, "You're all right . . . don't worry about anything . . . but if you need me, I'm here."

Naturally, Reed scored the first basket.

The circulation was still slow in his right leg, giving it a dull, numb feeling. Red Holzman motioned him to go down the court when the Lakers were shooting a foul. Willis ignored him. He sent Dick Barnett down instead and played for the rebound. Later in the evening, he would have to concede his body that one little point. But not then.

With only 2:30 left in the first period, his body started to sag toward the floor. He reached out a hand and steadied himself; using the court as a lever, he pushed himself upward. They called time-out. Over at the bench, Red was hollering, "Get the stuff." And Danny Whelan, the trainer, picked up the can of ethyl chloride, a kind of novocaine spray, and he looked at Dr. Parkes and the doctor told him to go ahead. He rolled back the top of Willis's shorts and sprayed.

When the horn blew, Chamberlain was up early off the Lakers bench. He turned and took a long look at where the Knicks were huddled. And then he saw Willis going out again and he stopped looking. The rest of the night was Willis limping back to the bench and Danny Whelan shoving the ice bag under his shorts and Dr. Parkes leaning over Whelan's shoulder and speaking softly to Willis. It was another 200 milligrams of carbocaine. It was, most of all, pain. But he played twenty-one minutes in the first half and he came back to play as long as they needed him in the second.

And in the second half there was this one, glorious instant . . . so quick that it went almost unnoticed. There was Wilt muscling with his back to the basket and Willis was leaning hard on him. Wilt put the ball on the floor and when he does that it means only one thing and that is that he will try to shoot it.

But Willis kept crowding and crowding and Wilt stood there frozen and Walt Frazier slipped in and stole the ball. Then Willis came limping back up the court.

Finally, they were sending Nate Bowman in to replace him and Willis was standing next to Bowman with the sweat pouring off him and his face twisted in pain and he was telling him, "Just lean on him, baby. Lean on him."

It was brutal courage. It was raw willpower. It was the thing that won it for this ballclub and the people who saw it will be a long time forgetting it.

WALTER'S GAME

APRIL 1987

NEW ORLEANS—It was a game whose memory time can never dim. In the deepest recess of his mind's eye it will remain evergreen long after the cheering stops and the backslapping ends and the springtime of his years stretches well beyond their appointed autumn. Nothing that happens here tonight when Greg Monroe and his Syracuse teammates meet favored Indiana inside the Daddy of the Domes for the national championship will alter its meaning.

It was the only game Walter Monroe ever saw his son, Greg, play.

Tonight, there will be the twin pep bands of Indiana and Syracuse and the vastness of the Superdome and its multilayered wall of people. Tonight, there will be a nonstop Niagara of noise and the coaches, Bobby Knight and Jim Boeheim, will stalk the sidelines with the manic tunnel vision that such moments always produce.

To win it would be the culmination of the kind of dream that every college kid—Greg Monroe included—nurtures in the passionate hope that one day the wish becomes the deed. To win it is to place personal sneaker-prints in the sands of history.

To be a part of such a championship team is predictably much on Greg Monroe's mind.

But no matter how much such a moment would come to mean, it will never replace Walter's Game.

Eight years ago, Greg was a freshman at Pittsford-Mendon High School in Rochester, New York. Walter, a city bus driver, had already suffered two severe strokes. But on the night Pittsford-Mendon opened its season, Walter was there. So were Greg's mother, Mary, and the four other Monroe kids.

"It's ironic what happened that night," he said yesterday. "In four years as a starter there, I'd set the school scoring record and we'd win a state title. But in all that time, I never played a game as well as I played that one."

"I'm not a big basketball man," Walter, who had played football and baseball very well as a kid, told his son a month or so earlier when Greg had made the team as a freshman starter. "I'm not going to give you any advice. All I want you to remember is to do the best you can, take it as far as you can go so you'll never have any regrets."

On that night in Rochester, Greg Monroe was spectacular. He scored twenty points. He kangarooed toward both backboards and came away with sixteen rebounds. He had no way of knowing it then, but through long, painful nights when he was alone and holding back the tears that would sear his eyeballs, he would remember Walter's Game. In a strange way that perhaps only fathers and sons can understand, it would become a silent bond between them.

"I am so grateful," he said yesterday, his voice barely audible as he dealt with a rush of emotion, "that I played that kind of game on that special night."

And then Walter was admitted to Monroe Community Hospital. Suddenly the strokes were secondary. The diagnosis was terminal cancer.

Mary Monroe became the head of the house. She was already working at Kodak, and, for her and the five children she had to raise, the world centered on holding the future together between nightly visits to Monroe Community.

"Basketball for me," Greg Monroe recalled, "became a way of finding something where I could try to forget for a while. I was so close with him. My mother is a strong lady. She kept her head up and she kept our heads up, too."

That freshman year in high school, Boeheim came over to look at another player. But, after the game, he asked the coach about the skinny freshman.

"He told me that Greg's father was ill," Boeheim said, "and that the doctors didn't think he'd recover. He told me he thought Greg was going to be a college player and he said whoever got him was getting a remarkable young man."

Walter Monroe fought like hell. In the beginning, Greg would tell him about the games he'd played and the things that were happening in school. When Graduation Day came, he told him he was going to Syracuse on a scholarship.

"For seven years," Boeheim continued, "his father was in that hospital dying. Greg carried that weight all the time. He kept his grades up, he made the practices, and he kept an awful lot inside."

"When you use courage in the real sense," a guy wondered, "would you have to say that makes him the most courageous player you ever coached?"

"All I know is that I've never known any athlete who had to cope with as much and did it as well as he did. Athlete? I never knew anybody else like him for that matter."

Walter Monroe kept on fighting. He was slipping badly. By Greg's junior year, he could no longer speak.

"We would send him tapes of the Syracuse games," Greg said. "And when I got to visit I'd try to tell him as much as I could. I'd look for him to blink because I couldn't be sure he understood what we were saying. Then I'd see him smile and I knew he was hearing me. I knew that if he would have spoken, that smile would have said, 'I'm okay. Don't worry about me. Take care of your mother. Do the things you have to do.' "

"We knew it," says Howard Triche, who, like Greg, is a senior co-captain. "We knew how hard it was for him but he didn't talk much about it. It was very tough for him."

During his sophomore year, Syracuse went over to Rochester to play in the Kodak Classic. "I remember playing those two games and knowing that my father was there in the same town dying," Greg Monroe said. "But my mother told me I had to be strong. The ordeal made all of us stronger."

Last year, as Walter Monroe fought his final battles, Boeheim would excuse Greg Monroe from practice twice a month and he would drive the three-hour round trip to be with him.

Walter Monroe died on June 9.

"Sometimes I get down," Greg said. "I wish so much that he could be here tomorrow, sitting with my mom.

"I was lucky to have him."

A LONG WAY FROM HAVANA

APRIL 4, 1980

MESA, Arizona—They had come out of the sunshine ghettos of Havana, or down from the primitive company towns that pockmarked the plush sugar-cane fields of Oriente Province, seeking the dream that so many Cuban kids had chased since the long-gone days when people like Dolph Luque and Mike Gonzalez had first left the island to earn a slice of baseball history.

Poverty and diet had combined to fashion the kind of hunger that pushed them far more than the traditional "extra mile." They were undernourished and overmotivated. To some of them, a signing bonus was the price of a glove and a set of spikes. Most didn't even get that.

They were shipped to the States in platoons and delivered safely to the minor-league camps of Florida. Few spoke any English. When the manager explained the pickoff play, they sat in the back of the group and nodded and didn't understand a damned word he said.

But when they went into the hole to field the grass-cutter at short, they dove like maniacs and made the impossible throw. Failure, they knew, simply left them nowhere else to go except back to poverty and despair.

Preston Gomez, who manages the Cubs today, and Cookie Rojas, the field marshal of Gomez's coaching staff, were the lucky ones. Each was fluent in English.

Gomez was out of the sugar-mill town called Preston. It was the mark of the times that with Gomez (a surname widespread enough to rank with Smith), American coaches and managers could not be bothered taking the time to personalize a transient relationship. They simply changed his first name to the town from which he came.

Tough as it was, there still remained the dream of major-league parks and money and identity. Then, in 1959, even that began to sour. Gomez, who managed Havana's International League franchise, saw it coming. He looked around and took a job running the Dodgers' Spokane franchise.

"Castro came to me that winter," Gomez said yesterday as he sat in the warm Arizona sunshine on an old metal folding chair near the dugout at the Cubs' camp here. "He reminded me that I was a hero, that I had won the Little World Series with Havana the year before. He did not think it right for me to go. But I knew him for some time. When I told him I believed he would do away with professional sports and that for me there was no future on the island, he did not protest. I left that year."

A year later, it came crashing down on the rest. By then, Preston had moved much of his family from Cuba. His mother, Elia, and his brother, Rafael, had stayed on. That year, in midseason, there were meetings of Cuban players all over the face of America. Rojas recalled that the Sugar Kings were in Richmond at the time and Gabe Paul flew down to represent the Reds, who owned the franchise, to announce that he was moving it to Jersey City. He told them it was painful for them, and he knew it, but he would let the team return to Havana that week.

Cookie's decision to stay was automatic. So was Gomez's. But a year later, another dimension cut into his life. For nearly two decades it would put lines in his face far deeper than those he acquired squinting across sun-drenched infields.

His brother, Rafael, had joined what was left of the Cuban underground after the Bay of Pigs. They caught him with a bomb and they sentenced him to that high-walled slice of penal hell that the Cubans call "La Cabana."

In 1969, Preston Gomez returned to Cuba by way of Mexico to give baseball clinics. He told a reporter the month before he went, "I am not political. And I will not beg. But I know along the way I will see him [Castro]. I know he will see me and be reminded of Rafael. We will see what happens."

Back in Cuba for the first time in a decade, he joined his mother and went along on her monthly visit to Rafael at La Cabana. "He had lost thirty pounds. My mother cried a great deal. He told me that some of his friends had been transferred to farm work on the Isle of Pines. But he didn't conform. He swore he wouldn't be beaten down.

"I told him that perhaps he was achieving nothing. I thought of the way my mother looked and how often she cried and the way it must be for him every day with nothing but those four walls to look at." Six months later, at Castro's personal order, Rafael Gomez was transferred to the Isle of Pines. For ten years, Preston Gomez shuttled between the United States and Cuba. Each time he saw his mother, her eyes were an unspoken plea to do something. Each time he saw Castro, the brother was never mentioned.

But now, Rafael Gomez has been released from prison and exiled to Los Angeles. He has a job. He speaks very little, according to Preston, "except when he runs into another exile. Then," Preston says, "he comes alive.

"Baseball is my life, but it is second to my seeing him alive and free.

"For my mother, it was the end of a nightmare. She died one month after his release. But she lived to see him free."

On The Road Again And Again And Again

THE SCENE

KUALA LUMPUR—Over in Kota Kinabalu, Borneo, last week, Mr. Soon Yin Fong, forty-five, father of seven, perhaps moved by the proximity of Malaysia's first heavyweight championship fight, went home to his wife, Tangina Binte. The thing Mr. Soon Yin Fong went home with was a big left hook, which he bounced against her chin with great force, which, of course, is how everyone got to court.

In any event, he told Chief Taib of the native court that he had no recourse but to seek a divorce, whereupon the chief ordered him to pay child support, $30 in cash and a pig.

Obviously, any country where a guy can get a divorce for thirty bucks and a pig is worth watching.

The visitors here have been watching rather closely. The East and the West, which Kipling insisted would never meet, have come together this past week in Kuala Lumpur with a certainty that has sent old Rudyard to the canvas for the mandatory eight-count and the feeling is that Mr. Kipling is not going to get up.

What kind of a week has it been?

Well, try this one on for size.

A Malay is explaining an ancient folk myth where a divinely inspired prophet was advised from above to strike out in a divinely powered boat and with God as his copilot he arrives at a beautiful uncharted land called Melaka. As he pauses, the P.A. system in the lobby of the Merlin Hotel resounds to the strains of a snappy instrumental version of "My Yiddisha Momma."

Meanwhile, Belinda Ali, the wife of the champion, is taking daily polo lessons, a beer company is running a poll to see whether Malaysians think the challenger or the champion is more handsome, and Muhammad Ali, in a masterstroke of understatement, tells Joe Bugner, "Aw, man, you can't wear white trunks. It will look like you don't have any clothes on."

And downtown, well, downtown Malaysia remains Malaysia.

The muddy waters of the River Kelang still rush through the heart of the city, where they form a confluence with the Gombak. On the pedestrian bridge above, outdoor barbers lean against their portable folding chairs, battered razor strops at a weary parade rest, waiting for the call to arms.

In hard-packed wooden stalls in the back alleys, instant shirtmakers bend myopically over their work, the hum of their sewing machines mingling in an *a cappella* chorus with the outdoor food vendors, the brummmph . . . brummmph . . . brummmph . . . of the motorbikes as they tool along the wide European-type boulevards and then suddenly wheel and disappear into the myriad alleys.

The air is heavy with the smell of the river and the acrid odors of Malay, Chinese, and Indian cooking. The upper skyline is a blend of stainless steel and functional lines. Halfway down the horizon, the minarets that mark Moorish architecture take over.

Yet as recently as 1830 there was nothing here . . . nothing but the jungle and the rivers and the tin. It was, of course, the tin that made this city possible. In 1830, Sultan Muhammad sent eighty-seven indentured Chinese laborers upriver under the command of his nephew and his brother to seek out the tin.

Malaria and the heat laid most of them low.

And if you don't think the heat is still around, then try this one on your air-conditioning set. For the past three days, Muhammad Ali has been telling everyone: "I represent America. Ain't no English fighter gonna beat the man who represents Joe Frazier, Ken Norton, George Foreman, Joe Louis, and Rocky Marciano."

All that was missing was Angelo Dundee and the Rockettes, tap-dancing across the ring to a snappy version of "Yankee Doodle Dandy" while Don King waved a Remember the Alamo sign.

Meanwhile if, as they say, "it ain't the heat, it's the humidity," enough of it must be hanging over the Bugner camp to float the QEII. "I have had a tougher upbringing than Ali," Bugner says. So when the champion talks to him and tells him that he is fighting the baddest man in the world, what will Joseph do? "I shall answer back," says Joseph, "and I shall tell him, 'Do settle down and pay attention to the contest.' "

He did not say whether or not he would stamp his foot.

In the face of all this, the local populace has reacted with remarkable sanity. This is no easy task, particularly since it had been on Don King–alert for more than a week. Mr. King, the co-promoter of this fight, has been known to whip through a town like a dose of blackstrap molasses through a ten-year-old.

But on Saturday, much to the despair of the local press, which had been desperately seeking a few thousand well-chosen words, no Don King embarked from the evening Malaysia Air Service flight. This is not to be confused with last Monday when he did not arrive . . . last Thursday when he again blew the plane . . . Friday morning when he missed yet another.

On Friday afternoon, however, Hurricane King blew through the lobby of the Merlin Hotel and into a reception committee that had been waiting for a week. It had been waiting for so long that the night porters had begun to sweep around them.

It was a modest entrance. Mr. King wore a white-and-yellow diamond-patterned leisure suit, a white shirt, yellow socks, and white shoes. Despite the rigors of the long plane trip, his Afro looked as though it had been newly electrified.

A girl in native costume burst forward and hung a garland of indigenous flowers around his neck. The blend of suit and blossoms looked like a chef's salad that had been left out of the refrigerator for a week.

"Would Mr. King have a few words to say?" a local Malaysian writer wondered.

Does the Mississippi have to be told to roll?

"I have knowledge," he told King, "that a secret Malaysian source is willing to pay three times the many millions of which other people speak if you can get Muhammad Ali to give up his retirement and fight Joe Frazier here. What do you say to that?"

"Ohhhhh . . . my brother," Mr. King replied, "you say the words that make me respond . . . you are making me tingle . . . let us leave all those other reporters as soon as possible and in private let us speak softly to one another about who this unseen brother may be."

Ladies and gentlemen, it is now post time.

LOOK OUT, WORLD

SEPTEMBER 1975

MANILA—The typhoon watch can't get a call anymore. In the wee small hours of the morning, the fuzz turns a gentlemanly back on the curfew-breakers along Roxas Boulevard who line the big, wide avenue by the bay to catch a glimpse of the fighters lumbering along through their roadwork. In the front parking lot at the Hyatt House, a tall, angular black man with a Bible in one hand hurls dire prophecies at the doorman: "I have seen God. He has told me that Joe Frazier is a mighty warrior. Joe Frazier has the power. You," he thunders at the doorman, "will not see God. You will not go to heaven. But I will. And Joe Frazier will be the Lord's instrument for a mighty miracle."

"Ask him if he'll lay 7-5 on that," a nonpilgrim says.

And welcome to the week that was . . . the week that is . . . the week that will be . . . whenever and wherever Muhammad Ali hangs his punching bag.

It is early morning and a steady rain washes the near-empty streets. There will be no roadwork. The hell there won't. "Let's us take a ride," says Muhammad Ali. Who else on the face of this planet would consider doing his roadwork from the driver's seat of an El Dorado?

The car lurches away from the Hilton parking lot like a tidal wave in search of a shore. The local security men are racing to catch up. Then the rain stops and he steps from the car to breathe deeply of the early-morning air. What he gets is a mouthful of carbon dioxide.

A brace of motorcycle cops roars up and politely asks to be photographed with him. After he obliges, he turns and says, "Now you got to take my picture." Now he has one cop's helmet and he is astride one of the bikes and there is a great roar and look out, world, that isn't John Shaft wheeling around the corner on that motorcycle.

Meanwhile, the daily training sessions grind along in the Folk Arts Center—more an exercise in ticket-selling than conditioning. Both fighters were long since ready for this. They do not figure to get any readier just because the countdown has begun in earnest.

Joe Frazier stalks across the ring with gloves the size of twin bedpans. He snorts and grunts and drives home a mild left hook into the belly of a sparring partner named Stan Ward. And from high above the arena comes the shrill cry, "Gooooooo-rillllllla . . . Gooooooooo-rilla."

On a narrow catwalk at the very top of the arena, the heavyweight champion is leaning over the rail. Every neck but Frazier's suddenly swivels toward the ceiling. Much to their disappointment, he did not descend aboard a fiery chariot.

"Well, I'll tell you," Frazier says later, "he certainly acts like a man who is losing his mind. Do they have some sort of mental-health clinic here? I mean I don't want them to throw a net over him before the fight."

In the span of a single frenetic week, Muhammad Ali has stood outside Joe Frazier's hotel room and aimed a cap pistol at the challenger, stalked across the stage during Frazier's workout, followed by a retinue of bodyguards who pose all the credibility of a platoon of Maxwell Smarts, and still found time to go out to Ortanez University to hear something called the official debut of the "Muhammad Ali Leadership Song."

The town, for its part, is not quite sure how to take him and you know that things being what they have always been, it is impossible to leave him. In truth, much of the grass-roots sentiment here seems to lean heavily toward Joe Frazier and nobody among this largest Christian population in all of Asia was particularly thrilled by Muhammad's statement calling this fight a "holy war."

Still, when it comes to the wagering of dollars and cents where two foreign fighters are involved, it is not difficult for the average Filipino to bet with his head instead of his heart. They are doing that in particularly heavy amounts and down at the old Central Market, where the man in the street finds his action, they have bet it down to even money.

Which brings us down to Bundini Brown. Mr. Brown is a member of the heavyweight king's court, a retinue roughly the size of the Houston police force. His function has been running the gamut from court jester to cheerleader to human voodoo charm.

The other day Mr. Brown wandered over to the Frazier camp in search of a little action. He insists he is still owed $6,000 from a member of the Foreman camp, and this time he was determined to find someone from whom he could collect.

"I'm betting a grand on the king [Ali, not Don]," he challenged Eddie Futch, Frazier's trainer. Mr. Futch did not rise to the bait. "Come on, chumps, somebody cover my grand."

"I'll bet you," an adolescent voice shot back, "but I only have $100."

"That's okay, young man," Bundini told Joe Frazier's son Marvis. "You betting on your daddy and that's like betting a million dollars—of course it won't do you no good."

"Did you bet that fifteen-year-old kid?" a guy wondered.

"Do a bear like honey? Hell, yes, I bet him."

And finally, there was the intrepid reporter who, covering his first fight, asked Angelo Dundee, "Do you think the weather will be a factor?"

"No," Angelo said. "After all, both men are professionals."

Yeah and, after all, both men are fighting indoors.

HEAVEN HELP US

JUNE 1988

And on the eighth day, God made the Tyson-Spinks match.

At least, that was the presumption yesterday as the mayor of Atlantic City, the Honorable James Usry, told a small, intimate gathering of 450 in a room large enough to hold the East Islip, New York, Demolition Derby, that "this is the greatest sports event in the history of the earth. To the winner goes the spoils."

And welcome to Sodom-by-the Sea, where your host Donald Trump rarely makes a mistake but he made a beauty this week. The sign at the Trump Plaza should not read "WELCOME MIKE TYSON AND MICHAEL SPINKS." What it should say is "WELCOME PSYCHIATRISTS INTERNATIONAL. You Have Come to the Right Place."

The longer the wait until fight night gets, the more the impression grows that someone has made a terrible mistake. We have not assembled down among the sheltering green-felt tables for a fight at all. Listening to the assembled cast of characters, which sat on a dais large enough to house the Mormon Tabernacle Choir in the Trump Plaza Theatre yesterday, you could be excused for coming away with the impression that Mike Tyson and Michael Spinks were going to fight from separate couches strategically positioned on the world's largest ink blot.

Consider, if you will, some of the folks and some of the rhetoric emanating from the dais, the live audience, and the electronic outposts linked together for yesterday's exercises, which ran the gamut from good old-fashioned paranoia to sophisticated "what did he really mean by that?" All that remains is for Larry Hazzard, the commissioner of the New Jersey State Athletic Board, to name Sigmund Freud as the referee and Dr. Ruth as the knockdown timekeeper.

Mike Tyson, the world champion, twice spoke pointedly about the way greed can spoil things. Butch Lewis, the promotional force behind Spinks, sat there dressed like the boy next door—

if the boy next door to you happens to wear a tuxedo, a large white bow tie, and no shirt to lunch.

"Why is he so quiet (at least quiet for him)?" a newcomer to this loony bin asked a veteran of the asylum.

"Not so loud. His chest just came back from the cleaners and I think he's praying for God to let him grow pearl buttons on it."

Hazzard, who is entitled to a little paranoia, considering what the International Boxing Federation (one of three useless sanctioning boxing bodies) has put him through this week, stared into space like a man on the way to an exorcism. Unfortunately, there was nobody to aim a silver bullet at since all three groups were represented by empty chairs. This was a shame but some folks said the empty chairs were an intellectual step up.

"I'm hell-bent that this fight will take place in New Jersey," he began, which seemed a fair assumption since they have already gone to the trouble of renting the arena for Monday night, "and I set the rules. Any problems and they have to come through me."

The way things have been going, if he can settle the problems bothering the supporting cast, he will probably be offered an appointment to the Menninger Clinic.

Bill Cayton, Tyson's manager of record or manager in transit, depending upon what hour of the day it is and to whom you are speaking, stood up and announced, "Boxing has changed. It has become a complicated and intricate business. I have been advised not to respond to any matters pertaining to the managerial situation." That was fine since nobody had bothered to ask him in the first place.

Don King? Well, Mr. King has his own psychological problems. As you know, he is a shy and introverted individual who constantly tries to blend into the background. Right now, he is struggling desperately to overcome that but it isn't easy. Some people say it all traces back to his boyhood when he was kidnapped by jackals in the hills of Cleveland and forced to eat an electric hair dryer.

Yesterday Mr. King gave a five-minute speech, which felt as though it lasted no longer than an hour. The thrust of his talk was the food, the rooms, and the gaming tables at the Trump Plaza and the genius of Donald Trump. Resident therapists agreed he was making great strides toward coming out of his shell, until a questioner asked him to describe Mike Tyson with a single word.

This is like asking the Chinese not to multiply. Mr. King was deeply shaken.

And then there was Kevin Rooney, who is Tyson's trainer. Kevin added his form of restraint to the proceedings when he explained, "We're here to kick a little ass."

"Yes," one of the pilgrims whispered to a fellow communicant in the next pew, "but what does he really think?"

Among the other psychiatric highlights, Mike Tyson lectured on the administration of pain and Michael Spinks explained why "a little terror in your life" is a very good thing.

"But what about the styles involved here?" somebody asked Tyson, seeking and getting a great insight.

"Style," Tyson scholarly responded, "is just crap. I just want to fight."

Psychologically, there was something here for everyone yesterday, as witnessed by Michael Spinks's answer when he was asked because of the task at hand, did he have a secret weapon.

"Yes," Michael responded, "it's inside my boxing trunks."

Even the Freudians chose to let that one pass.

ON THE ROAD

He is twenty-six years old and the skin around his eyes is puckered into that eternal, honest squint that is a blend of high cheekbones and years of gazing into the flatland sunshine at the cattle that comprise so much of his life. Last Sunday night, he sat down to dinner with his parents on the Blackfoot Indian Reservation in Montana and, somewhere during the meal, his father looked up and asked, "You going down to Cheyenne for the rodeo?"

"Yeah," Mickey Running Fisher said. "Mike and Smiley and me."

John Running Fisher nodded. He is forty-nine years old and once, when his youth had room for dreams, he rodeoed and he won some money and he stored some memories, but that was in another world.

"Listen," John Running Fisher said, "you go down there and you do yourself some good. You can win a little. You ain't exactly a stranger when it comes to horses."

Nothing much else was said about it. John Running Fisher never did get to the big rodeo in Cheyenne, although he had always wanted to go. There is, Mickey Running Fisher will tell you, a quiet but strong understanding between father and son when it comes to horses. It goes back so far and so deep that Mickey Running Fisher cannot possibly recall the day his father first leaned down from the saddle, scooped him out of his mother's arms, and gently placed the reins in his small, brown hands.

Mickey is single and young and strong, and all over the reservations that dot the western slice of America there are Blackfeet and Sioux and others just like him. During the week they mend the fences and wet-nurse the cattle and chop the wood and they whisper to themselves, "Lewiston next week or maybe Columbia Falls."

None of them get rich. All of them dream. All of them can point to a man named Kenny McLean, who is part-Indian and who for eight of the past eleven years has been among the ten best bronc riders in the world. Kenny McLean is not what keeps them going. They go because there are horses to ride and challenges to face. Kenny McLean is merely proof positive of the pride.

At 2 A.M. Monday, Mickey Running Fisher nosed the Chevy out onto the paved road leading out of the reservation. Smiley Kittson was with him and so was a kid named Mike Gilliam. Smiley is nineteen. Once he gave it the big try, roaming as far south as Arizona, leaving the reservation for nine months. But he didn't make much money and he will tell you in much the same words Mickey Running Fisher uses that the reservation is home and free and, for him, a good place to be.

They went roaring out into the Montana night. Sweeping through the flat tabletop land and bending down through Great Falls and on into Helena, past Canyon Ferry Lake, across the Great Divide, and on into Wyoming. They drove in shifts. While two tried to sleep, the third pushed the car against the 850-mile timetable they faced, half-listening to the hard-rock music on the radio, which never seemed to change from station to station or town to town.

This is the way they travel on their own minicircuit, which bumps only tangentially with the far-more-lucrative Rodeo Cowboy Association schedule. All three were entered in the amateur saddle bronc riding at Cheyenne. The magnitude of the rodeo and the number of kids like them determined to try it made this one of the few spots along the way where an amateur could make some real money.

They hit Cheyenne at 11 P.M. on Monday. In their way they are latter-day Essenes of the road, sharing expenses, living each for the other during these periods, dividing each from his ability to each according to his needs. Automatically, they headed for the greenery near the rodeo grounds. They took the sleeping bags out of the trunk and bedded down there in the park. The night was cool and the stars were bright, and from the nearby fairgrounds they could hear the sounds of the midway.

They fell asleep, each wondering what kind of animal awaited him the next day.

Mickey Running Fisher drew first. The horse was named Witch Doctor. He was more lover than fighter. That afternoon, when Mickey went into the chutes, Smiley and Mike were there watching. "And now," the announcer said, "here's Mickey Running Fisher from South Dakota." All three of them are from Montana. But the program listed Mickey from South Dakota, Mike from Wyoming, and Smiley from Kansas.

"I've never even been in Kansas," Smiley told a man.

It was a small matter. Anonymity is a way of life for them in any case. They were more concerned about Mickey. Witch Doctor was a quitter. He wouldn't come out. Then he wouldn't buck. Then he tried to sit down, so they flagged him. And Mickey Running Fisher thought, "All those miles and all that time and now . . . nothing."

But the judges vote him a re-ride the next day. "If I can't do anything tomorrow, we'll hop in the car and drive back to Lewiston. That's 600 miles but they got a little rodeo there and maybe we'll have some luck. The next day, we could go on to Columbia Falls and catch another one."

Smiley and Mike came up empty. They bucked off. The next day it rained. If this, as they claim, is the daddy of them all among the rodeo set, then the rainstorm was its great-grandfather. There was mud and slop, but when they banged the chute door open, Mickey put his body into a horse named Tango and thought, "I don't want to go to Lewiston. I want to be here. I want to win for a change."

He gave it a hell of a ride. It looks like he's going to make some money. He can't wait to tell John Running Fisher about that.

LOVE'S DREAM

FEBRUARY 1983

ST. LEONARD DES PAIC, Normandy—The road to Romeo's house is lined with frostbitten hedgerow. It stretches westward for 160 kilometers, out through the Bois de Boulogne, out from Paris, and out past a small village that a man named Charles Landry made into a major tourist attraction forty years ago by incinerating several wives out of boredom and economic need.

It rolls on into the heartland of Normandy, sweeping in gentle arcs past winter-bare farmland. It ends at a 700-year-old chateau fronted by 800 acres of pure joy. Here the sky may be gray. Here the January frost warms blue-white patterns on the fenceposts. Here the birds have left for the South of France. But here waits eternal spring. This is the place where Romeo lives.

In French it is called Haras des Rouges Terres. In English, the Stud of the Red Earth. But in all languages it is the same.

Romeo's square name is Jamin. He is sixteen hands high and once he was the world's premier trotting horse. In 1958 and again in 1959 he won the $100,000 Prix d'Amérique at Vincennes. That second year he went across the ocean to Roosevelt Raceway and won that track's first International Championship. Two weeks later they shipped him out to Du Quoin, Illinois, where he trotted the year's fastest mile and beat the hell out of the clock in a time trial.

He was so good they called him "Creeping Death," and when he came home to France, he came amid the sounding of brass and the cheers of a nation.

But today, there are no crowds. Today, there is no rose-strewn winner's circle. Today, there is only romance—day after day after day, and mare after mare after mare. Jamin is France's highest-paid four-footed gigolo.

Yesterday, they led him out onto the private cinder-topped exercise track here and he stood there nervously until they let him go. Then he swept forward, high gaited in the morning cold, and as he took the far turn he looked much the same as he had that night five years ago when he became the symbol of international harness racing.

This was no small accomplishment. Strong men who have been called upon to perform similar tasks lose their vigor and their hair. The road to Jamin's new profession is fraught with trauma.

"It was not easy for him," André Rouzaud explained. André manages the stud farm as well as one of the world's largest champagne companies for his employer, Madame L. Olry Roderer. "We tried to help him as much as possible."

In 1961, the people at Haras des Rouges Terres decided to turn Jamin out to stud. When they announced the decision, it was discussed with much emotion in the French press. All over France, people waited and debated. Anyone can win races. The true challenge was still to be met.

This became clear to André Rouzaud, the manager; Francis Riaud, the master of the stud; and Jean Riaud, the driver, when a letter from a two-franc bettor arrived for Jamin. It wished him "Bonne Chance" and then it reminded him that always now he must remember to work hard for the *"gloire et honneur"* of his country.

Jamin was then a tender seven years old. Always there had been grooms and fences and the lonely celibacy of segregation. Innocence thus protected for seven years is not lightly cast aside. After exhaustive interviews, the board of strategy selected a worldly wise mare named Soulaine. She was twenty-four years old.

But a funny thing happened to the bridegroom on the way to his wedding. He was still racing at the time and the gang got together for a bachelor party at Vincennes. With boyish enthusiasm, Jamin sprained his leg. Innocence received a two-month reprieve.

All of France waited . . . . On April 1, 1961, before the secret but highly vocal wedding party at "Red Earth," romance and Soulaine came shuffling forth to meet Jamin. At least everyone thought romance had, until a month later when Dr. Pouret, who is expert at such matters, examined Soulaine.

"But no," André sighed, "the doctor looked at her and shook his head. Then he looked at us and shook his head. It was so sad."

In Paris they said, "Perhaps the different ages . . . these things are most delicate." And again France settled back to wait. So did Abner, who is Jamin's daddy, and who stood at stud himself three miles down the road. This was an affair of family honor. Abner still made the price 6-5 on junior.

The Republic sipped its Cognac and wondered. Indo-China was gone. Algeria was crumbling and Italy was hot to steal the tourist trade. Nineteen sixty-one was not a vintage year for France. But Jamin was still a champion. He was all heart and the Republic sighed once more as he lost that to a four-year-old mare named Nyssia.

When Dr. Pouret clinically announced the Triumph of the Great French Dream, they broke out the Calvados all over Normandy. Calvados is the native white lightning. It is a sort of Sneaky Pierre—half cider and half molten lava.

Yesterday, André Rouzaud neatly tossed off three fingers of it and explained that Jamin's original $2,000 stud fee is monumental by French standards. "His colts will prove themselves soon and the fee shall grow higher."

"Well," a tourist said, struggling to keep a belt of Calvados from spurting out of both nostrils, "you must have been worried when nothing happened with Soulaine."

"No, no," André said. "You do not understand. Sad? Yes, because, well, you know how those things are. But never worried. Jamin is a French champion. We knew he would succeed. All of us knew it."

In such matters, the Republic remains undefeated.

THE BIG WHEEL

FEBRUARY 1963

LONDON—On the sands at Mablethorpe, Percy and Maud Harrison, England's newest folk heroes, snuggle side by side in beach chairs. Maude is a matronly fifty-three and Percy is battling an expanding waistline. They could be your next-door neighbors—except that Percy put down a penny bet in the English soccer pools and came away with the equivalent of $946,400 tax-free.

In fashionable Berkeley Square, a charwoman dusts the headlights in a posh luxury-automobile showroom with one eye on the feather duster and one eye on the clock. She has already bet 2s. 6d. on a horse that subsequently won out at Salisbury and is anxious to collect her winnings and head for bingo before her old man comes home and drags her off to the greyhound races.

In Hanover Square, a Cuban exile stands in front of a roulette wheel while a cluster of students takes careful mental notes. Final exams are due soon and if they don't pick up all the nuances they are not going to get their diplomas. As every London schoolboy knows, a croupier without a gambling degree is an unemployed croupier.

Down at places like the Victoria Sporting Club and the Olympic, they are counting out chips in neat little stacks in preparation for the evening's work. But over at the Charlie Chester Casino on Archer Street, they are already emptying ashtrays because Charlie Chester goes full blast, twenty-four hours a day.

And welcome to historic London-by-the-Thames. England swings like a pendulum do, and the rhythm it swings to is win . . . place . . . show and five, the point is five . . . and gin, baby, gin.

Nowhere on the face of this hustler's earth are you going to find a country where more people bet on more things than on this tight little island. A man who runs one of the gambling casinos, which came into the realm of honest society with the

1963 enabling act, puts it this way: "I have been here for twenty years and in all that time I cannot honestly say I have met a person who does not bet on something. What Parliament did when it legalized gambling casinos was to take games of chance out of the back streets or the elite private clubs. But they were always here. The law itself is vague and should be more concise but the principle is clearly in keeping with our way of life.

"In short, if we think we can make a buck out of gambling—and who doesn't really deep down think that way?—we gamble. We love it. We thrive on it. Hell, even the government gambles. It issues premium bonds and if your number comes up, well, you win. Frankly, it's human nature and the English are the most human people in the world. It is different in your country."

"Well, a little bit," the visitor admitted. "I mean you can't book horses unless your silent partners are on the public payroll and then it's still better not to get caught."

"Exactly," the man said. "Our turf accountants are respected businessmen. In your country people call them gangsters. Well, I say if a man pays you what he owes you when you win, if he quotes an honest price, if he works with a pencil instead of a gun, he is hardly a gangster."

The turf accountants are the shining jewel in the gambling binge that daily sweeps this country. The casinos are in a bit of difficulty right now, but the bookie joints are making money for both themselves and Her Majesty's Government, because they have hit every stratum of British social life, which is either good or bad, depending on your moral viewpoint. It is all good, however, as far as Her Majesty's Treasury is concerned. As a case in point, the casino man and his visitor went down to a turf accountant's joint near one of England's larger hospitals in time to bump into a leading cancer-research man, whom the casino man knew.

"Arthur, what the hell are you doing here?" the casino man asked.

"On my way to work. I thought I'd pop in and put one down."

"Next thing you'll be telling me," the casino man said, "is that your boss over at the hospital is on his way here."

"Jolly well better had be," Arthur said, looking at his watch, "else he's going to be shut out."

LITTLE BOYS LOST—I

SEPTEMBER 1974

TRIER, Germany—If you didn't know better, you'd have sworn the whole damned trip had been planned as Richard Nixon's farewell gift to the American press corps. On Sunday night the flora, fauna, and ragweed of American sports journalism went winging out of John F. Kennedy Airport under the impression that it was headed for Kinshasa, Zaire, Africa, George Foreman, Muhammad Ali, and the Great Rumble in the Jungle.

As every schoolboy knows, the shortest distance between two points is a straight line. Unfortunately, this group is fresh out of schoolboys. It is also fresh out of patience, sleep, money, and navigators. In the past twenty-four hours, it flew to Iceland so that it could get to Luxembourg so that it could get to West Germany so that it could get to the lobby of the Hotel Merian.

Getting to the lobby of the Hotel Merian was of great importance. If you didn't get there in time, how else could you stand around from noon to 3 A.M. so that you could call New York to find out what was happening in Kinshasa?

And at 3 A.M., the lobby of the Merian had all the charm of an unmade bed. So did its occupants.

"That kid of mine," Murray Goodman was saying, "how is it he can call me from Caracas when he needs money and can call me from Kinshasa when he needs cigarettes and now—nothing."

Mr. Goodman is the Lord High Chaperon of this group. As he spoke, he was tastefully attired in an open-throated sport shirt, a large cigar, and a set of matching bags. The bags were suspended from beneath each eye socket.

"A son should call his father," a guy said, opening his eyelids to half-mast and neatly elbowing one of the flora of American sports journalism in the ribs because he was snoring in his ear while both of them were draped over the hotel's reception desk.

Bobby Goodman is somewhere in Kinshasa and he is Murray's

link to the Ali-Foreman promotion. Murray is the flora, fauna, and ragweed of American sports journalism's link to Bobby. Then a telephone operator who had been handling more action than OTB on the eve of the Kentucky Derby announced between yawns that the hotel switchboard was nearly as broken as his English.

"It can't be broken," Murray said.

"Thank you very much," the operator smiled.

"Get the damned thing fixed."

"Thank you very much."

"Damn it, we got a plane halfway between here and Kinshasa, we got the heavyweight champion of the world with an eye cut, we got the democratic president of a one-party country sore as hell, and we got eighty guys sleeping in your lobby and all of them are waiting for this telephone call."

"Thank you very much."

The trip had begun innocently enough. An hour before its start, somebody discovered that the plane was going to Iceland.

"Why are we going to Iceland?" a suspicious traveler asked.

"I don't know," Murray said. "Maybe the pilot wants to squeeze in a game of chess."

After Iceland came Luxembourg. And in Luxembourg came Casper.

Casper was beautiful. Casper is the president, vice president, guide, secretary, and information minister of something called Trans-Touring. He was waiting on the runway. It was a triumphant moment.

The ground crew schlepped over a set of stairs. The ground crew at Luxembourg Airport has a very strong union. It moves at least an inch a minute. The air-conditioning had been turned off by then. At suffocation-minus-five, they finally got the door open. Sunlight streamed in. The flora, fauna, and ragweed cheered. It moved majestically down the ramp.

Then a guy from *Sports Illustrated* stepped in a hole in the ground and broke his ankle.

Somewhere there was a message in that.

Outside the terminal, Casper was happily slamming luggage around. He boarded the bus, reached for a portable hand mike, and said, "Hello and welcome. I am your guide. I am to take you to your lodging for the night. I have here a copy of your travel plans. Does everyone have one?"

Everyone did not and Casper disappeared to get more mimeographed instructions. When he returned, he handed the lot of them out and then said, "Good. Now you all have one. Now I must tell you that they are no good. The plans are changed but you may keep the folders."

Somewhere there was a message in that, too.

And then the bus pulled out, made a turn onto a highway, and began to roar past lush, green farms. The driver leaned over and switched on the radio. It blared forth with the semifamiliar tones of "The Yellow Rose of Texas." The reason the tones were only semifamiliar was that they were being sung in German.

And somewhere in that was the largest message of all.

Ten minutes later, a guy was lifting a barrier that looked as though it belonged at a rural Ohio grade crossing. The big sign under the eagle on the pole read, BUNDERSREPUBLIK DEUTSCHLAND.

"This isn't happening," a guy said when a guy in a Good Humor suit and a white yachting cap with an eagle on it came on board to check the passports. "I am just going to sit here and wait until I wake up. If I take all this seriously, somebody is going to walk over, tap me on the shoulder, and say that George Foreman has a cut over his eye."

He was wrong.

That didn't happen until three hours later in the hotel elevator.

"I think," Mr. Goodman had said at 1 A.M., "that we have to take a vote and see whether to press on or rethink our itinerary. Then when Bobby calls . . . ."

"The phone is broken," a guy said.

"Thank you very much," the hotel operator said.

But at 3 A.M., Bobby did call. Murray listened carefully for a minute.

"The hell with your cigarettes, what's happening? . . . You think it's off . . . . they want us to come . . . they say it's on . . . they want us to come . . . they don't know if they sent the plane for us . . . they want us to come."

"Thank you very much," the operator said.

"Gentlemen," Mr. Goodman said, gently recradling the telephone, "I think we have a problem."

257

LITTLE BOYS
LOST—II

SEPTEMBER 1974

LUXEMBOURG—The last time we left the flora, fauna, and ragweed of American sports journalism, it was draped over varied pieces of furniture in the lobby of the Hotel Merian, just across the border in Trier, West Germany. It was 3 A.M. None of them had changed their clothes in the past forty-eight hours; stale cigarette, cigar, and pipe smoke hung over the room like a mushroom cloud; and an enormous pyramid of empty beer bottles was threatening to cascade down on Murray Goodman.

Since two heavyweight fighters, the Republic of Zaire, and a number of long-distance telephone receivers had come crashing down on Mr. Goodman in the past forty-eight hours, a wise observer would have to make the beer bottles an 8-5 favorite.

Mr. Goodman was trying mightily to explain the course of events as he interpreted them from the moment The Last of the Great Aerial Circuses had begun to touch four separate countries on the same flight until George Foreman reached for his Band-Aid. He is the promotion's chaperon on this journey into the Twilight Zone. You could make a reasonable case for the theory that Ulysses had more fun.

"As I said, gentlemen," Mr. Goodman sighed, "I have just spoken to Kinshasa again and it appears we have this problem. The one encouraging thing is that President Mobutu insists that George's cut is being overdramatized."

"All things are relative, Murray," a guy said. "The president means it is overdramatized if you compare it with the one he wants to lay across George Foreman's neck."

As the dialogue continued, a hotel porter desperately tried to clean up the lobby. It was the greatest challenge since earth day.

"I think we should take a vote on whether to go on to Kinshasa or go back home," Mr. G. suggested.

"I think we should press on to Kinshasa." a guy said. "Trying to find out what's happening from here is like covering the Battle of Ethiopia from Norway."

"I think you have a point," Mr. Goodman said. "They seem to want us to get down there as soon as possible."

"I think that's exactly why we shouldn't go," another guy said.

"I think it's about time we all took a shower," somebody else offered.

The hotel porter tripped over a beer bottle and muttered something in German. Loosely translated, it sounded like, "I agree with the last guy."

"You know," another guy said, "it's not so bad being here. Did you know that the Romans passed this way in 15 B.C.?"

"Yeah?" Mr. Goodman replied. "See if you can find out how they got out."

"And it is also the birthplace of Karl Marx," a guy continued, brushing aside a fallen comrade who was drifting off to sleep and burning a cigarette hole in the speaker's jacket at the same time.

And then the telephone rang.

The telephone had been ringing since the flora, fauna, etc., had arrived. It had rung from Kinshasa and from New York and from Chicago, Oakland, and Luxembourg. This time it was Kinshasa again. As Mr. Goodman reached for the reservation clerk's telephone, the elevator door suddenly burst open at the other end of the lobby and a guy ran screaming down the hall.

"Fire . . . fire," he yelled. "I just plugged my electric razor into one of those funny-looking wall sockets and it blew up. There's a lot of smoke . . . . "

"Good," a guy suggested, "if the Romans can't get us out of here maybe the Trier Fire Department can."

And across the room, Mr. Goodman was saying into the telephone, "Yeah . . . I see . . . you really think so . . . stay in touch."

The room immediately got so quiet you could hear a beer bottle drop.

"They say in New York," Mr. Goodman began, "that they have spoken with Kinshasa and they believe there is a chance the fight might even go on as scheduled. They suggest we go to Zaire."

Which is why the troops were assembled several hours later

at the Luxembourg Airport. They were met by a representative of Air Zaire, who had arrived from Brussels along with President Mobutu's personal airplane. He was tall and angular and he was dressed in what looked like one of Mao's old jackets. He wore sunglasses and as he spoke, he kept looking around. Clearly, nobody—but nobody—was going to sneak up and steal the president's personal plane with him on the job.

"The fight shall be postponed for perhaps eight days," he said in French. "Everyone should come."

"I don't know," another guy said. "Look at this." He was waving around a newspaper that featured a picture of George Foreman and his $10 million cut. "That looks as though he won't fight for six weeks."

"I don't believe it," an Associated Press photographer said. "After all," he added, as though he had just solved the mystery of the Dead Sea Scrolls, "that's an English newspaper."

"What frightens me," another guy interrupted, "is that I'm standing here nodding my head as though all of this makes any kind of sense."

It was then that yet another guy arrived with the news that the fight was definitely off for more than a month.

"That does it," one man said. "That hard guy in the Mao jacket can stand there looking to guard the runway, you guys can fly down there and cover a rock festival. I'm going home. At least when the plane stops in Iceland I might catch a quick chess game."

He was nearly trampled in the rush toward the New York-bound ticket windows.

THE SIEGE OF L.A.

JULY 1984

LOS ANGELES—And now the siege has begun in earnest. Some 625,000 tourists began falling out of the skies over the City of Angels this week, the freeways belong to the devil, and heaven help those caught in between.

Bracketed by massive billboards extolling the virtues of Toshiba products, Fuji film, and down-home Kirin beer, the Olympic Games have returned to the U. S. of A. Well, nobody is perfect and, in truth, who is to say that one of the lesser events won't be staged in the very shadow of one of the above's home offices?

After all, half the soccer games will be played 4,000 miles away, in the old-line Los Angeles suburbs of Annapolis, Maryland, and Cambridge, Massachusetts; 200 square miles separate the southern tip of the competition down in San Diego from the northern outpost up in Santa Barbara; the twenty-three competition sites are cleverly sandwiched together in a small, intimate area of 4,500 square miles, roughly the size of Connecticut; and the Olympic Villages are locked up so tight we may learn tomorrow that all the athletes have left for Sardinia.

Considering the fact that ten separate suburban communities were under Class A smog alerts by day's end, who would notice?

So how did it go yesterday on D-Day-minus-three here in the only city on the Continental Land Mass where the phrase "trust me" translates from the native argot as "protect your vital organs at all times"?

This town, which made a business out of love as far back as Rudolph Valentino, has embraced the Olympic Spirit with a violence not seen since the Sabine women—and you know how much love they got. By high noon, love and the Olympic Spirit were locked in the kind of embrace that tempts irritated homeowners to throw cold water on overfriendly pairs of collies.

Down at the main press center, little kids were giving out flowers to the world's press with irresistible smiles and an occasional "what do you mean you don't want the damned flower, mister?" Meanwhile, somewhere in the great city, teenaged antigraffiti squads, numbering 1,000 members, were splashing pastel paints over everything that didn't move and took only four letters to spell; thirty cops on horseback were sweeping the downtown area of ladies of the evening (afternoon and night) along with their booking agents; and a cast of 12,000 tooters, hooters, dancers, prancers, and only David Wolper knows what else, were practicing for the opening ceremonies.

"There has never," Mr. Wolper will tell you in the tradition of this city's knack for understatement, "been anything like this— except maybe D-Day." Toward that end, some 4,000 pigeons have been shipped in for the climax. Let us all pause and thank God that statues cannot read. They'll find out soon enough.

Yesterday, out in a town called Rialto, a man named Jim Souza walked softly through his work. Mr. Souza damned well had better walk softly, since he is the custodian of enough heavy artillery to change the balance of power in Southeast Asia. At the conclusion of Saturday's opening ceremonies, he will be the man who will set off the fireworks. Dearly beloved, from what we have been told about this, let us all pray that the San Andreas Fault elects to go out on a very long lunch break.

And then there is Edward Keen. He is the reason that you cannot buy a nail, a hammer, a board, or a roll of gaffer's tape anywhere in Southern California. He is the official construction superintendent of the Olympic Games and yesterday the hammering was spectacular. Things moved so fast it was unclear whether he was employed to put the game facilities in order or finally finish building this city.

Certainly there is one piece of information you can take to the bank. Whatever it is that he is doing, nobody is going to work. We are, indeed, going to interrupt him. After all, the city is ringed by a security force that includes 20,000 men and women from fifty jurisdictions, 300 state highway patrol cars, eighty helicopters, and a couple of blimps.

There is also a 399-foot U.S. Coast Guard icebreaker named the *Polar Star*, berthed up the freeway in Long Beach, which should destroy forever the nasty rumor that the Los Angeles Olympic Organizing Committee never received the news about the *Titanic*.

One does suspect, however, that it might not have gotten the news had it depended on the goodwill generated by its relationship with the United States Olympic Committee. By noon yesterday, the USOC publicity staff still had not received the necessary credentials to gain total access to the Olympic Village, which ought to tell you how nicely communications are moving between the two groups.

In short, these are the Olympics with which Leonidas of Rhodes might have had a little difficulty. Known by historians in Newark, New Jersey, as Lenny the Runner, he scored footrace triples in four successive Olympiads between 164 and 152 B.C. Clearly, he would be out of place here because nobody ever set up a trust fund for him in the Western world and nobody ever gave him an apartment, a car, and a stipend as a hero of sport behind the Iron Curtain.

Well, times do change and they surely have in the time warp between Lenny the Runner and the 7,800 athletes who are still arriving for this one.

But some things are constant. In Lenny's time there was a city in Greece called Pisa (and before you start writing patronizing letters, it predated the Pisa of Italy today). In any event, Pisa held several Olympiads and wanted more. It started a movement to make itself the permanant home of the Games. Some folks disagreed. They came to town wearing armor and throwing very sharp spears, as they should've. They burned the joint to the ground. Some other folks insist they might actually have been residents of Pisa in disguise.

Somewhere in that there is a lesson.

Fortunately, the taxpayers of Montreal '76 have never read it.

Whatever application there is for the taxpayers of Los Angeles in particular and the United States in general still remains to be seen.

Meanwhile, let the Games begin.

NOBODY'S A WINNER IN DERBYTOWN

MAY 5, 1978

LOUISVILLE—The sign on the motel wall read, "If you live a good life, go to Sunday school and church, and say your prayers every night, when you die you'll go to Kentucky."

Considering the ultimate reward promised, it ought to be followed by another line: "The preceding was a paid announcement by the devil."

This is a city in crisis but with single hotel rooms going as high as ninety bucks a night for the Thursday-Friday-Saturday treadmill euphemistically called "The Derby Package," one strongly suspects it will spot the tourists two touchdowns and a field goal and still finish well in front.

Last night the airport was packed with arriving sportsmen of the day, ladies of the evening and hustlers for any hour. Today the taxis hood their meters and start operating on flat rates high enough to underwrite the movements of all the rolling stock under General Patton.

Still, for a brief instant, there had been tiny signs that perhaps Pegasus, or whatever other pagan deity oversees the operation of that slice of Twilight Zone known as the Kentucky Derby, was going to break his 104-year silence and lend a helping hoof to the good guys.

They began to surface a week ago with the twin announcements that the spring frost had imperiled the mint (as in mint julep) crop and that somebody had swiped a mutuel ticket machine from nearby Keeneland.

The former threatened to seriously limit the ritual of destroying perfectly good booze by mixing it with grass. The latter was more of an economic threat than a religious one. The missing mutuel machine, which was described locally as three feet high and a foot and a half wide (leading one to wonder why they left out "armed and dangerous"), has the ability to print mutuel tickets. With the right kind of paper, it could raise all kinds of hell here on Derby Day.

It was a hope but hardly a promise.

As a local pointed out yesterday, "In the first place, they can't get the right kind of paper. And as for the mint in the mint juleps, have you ever seen a Derby crowd? It will be so stoned by post time that you could garnish the bourbon with lox and bagels and they wouldn't know the difference."

Yesterday, in keeping with this return to reality, dawned wet and lousy. By the dawn's early dew, a couple of local hardboots were discussing the breeding factor that makes Kentucky Derby winners. You have to understand that in this business, there is a great emphasis on sex. Someday, somebody is going to point to one of the tiny jockeys and explain that he is by Toulouse-Lautrec out of Minnie Mouse. In any event, the obsession here is so great that to have a non-Kentucky bred win the race is considered a crime on a par with forgetting that the national anthem begins with the words, "Oh, the sun shines bright on my old . . . . "

"Well, we've got five Kentucky breds going," the first hardboot said.

"Yeah," the second replied, "but that Affirmed, he's Florida bred." He said the word *Florida* with the kind of reverence that cons generally reserve for San Quentin.

"I know," the first one countered, "but he was conceived right here in Kentucky."

It's enough to make a man want to open a breeding farm in Passaic.

In any event, yesterday the outsiders in this race could still harbor dreams of glory, serene in the knowledge that they can keep on living in Fantasyland right up until post time tomorrow. Down by Barn 33, a good-looking gray colt named Chief of Dixieland was standing in the rain. Steam rose from his lathered flanks. Perhaps twenty feet away, Jake the Rake was saying, "If I didn't think we belonged here I wouldn't have come. You can talk about the race all you want. Eventually you have to go out and run it and that's when we'll really find out."

Jake the Rake wore a green turtleneck sweater, dark slacks,

a leather jacket, and a checkered sports cap. His square handle is Jake Morreale. He is the trainer and part owner of Chief of Dixieland and has never had a horse in the Derby before. To say he is training a longshot is to claim the obvious. Still, one suspects Jake has been around a little.

"The reason they call me Jake the Rake is one day I cashed a bet on a horse called Mr. Pak at $144 for $2. The exacta paid $1,800 for $2. I cashed that, too. Black Cat Lacombe, the publicity man, thought I should have suggested the bet to him. He said if I kept things to myself, I'd keep on raking in money."

Jake the Rake paid $15,000 for Chief of Dixieland. When one of his neophyte owners earlier handed him a check for $20,000 and said go out and buy a Derby winner, he was shocked when Jake told him he doubted it was enough. "You could buy a whole herd of horses for that, it would seem to me," said the man who is named Aubrey Pate. "Hell, I just bought my kid a horse for thirty-five bucks."

"Don't run it in the Derby," Jake advised.

In any event, he is here with this rank outsider and he believes he has a chance.

"Some chance," Jack Price said later in the day in the press box. Price was the owner-trainer of Carry Back, the 1961 Derby winner. "It takes planning. What guys who train horses like that have to do is give the jockey explicit instructions."

"What kind of instructions?" a guy wondered.

"Well, the best thing he can tell him is to wait until six other horses fall down."

Go argue with that.

266

Index